FORBIDDEN CHILDHOOD

RUTH SLENCZYNSKA

AND

LOUIS BIANCOLLI

Doubleday & Company, Inc., Garden City, N. Y. 1957

Just as my fingers on these keys
Make music, so the self same sounds
On my spirit make a music too.

Peter Quince at the Clavier, Wallace Stevens

THE fact that I made my concert debut twenty-eight years ago puts me in a rather odd position. People recall me as an old-timer. I am someone they heard far back in their youth. Yet I am only thirty-two. Time and again they have come up to me and said, "I remember you when . . ." as if I were twice my age. Wherever I go there is always somebody who heard me play as a child. They come backstage, wait in the hall, walk up to me in hotel lobbies. There was the dainty little lady in London two years ago who came backstage to show me a copy of the very first program I played there at twelve There is the lady who walked into a rehearsal in Boston in 1954 and waited to tell me that she remembered me as a girl of four at a party in Philadelphia. It seems she overheard a conversation between me and a little boy. The boy had said to me after I finished playing, "You know I play the piano too," and I had replied, according to her, "Yes, but do you make music?"

They remember me from Copenhagen or London or Oakland or New York or Paris, and they always begin by specifying how old I was at the time, twelve or eight, six or four. . . . After witnessing still another of these backstage encounters Arthur Fiedler of the Boston "Pops" Symphony turned to me in mock anger one day and said:

"When is somebody going to come up and say he heard you when you were six months?"

Ruth Slenczynska

FORBIDDEN CHILDHOOD

LONG before I was born, even before he met and married my mother, Father had it all worked out in his mind: I was going to be a musician.

It didn't much matter whether I was a boy or a girl. It mattered even less what Mother wanted and what she might want me to be when I finally appeared. Girl or boy, I was solidly booked for music. It never even entered Father's mind that I might have something to say about it. I was his, to do with as he saw fit. Mother happened to want a boy, which was probably the last time she had any reason to hope one way or another about my future. Father was just overjoyed to have a child, so overjoyed, in fact, that for the first and last time in his life he brought my mother flowers.

I was two hours old when Father first saw me. Mother said he gave one look at my hands and burst into tears.

"Look at those good sturdy wrists!" he said between sobs. "Notice the way her thumb is separate from the rest of the hand! Look at the tips of her fingers! I swear to you, Mamma, that's a musician!"

He never once raised his eyes to my face. As he went on muttering to himself about what he saw in my hands, Mother though he was mad. Josef Slenczynski beheld the future that day in a maternity ward in Sacramento, and it was in his own image.

That day my destiny, almost my doom, was sealed. Father

read my hands and I became—and, in spite of Father, still am—a musician.

What he then noticed was later to be pointed out again and again as a special peculiarity of my fingers. The top knuckles can't be bent back, and the tips of my fingers are solid as iron. That fact never stopped fascinating Father.

I was born in the Sister's Hospital in Sacramento, California, on January 15, 1925. I have since found out that it was staffed by members of the Catholic Order of the Sisters of Mercy. I know this because shortly before I went back to the concert stage in 1951, I worked as a piano instructor with these selfless and dedicated ladies at the Mercy School of Music in Burlingame, California. It seems that visiting colleagues from Sacramento told the sisters one day that I was born in their hospital.

I was only twelve days old when Father made his first public announcement of my future. It was at the home of Herb Caen, the San Francisco columnist and author. His sister, Estelle Caen, only a little girl then, used to play accompaniments for Father, who was very particular about who played the piano for him. Mr. Caen tells me that my father said to his parents that if he had little Estelle as a pupil he would make a great artist out of her. Pointing to me, he then said:

"You see that tiny thing there. Someday that little baby is going to be one of the world's greatest musicians." Mr. Caen says they all laughed at that, although he admits that four years later, when I gave my first public concert in Mills College, they weren't laughing so hard any more, and that ten years later, when I was soloist with almost every big orchestra in the world, they weren't laughing at all. They began to think that maybe my dad knew what he was talking about.

Father never meant me to be a pianist, not at first. The

word he used about me was "musician." What he meant by that was violinist, because he himself was a violinist, and what he had in mind for me was to become the "world's greatest violinist." From looking at my thumb and fingertips he was convinced I would someday make the world forget Kreisler and Heifetz. Now, when I quote my father, I would like to make it clear that he was always using the superlative. The positive and the comparative, the great and the greater, didn't exist in his grammar. Such degrees of worth were of no consequence to him. Things or people were either the worst or the best, the smallest or the greatest. There was nothing in between. The superlative was the only form of the adjective he knew. That may have been because, being a Pole and educated in Europe, he never spoke English like an American. It was probably a clue to his psychology, too. Nothing was ever merely good or wonderful or fine. It was the greatest. If he heard a voice, it wasn't just beautiful, it was the greatest voice he had ever heard. If the voice was bad, it was the worst voice he had ever heard.

That his twelve-day-old daughter was destined to be "one of the world's greatest musicians" was merely typical. People soon came to know my father's limitations in English, and those who didn't were inclined to suspect that all musicians were a little rattled and not to be taken too literally.

Father must have been a restless sort of person in his childhood and youth. Like his younger brother, who settled in Brisbane, Australia, he ran away from home as a boy. The brutal beatings administered by a tyrannical father may have explained his flight as much as wanderlust and a desire to escape being drafted into the Polish army. I was about eight months old when my uncle in Brisbane invited us to join him in Australia. Father agreed, and the three of us undertook that long journey. We remained in Australia exactly five days. In that time Father had one stormy quarrel after another with his brother, the result being that we were soon back in California, this time in the Bay Area around Oakland and Berkeley, where much of my early life was spent.

Wherever he set up house, Father always managed to round up enough violin pupils for a comfortable living. Oakland and Berkeley were no exception. I am told I was only sixteen months old when I began to manifest the signs my father was so certain would appear when he first beheld my fingers as a newborn baby. Father used to give lessons every day in the living room, which also served as studio. I was evidently within earshot of those sessions because both my father and mother insist that I was able at sixteen months to hum all the melodies of the violin pieces being studied. Hum them, moreover, in the right key, not haphazardly.

Who can say when music first became a living reality to me? Father used to insist I was born with absolute pitch. That I doubt, but he swore to me and everyone else that at five months, long before I learned to say "Mamma," I once hummed a phrase in perfect key. Maybe that isn't so astonishing as it sounds. My ears had been flooded with Father's violin since the day Mother brought me from the hospital. I was already sensitized to music. Mother told me that when I was fourteen months old the sound of a police or ambulance siren would drive me frantic. I'd burst into tears and try to hide myself. Later I concealed my pain out of shame when I saw other children dash to the windows as the fire engines went screaming by. Music was something else. I always wanted to get closer and closer to it. It was at first a fairyland that became a private world and a refuge.

The music was also like a light that turned on pictures in my mind; they just flashed there as if at a signal from the keys. I saw beautiful green hills in the music. I was three and a half at the time. The music was a Mozart minuet. For days, when I was six, I had the distinct image as I played of a beggarly little woman, standing on a street corner, shivering in a thin ragged coat, her children huddled about her. That was the second movement of the F minor concerto of Bach. Even now when I play the opening part of Mendelssohn's "Rondo Capriccioso," with its serene, warm beauty, I am inside the Madeleine Church in Paris, the sun glowing through the stained-glass windows, making colored shadows on the wall.

My own earliest recollection of any kind is rather significant, I think, for two reasons. First, because it dates back as far as it does, and second, because it involves the piano. I was two years and three months old at the time. We had moved to Claremont Avenue in Berkeley, and the time was Easter, 1927. My sister Helen was a brand-new baby in the house. Our upright piano stood in the living room. Gathered there that day were my aunt Rose from San José and her two boys. Some chocolate Easter eggs lay on the kitchen table, and my aunt was methodically slicing them for distribution. When Father saw that my aunt was planning to give me one of the pieces, he cried out:

"No, no, no! Ruth doesn't get any—not until she goes in and plays her piece on the piano."

And I remember wriggling up on the chair, reaching for the keys. While they all sat around as quiet as they could be, I played some little melody that I had heard my father teaching to one of his violin pupils. When I finished, they all clapped their hands, and Father allowed me to eat my piece of chocolate Easter egg.

This episode didn't mean that Father had changed his mind about me. In his eyes I was a violinist in the making. The piano was just a plaything and an exhibit on which to show off his daughter. But the pattern was already being formed. Father's word was law; what he wanted me to do I did. There were already ways of punishing me if I didn't obey slavishly. Very early I thus knew the difference between right and wrong. If I did what my father told me to do the way he wanted me to do it, I was being a very good little girl. Any other behavior was wrong. My mother must have secretly dreaded what lay ahead of me from the very start. I remember overhearing a conversation in the back yard between her and her good friend, our Greek neighbor Maria Pappas, whose daughter used to play with me.

"He keeps telling me," said my mother, "that our little girl is different from everyone else, that she's going to be known all over the world. 'Just wait and see!' he says. That's fine with me. But I wish he wouldn't be as sharp with her as he is. He expects too much of her."

Sometimes my mother would cry over it. . . .

Shortly after this we changed residence once more, to Etna Street in Berkeley. The family needed more room because my second sister, Gloria, was expected daily. The first thing I recall about our new home was that a large family of bees moved into it with us. They seemed so tame and friendly that I wasn't at all frightened when one little bee settled on my finger. I suppose I was looking at it between my thumb and index finger when suddenly, to my great surprise, it stung me. I gave a loud yell, which brought Father rushing to my side. That mishap must have become symbolic, because ever afterward I can remember his saying again and again:

"Don't do bad things with your hands, like squeezing a bee or getting your fingers caught in doors. Those hands are precious. You're going to be a musician. Watch those hands every minute of the day."

I was just about three then. In our new house on Etna Street we had a pair of sliding doors separating the living and dining rooms. Among the latest additions to the furniture was a toy piano on which I played in the kitchen. It was purchased with the idea of preventing me from climbing up on the bench and banging away at the big piano. When my dad was giving a lesson, I would cross the dining room and alternately put my ear and eye to the small opening between the sliding doors. If the doors were shut tight, I would open them just a wee, wee bit, not quite enough for him to notice I was standing there. I was fascinated, watching all these grownups playing pieces over and over again as Father scolded, corrected, and encouraged them. How proud I felt when he would take the violin in hand and show them the right way. I would stand there by the hour. When Mother called me, I pretended not to hear. That was my favorite little spot. It took plenty of coaxing to drag me away. In the kitchen I would sit at my toy piano and finger out the tunes I had heard through the sliding doors.

"That's Mr. Campilli's exercise," I would say, reconstructing it as best I could on the tinkly keyboard.

"I wouldn't mind," my father would say, "but you play the same mistakes he does."

Then I played Miss Ellinwood's latest piece and some other pupil's, always as I had heard them, with the same slips and peculiarities. That little toy piano was awfully frustrating because it had only white keys, with black keys painted on them. I communicated my feelings about the toy piano to Father.

"When am I going to play on the big piano?"

"You keep away from that piano!" Father snapped back. "Wait till you have enough sense. I don't want you to get it out of tune."

So I went back to the kitchen to my toy piano and all its frustrations.

I must have suddenly acquired "enough sense" in the spring

of 1928, when I was a little over three years old. Father then gave me my first official music lesson. This was how it came about. My sister Gloria was being born at the hospital. The night before, while doing the dishes, Mother gave a sudden cry of pain. After hurriedly putting me and my sister Helen to bed, she and Father left for the hospital. The moment I awoke the next morning I asked my father, "Did the baby come yet?"

"No. Don't bother me. Go back to sleep."

I went back to bed, and pretty soon was up again asking my father, "Why hasn't the baby come yet?" You see, I wanted a new baby in the family very badly. My mother had me and Helen ask God every night before we went to sleep to give us a baby brother. She had been disappointed twice, and now Gloria wasn't going to be a boy either, at which point Mother became philosophical and decided to quit. My reason for wanting another baby in the house was quite simple. I loved the idea of having another friend to play with. I had my own ideas of what a new baby meant. I thought a baby was born according to specification. You named the age and size, and there it was. When Gloria finally arrived and she was just another infant, my mother saw the look of disappointment on my face.

"What did you think it was going to be?" she asked.

"Oh, about nine or ten years old . . ."

Well, here were Father and I waiting for Gloria to be born. "Can I have crackers and milk?" I asked him when I realized he didn't like being asked any more questions about the new baby. Father showed no interest in me at all. He just paced up and down the living room, as if he were the only one there. My eyes suddenly wandered to the big piano and the chair in front of it. I don't know what prompted me, but I climbed into the forbidden territory and began striking the keys. The pacing suddenly stopped behind me.

"If you have to play the piano, you might as well play it right," I heard my father say. "I'm going to teach you to play a C major scale, and if you're a real good girl and you play the C major scale in the right hand alone in one octave, then we will tell Mamma in the hospital."

I applied myself and learned how to do it.

"All right," said my father, "now you learn how to play the C major scale in the left hand alone, and we'll tell Mamma in the hospital."

And I mastered that in no time flat.

"Now you've got to play the C major scale with both hands together," said Father, "and we'll tell Mamma in the hospital."

That was a little harder, but I learned that, too.

"Now can we go to tell Mamma?"

My father said, "No, it isn't time yet. You must now play the C major scale in four octaves, both hands together and we'll tell Mamma in the hospital."

And I did. That was my very first lesson. I had mastered it, and I felt a keen sense of pride in being able to go from one end of the keyboard to the other without making a single mistake. I found it great fun, too, because I could lean away over on one side. I made it a sort of game, to see whether I could lean completely on one hip, legs dangling, and then on the other, and go all the way back and forth.

It was now time to go and tell Mamma. So Father gave me my crackers and milk, packed Helen and me in the back of the car, and off we went to the hospital. I was heartbroken when the nurse told us that children were not allowed in. When Father went in alone to see Mamma, I shouted after him, "Don't forget to tell her about the C major scale!"

Outside I waved to my mother when she came to the window. Finally my father returned, and the only thing that interested me burst from my lips.

"Did you tell Mamma about the C major scale?"

As my father picked me up and waved to Mamma, who was watching from the window of her room, I could tell from her face that he had told her. That was all I wanted to know. I had completely forgotten to ask him about the new baby.

ALMOST the first result of the new arrival in the household on Etna Street was a hunger strike. Mother seemed so occupied with our little sister that Helen and I began to feel neglected. We became intensely jealous of all the love and attention being showered on Gloria. So the two of us stopped eating. Mother was particularly worried about me because I was always a fat, hungry baby. Now I wasn't eating at all. I was listless and pale and moody. The doctor prescribed a tonic to sharpen our appetites, but of course the malady went deeper. Helen gradually came around. I held out longer, cutting myself off from everything and everybody. It was then that the piano became my sole interest. I noticed that Father didn't order me away from it as he used to. And that more than anything else broke my hunger strike. I had found a new companion. Pretty soon I was going to the piano every day, encouraged by my father and the little lessons he gave me. Years later Father used to say to people that I wouldn't eat until I got the piano. I was no longer jealous of Gloria.

Father's first lessons lasted from twenty minutes to a half hour a day. There was no special time for them—only whenever I had the time or whenever mother was attending to the new baby. They grew into a regular little habit. I was three and a half years old. Mother, meanwhile, started to teach me the alphabet and how to read and write and count. I was soon being thought of as rather advanced for my years. I think precocious children are obnoxious, and I was one. My daily walks around the block with Father became a ritual of mental exercise, too. Father would ask me how to spell "play," "day," "house," easy words that he had overheard Mother teaching me to spell. Helen, who was all of one and a half, would mimic me: "D—A—Y spells 'day,'" she would say, lisping the verb as "thpellth." Everybody in the neighborhood thought we were very bright youngsters, especially Helen. She seemed to know as much as I did, and she was two years younger!

The walls of our kitchen were festooned with two large maps. I remember feeling strangely important the day Father put them up with a few thumbtacks. One was a map of the Holy Land. The other was a map of the world in bright colors, blue and pink and green, the green representing the ocean. When Mother showed me where California was, I was amazed at what a great big place the world was and what a tiny little corner of it we were in.

"Will I ever see more of this great big world with all the beautiful colors on it?" I asked Mother.

"Well, you've already traveled a lot. You've been to Australia and back."

"But I don't remember that. I want to see more." Then Father chimed in, "If you're a smart girl and practice hard, and do everything I tell you to, you will get to see all of it," and he waved his hand over all that blue, pink, and green.

After supper, when Gloria was put to bed, Father, if he was in the right mood, would open up his violin case, take out his violin, and play for us right there in the kitchen. Mother was never a musician and could not play one note on the piano. Father, who never spared her feelings if he could help it, would take special delight in reminding her that in Europe she would not have been considered educated at all because she lacked musical training. That gave Mother an inferiority complex about music that she hasn't outgrown to this day. But she always loved to listen. We would sit around the kitchen table and drift into dreamland as Father played the violin. Striding up and down the kitchen, he would play things by Kreisler and Bach and Paganini, themes from the Beethoven concerto—all the pieces he had studied as a young man in Warsaw and Berlin and Vienna. We thought he was wonderful.

Father's big idol was Mischa Elman. The proudest document in his possession was a letter someone had written to him after one of the small studio recitals he used to give before he married Mother. The writer informed Father that she had enjoyed his performance of a certain composition as much as when the great Elman himself had played it in Carnegie Hall. That letter was in Father's wallet to his dying day.

Evidently impressed by my progress in music and three R's, Father one day promised me a great big surprise. I couldn't imagine what it might be. There was no birthday immediately ahead, and Christmas was still a long way off. I kept pestering him about it, but he became more and more mysterious about it; just smiled secretively, wagged his finger, and said, "Ah, you're going to love it! You'll be in heaven!"

Well, I was already playing on the big piano, and that was surprise and heaven enough to me. I had started to learn what the black notes meant. I think it might be interesting to recall here how Father explained to me what the sharps and flats were, a subject that long baffles children if wrongly taught at the outset. It is necessary to keep in mind that I was just three and a half years old and that I did not know the meaning of the terms "left" and "right" yet. So at first I was just sitting before the piano and I was told to pat the chair with my right hand and say "right" and pat the chair with the other hand and say "left—"Right, left, right, left." Pretty soon I got the feeling of which was which.

Then Father told me that the distance between any note on the piano and its nearest neighbor, whether it was white or black, was called a half-step. You see, Father was clever enough not to emphasize the fact that some of the notes were black and some of them white. The day that he taught me my C major scale I first learned the names of the notes—C, D, E, etc. Now he told we that any note a half-step to the right of any of these basic notes was simply called C-sharp, D-sharp, and so on, and any note a half-step to the left of them was called C-flat, D-flat, etc. There never was any question in my mind about it from the very start. It was a very simple lesson, yet its importance deserves stressing here. It shows how easily a three-and-a-half-year-old child can be made to grasp that hard point. Yet I have seen adults who, because of faulty training as children, failed to comprehend the meaning of E-sharp or C-flat on the piano simply because these sharps and flats fall on white keys instead of black.

Double sharps and double flats were learned exactly the same way, simply by adding the concept of a whole step, which in my vocabulary meant two half-steps. When I had fully grasped the idea of sharps and flats, my father taught me the G major scale in exactly the same way as he had the C major scale. Now it is interesting to see why he did this. A violin is tuned in fifths. Father, you see, was thinking in terms of a violin rather than of a piano. The G string is an open string on the violin, and as I understand it, it is possible to play a G major scale without going into positions. Hence it is the first scale that most violinists are taught to play. At least that is the method Father advocates in his book, *Scale Development for the Violin*, which he wrote in 1919,

Of course the G major scale has only one sharp in it, which was another reason why Father taught it to me when he did. Having mastered that scale thoroughly, with both hands together in four octaves, I next learned the D major scale, which has two sharps, and so on and on until I had mastered the F sharp major scale, which has six sharps, followed by the C-sharp major scale, which has seven. This is how I tackled the scales on a day-to-day basis. The easier ones—up to, say, E major—I learned at the rate of one a day. Then it would take two or even three days to master a new scale. At length, I was playing seven scales. It was like building a pyramid. Each day I started with the C major scale. When that was perfect, I would play the G major scale, then the D major, and so on, and every day I would do all of them, and my practice period gradually lengthened.

All of this was such a gradual process that I was never conscious of its taking place. When we finally arrived at the scale with the seven sharps, Father delivered a favorite pun of his which was a little over my head at the time.

"Now that we are through with the sharps, we shall move into the flats."

I remember he laughed and tried to explain his little joke to me, but it was hopeless. Mother wasn't very helpful when I appealed to her later.

The flats were a little more difficult for me to learn than the sharps. Let me try to explain why. When Father was showing me that each scale had one more sharp than the previous one, he also taught me the meaning of the interval of the fifth. I was able to figure out on the piano that a fifth above C, counting C, was G; that a fifth above G was D, and so on, up to C-sharp, which was the scale with the seven sharps. Trouble set in when I began figuring fifths from that point on. From C-sharp to G-sharp was a fifth. Now why couldn't we call that G-Sharp major? That puzzled me a little. So Father started all the way from C again, showing me a brand-new interval which was called the fourth. From C to F was a fourth, and F major had one flat, B-flat. In my mind it was a short of sharp except that the term "flat" had already settled in my consciousness as a half-step to the left rather than a half-step to the right. There was no confusion there. After F major, it was simple to figure out how a fourth above F was B-flat, and a fourth above B-flat was E-flat, and so on, until we reached the joining point. This was either C-sharp or D-flat, whichever you chose to call it.

All the while this was going on, my mother was teaching me to write the letters of the alphabet and put them together into words. About this time I also learned to write notes. Each time Father taught me a new scale I would write it down in a little notebook with the little signature right after the clef sign. That way I became accustomed very early to the look as well as the sound of all the scales I was learning. Now, when Father saw that I was able to play the twelve major scales properly, he introduced me to something new. The minor scale. So, now, each time I played the C major scale, I would follow it with its relative A minor scale, and that way I learned the interval of the minor third. As I mastered each of the twelve minor scales, into my little notebook it went with its signature, in my own handwriting. I had learned both the harmonic and melodic minors. I dwell on the way and the order in which I learned these things because I think they help explain so much that follows in the ease and speed with which I grasped more complex matters later. My training as a small child in this question of scales and scale signatures was completely free of confusion. In a very short space of time Father had given me a good foundation in scale structure. I think it safe to say that at three and a half I knew the piano keyboard.

During all this time Father never let me forget about the tremendous surprise he had in store for me. The time was now about the end of August, coinciding with the last of the twenty-four scales. The air was a little chilly, because I can remember blazing logs in the fireplace in the living room. It was on one such afternoon, chilly outside, a warm glow in the fireplace, my curiosity at the breaking point, that Father announced, "I'm almost ready for the surprise." I was as much mystified by the why as the what. Finally Father let me understand that if I was able to do all twenty-four scales (by this time they were really thirty-six, because I was doing one major and two minor scales on each of the twelve keys) the big surprise would be mine.

"They must be absolutely perfect," Father said. "Both hands together, four octaves."

Now I was most eager to do it perfectly, because, besides having the incentive of the mysterious surprise, I wanted so much to see the beaming look on Mother's face when I received my reward. So I got going on my marathon of scales, and could hardly wait till I finished the last B minor scale. The fact is I slid off the seat and finished standing up, whereupon my Father flew into a rage and shouted: "Just for that I'm not going to give you the surprise"

I burst out crying.

"I told you you had to do it perfectly," he yelled. "Playing the piano perfectly means that you sit there until you are completely finished."

That made me cry even louder. I now realized that Mother, who always wore such a nice smile of pride after I had done something to please Father, wasn't going to see me get the surprise, after all. I was expecting them both to make a great fuss over me for being such a good little girl, and I had bungled it all. My crying must have impressed Father, because he quickly relented. I have an idea he was as anxious to give me the surprise as I was to receive it. Well, he called Mother into the living room. Very ceremoniously he seated her in a big chair with the baby in her arms and little Helen at her side. I stood bowed and sniffling beside the piano, because the piano was my friend and Father had just given me the dickens for doing something wrong. I was a little wary, too, not knowing quite what was in the wind. The great big grin on my father's face wasn't very helpful. Finally he climbed up on a chair and reached for a large package that had been placed on top of a closet. This he now set on a table and unwrapped, producing a tiny violin case, the tiniest I have ever seen. All curiosity, I walked over to the table, staying a bit clear of Father because I was just a little afraid of him at that moment. Still, I was curious. I was now standing on tiptoe, craning my neck, as Father carefully took an adorable little violin out of the case and gave it to me. I didn't know what on earth to do with it, not even how to hold it. Not knowing what to think, I picked it up clumsily. All this while Father kept talking: "Isn't it beautiful? Isn't it gorgeous? Think of all the wonderful music you'll make with it! Soon you'll be playing for mamma and the baby and Helen. . . ."

Father paused a moment. "Pick it up," he said. "Put it under your chin—like this." He handed me a little bow. And that's as far as he got. For at that moment he received what must have been one of the greatest shocks of his life. Instead of beaming and gurgling with joy, I burst out crying all over again. I didn't know what to say. Great big tears rolled down my face. Here was the violin tucked awkwardly under my chin, my left hand holding it, a tiny bow in my right hand, Mother looking on expectantly, Father waiting for some sort of miracle. I didn't know what to do with the thing. All I knew was that I didn't want it, and I bawled louder and louder, till Father shouted at me furiously:

"What's the matter with you? I give you a big surprise, I go to the trouble of finding a nice little violin for you, and here you are crying your head off instead of being happy." Then a thought came to him. "Or are you happy? Is that why you're crying?"

I just went on wailing a blue streak. Finally I gripped the violin with my right hand and with a piercing scream flung it across the room, where it hit the wall and fell to the floor in pieces. I went on screaming and stamping my feet, and between sobs managed to say: "I want the piano! I know how to play the piano! I like the piano! I like to play the piano! I don't want the violin!"

That was my first real tantrum. Father must have been utterly crushed. His big dream had been to teach me the violin, to make of me the future female Elman. The hope that had begun in his bachelor days was shattered beyond repair. He stood there bewildered, speechless. Mother and Helen were silent, and now the baby began to cry, adding to the tension. The whole evening passed in that strained and miserable silence. I distinctly remember noticing that the cover of the keyboard was lowered on the piano. That was ominous, because it might mean that I would not be allowed to touch the piano again. I felt more wretched than ever. I don't remember having supper that night. All that comes back is the stinging misery—Father's sullen mood, the mute pain on Mother's face, the closed keyboard, the crying and crying, and Mother coming to me in bed and saying, "If you don't stop that noise, I'll put you on the floor." It was a black night.

The following morning Father pulled the blankets off me at six o'clock. That started it. From that day on, for as long as I lived at home and toured with my father, until my career as a child prodigy ended, I was dragged out of bed by Father at six o'clock every morning. That very first morning he said quite simply but very firmly:

"Come, Ruth, it's time for you to get up. Yesterday you told me you wanted the piano. That's fine with me. You're going to have the piano. You're going to have it for the rest of your life. I'm going to make you the finest pianist in the world. I wanted you to be a violinist. But you didn't. You like the piano. All right. It makes no difference to me which instrument you want. If the piano makes you happy, the piano it is."

Still in my nightie, without slippers, in an ice-cold house, I took his hand and walked out of the bedroom with him. My two little sisters and Mother were sound asleep. Father turned out the bedroom light and took me to the bathroom. Brusquely and matter-of-factly, he washed my face with cold water to make me fully awake. "Your mother will clean your teeth and fix you up later," he said. Then he took my hand again and led me into the living room, where he lifted me to the piano seat— he evidently couldn't wait for me to climb up as usual—raised the lid of the keyboard, and said: "All right, let's go through our scales."

I watched him remove the top off the metronome, and for the first time set it in motion for me.

"Play one note to each beat."

That was pure agony for me, trying to play one note to each beat, both hands absolutely together. Much as I tried and much as I wanted to please Father, I just couldn't do it, not for a while, anyway. One result of my clumsy efforts was that Mother was roused from her sleep and burst into the living room: "What is this? What's going on here?"

Gently but gravely Father shoved her out of the room through the sliding doors. "Go back to bed," he said. "We've got work to do!"

Poor Mother was soon back with a little robe and slippers which she put on me without a word. On her face was a frightened, bewildered look. Father only said: "That robe won't stay on long. She'll be warm all over in a few minutes. You'll see." And of course he was right.

Back to the ordeal of the metronome. It went slowly and painfully. Father never gave up. He knew exactly how to handle the new situation. Every time I made a mistake, he leaned over and, very methodically, without a word, slapped me across the face. I knew then I wasn't going to be coddled. It wasn't a matter of fear so much as astonishment with me. Father's behavior seemed so strange. He was a stickler for perfection. If I slipped in the middle of the C major scale, I would have to start all over again. And for each slip a matter-of-fact slap, till, I suppose, I came to accept it as part of the natural order of things. An hour after we started, Mother came in and proposed breakfast. Father merely growled at her:

"Go feed the other children. Don't you see we're working."

Mother and I exchanged startled glances. Yet I suppose I was happy in a way because I was being allowed to play the piano. And gradually the metronome and I became friends. Maybe it was because of Father's slaps, maybe it wasn't. It was past noon when Father finally indicated he was satisfied with my work. He hadn't even let me go to the bathroom during the six-hour stretch, and I am ashamed to say I made a few little mistakes of another kind right there at the piano.

"Go and get something to eat," said Father. To Mother, who complained that I must be starved, he snarled, "You mind your own business! This is my job and don't try to interfere. I know what's best for her. You just keep out of it."

Mother washed me and gave me some hot cereal.

Every day of his life Father used to take a nap after lunch between two and three o'clock, awakening with renewed vigor. That was an old habit from his European school days, accord-to him. After feeding me, Mother asked if I wanted a nap too, suggesting that I must be tired.

"I'm not the least bit tired," I said. "I'm a big girl now, not like those babies. I don't want a nap."

"You're going to have one anyway."

So she put me to bed, where I lay awake going over the morning's events. I felt strangely happy and proud that I had made the grade. I had tackled something that was pretty difficult. I knew this because Father had used the metronome with his grown-up pupils. I had the distinct feeling that I wasn't so dumb after all.

Yet it never dawned on me that it was highly unusual for a girl my age to be learning to play scales with the metronome in a sort of do-or-die routine with a punitive father. . . .

The moment the clock struck three, Father got up from his nap, took me out of my bed, and said, "You'd better not put your dress on—the perspiration will ruin it."

So I practiced in my petticoat, and to the day I was married I never wore a dress while practicing, always a slip. There were embarrassing moments when people called unexpectedly and found me in the living room at the piano in my undergarments, even when I was fifteen and sixteen. I felt it acutely, even though it was an old habit with me. Father never saw anything ridiculous in it. So, at precisely three, it was back to the piano and the metronome for me. Father had a sound way of improving keyboard technic at that point. After I mastered all the scales one note to a beat at, say, an eighty-reading on the metronome, he had me start all over again at eighty-four. When that was perfect, he set the metronome at eighty-eight, and so on, always with the metronome at a higher rate of speed.

It was six o'clock and dark when we finished. Finished the afternoon session, that is. After supper I was allowed to play for a few minutes with my two baby sisters. Then Father snatched me up again and plunked me down on the piano chair.

The living-room lamps were lit. Once again I went through the scales with the metronome. At intervals Mother would poke her head through the sliding doors to ask when I could be put to bed.

"As soon as we're through," Father replied, almost as if she had ceased to exist.

Finally it was over and I was bundled off to bed, a very self-satisfied and triumphant little girl, in spite of my smarting cheeks. This must have happened on a day that Father didn't have pupils. I remember the next day our practice sessions were more broken up. Because of his hasty tongue, Father never kept pupils for very long, nor were the lessons long either. When a pupil made a mistake, Father cut him down with biting words. The slaps were reserved for me alone. I guess it was soon after he saw what he could do with me that Father decided gradually to give up teaching others. He was no longer dependent on his pupils for a livelihood. Good revenue was coming from several property deals, and he must have already seen the promise of still higher dividends in me. Father was no slouch when it came to money matters.

ONE night, after supper, our little walk around the block came to a sudden halt at the end of our street. Father kept tugging me, but I wouldn't move. "Don't you hear music?" I said. "Oh, that's Miss Ellinwood's house," he replied, referring to one of his pupils. Still I wouldn't budge. I had never heard anything like it before. It was my first taste of chamber music. Up to then I had heard piano music and violin music and I knew what they sounded like together. This larger group of instruments offered a new and fascinating experience. I stood in front of the house in a spell, oblivious of Father and passers-by, saying over and over again, "Oh, how pretty!" At length, Father took me by the hand, and up the steps we went to ring the doorbell. "Excuse me," my father said to Miss Ellinwood, who came to the door. "My little girl heard the music and wondered whether you'd let her come in and watch." We were cordially invited in. The foursome consisted of Miss Ellinwood, her sister, her brother, and her mother. As they resumed playing I watched and listened with eyes, ears, and mouth wide open.

"Will I ever play with other instruments like that?" I asked Father when we walked back to our house.

"Better than that," he said. "You're going to play with a whole orchestra. Do you know what they call music for a piano and orchestra? They call it a concerto. Someday you're going to play lots and lots of concertos." I remember how the idea of playing wiith many musicians excited me. Because of that impromptu visit, Father engaged Miss Ellinwood's sister to come in for an hour every day to give me a little more formal instruction in the things Mother was teaching me. In exchange, Father gave her free violin lessons.

My progress must have been quite rapid. My scales were now moving at a very nice rate of speed on the metronome. I was already playing two notes to the beat with a metronome, and eager to move on. Father must have become perplexed at that point. Having expected me to be a violinist, he was now evidently at a loss what exactly to do with me as a next step on the piano. So he inquired around town for a piano instructor. The most recommended name was a Mrs. Ball. So over to Mrs. Ball's house we went one fine morning, and I shall never forget how startled that dignified lady was when Father, holding me by the hand, announced:

"My little daughter is ready to take piano lessons."

You have to realize that even now I'm not very tall. As a child I was about the height of a none too large doll. I was round and fat but extremely short. Mrs. Ball looked down at me from her great height.

"I think she's a little young. You'd better come back when she's six or seven years old—let us say, when she starts school."

Father said: "She already plays very well, and what's more, she can read and write and do arithmetic, too."

Mrs. Ball, obviously incredulous, said: "All right, let her play something for me."

"Go through your scales, Ruth," said Father.

I then proceeded to receive the second severe shock of my young life. I was used to practicing on our upright. Mrs. Ball's piano was a grand. Since Father had neglected to place me exactly at the middle of the keyboard, I was a little at a loss to find middle C. Unable to start, I only got more and more flustered.

"Go ahead, Ruth," Father commanded.

I recognized the stern note in his voice. It meant a good healthy slap was coming if I didn't get going. Mrs. Ball must have guessed what was ailing me.

"Do you know where middle C is, dear?"

I looked at the keys. Thinking desperately to myself, "Where is middle C, where is middle C?" I found another C and by the sound of it knew where I was sitting, and the whole thing came into focus. I was able to proceed with my C major scale. I tell this anecdote in detail because I know many other children are nonplused when they make the first change from the piano they play on at home and the piano they try at a friend's home. Parents are often troubled by this. Actually it is nothing to worry about. It is a minor adjustment we all learn to make, like getting used to a new bedroom or motorcar. I was also awestruck by the different size and shape of the grand piano. Mrs. Ball was more than a trifle surprised when I finished the C major scale.

"Can you play another one?"

Father said: "Go ahead, Ruth, play the A minor one."

I could see that he was proud of me, and I felt happy that I was able to please him. He wasn't an easy man to please, and praise to one's face came rarely and grudgingly from him. The A minor scale was followed by the G major and E minor scales, and so on down the line, till Mrs. Ball was quite overwhelmed.

When Father told her I knew all the scales and could do them perfectly with the metronome two notes to a beat, that I could read and write music and kept a little notebook in which I jotted down key signatures and so forth, Mrs. Ball was prepared to believe anything.

"What do I do with her now, Mrs. Ball?"

As answer, Mrs. Ball brought out some real piano music, simple, early-grades material, which she put on the piano rack in front of me. It was a duet with first and second parts, the easier part intended for the pupil, the other for the teacher. "Let me see you read this, Ruth," she said.

I had never really coped with printed music before, only what I was taught to write down myself. The first part gave me a little trouble at first, but the second time I was able to read it quite easily. Then Mrs. Ball sat down and played with me. I already understood something about rhythm because of the things I had been jotting in my notebook. So while she played the teacher part, I played the pupil part, and when we finished I said: "Now let me play the hard part." Mrs. Ball replied, "I don't think you can."

I looked at the music and saw that the "hard" part was written for two hands. I figured the right hand first and then the left, and then I put both hands together. Again I made a few little mistakes and again I caught that ominous note in Father's voice, "No, Ruth, No!" and I didn't much relish the idea of being slapped in front of Mrs. Ball. Flustered as I was, I worked the thing out and asked Mrs. Ball to play the easy part, and the duet went beautifully. She was completely sold. Father saw this and came right to the point:

"Mrs. Ball, I'm not interested right now in having you give my daughter lessons. I can teach her myself. What I want you to do is go with me to a music store and pick out some music for her. I'm a violinist. I don't know piano music."

Only somebody who knew my father can appreciate the importance of his admitting openly he didn't know something. Mrs. Ball, no doubt taken aback by his crude directness, got her hat and coat, and together we went to Tupper and Reed's music shop in Berkeley. Father wasn't too happy about the music Mrs. Ball picked. "Baby stuff," he protested. "My daughter is going to be a great artist." To which poor Mrs. Ball, who by now didn't know who was more baffling, me or my father, said, "But this is beginner's material, and your daughter needs it. Otherwise you'll be working her too fast." Father yielded grudgingly, and of course I made them both hum each of the pieces to me right then and there.

Now the reason that people were startled at what I could do at the piano was quite simple. Father was now making me practice nine hours a day, every single day of the week. No mistake ever went unpunished. The moment I missed a note I got a whack across my cheek. If the mistake was bad enough, I was almost hurled bodily from the piano. If it was even worse, I was banished from the living room for five minutes, during which time I would remain whimpering behind the sliding doors, wondering what black thoughts were crossing his mind. I would pry the doors open a little and see him smoking a cigarette and cursing away as he strode about the room. Catching sight of me, he would mutter an oath and then slam the sliding doors together. There I stood, shivering in my nightie, whining for my piano, in complete disgrace with my father. Finally the doors would open and he would say: "Are you going to be a good girl now?" When I said, "Yes," he went on: "You're going to do what I say—not make any more stupid mistakes. I hate dumbbells." He was to call me "dumbbell" so often that sometimes I had the feeling it was my nickname. It was a very grateful and apologetic little girl who toddled back to the piano.

I imagine there were two equally important drives in my life at that time. There was, first, the pure joy of being able to play the piano and there was the overpowering desire to please my father. Now pleasing Father was almost a superhuman achievement. Little that Mother did ever satisfied him.

He criticized the roast, the way she dressed, the way the house looked. He was forever finding fault with how the neighbors raised their children. For his pupils he seemed to have only a cold contempt. So, because his normal state was displeasure, I was in ecstasy when he so much as nodded approval of my playing. Being a good little girl meant learning as fast as possible to do things the way Father wanted them done.

That was the atmosphere in which I grew up, Father's critical attitude to everything and everybody, his fanatic perfectionism and dogmatism. I came to accept it as perfectly normal. There was, for example, his attitude toward dolls. They were anathema to him. I remember a discarded rubber doll whose head little Gloria had bitten off. Father caught me in the act of picking it off the floor to play with one day. In a voice of scorn he said: "What do you want to play with that for? It hasn't any brains. You can at least talk to one of your sisters. A doll is a stupid waste of time." I never lost my yearning for a doll of my own, and was always ashamed to admit it.

My other schooling was progressing nicely with Miss Ellinwood, who gave me an hour's reading and writing every day. At Christmas time I remember she brought some paste-ups for me to make a calendar for Mother. "But what shall I make for Daddy?" I asked, and she said, "What would you like to make for him? Another calendar?" I shook my head. "Oh, no, my father must have something musical." Miss Ellinwood thought it would be hard to find a musical calendar. "That isn't what I meant," I said. "Maybe I could write something myself." Miss Ellinwood suggested a song, and I tried ever so hard to make up a tune I could put down on music paper. Nothing I tried sounded like the kind of song to give Father as a Christmas gift. So I got Miss Ellinwood to help me write down "London Bridge Is Falling Down." It was all in my own handwriting. I went to the piano to be certain that the timing was absolutely correct. I didn't quite trust Miss Ellinwood's judgment when it came to writing music. I remember I argued the point of writing a quarter note with a dot, followed by an eighth note and two more quarter notes for the first measure. She wanted me to write four quarter notes. We struggled and struggled and I won. For some reason, I can't recall what Father's comment was or whether I ever gave him his gift. What stands out is the way I worked on it and the dispute with Miss Ellinwood.

How did Mother take all this? I suppose she concluded very early that, much as she might want to, she was helpless to stop it. Father had assumed complete control of me in the living room. That was his domain. Any protest of Mother's about the ordeal of practice or punishment he took as a form of trespass. In time she ceased making any attempt to interfere. She became meek and resigned, perhaps even awed by the results Father achieved with his driving persistence. She would say, "Why do you do this? Why didn't you warn me what this would be like? Why, why?" Stunned, amazed, even horrified at times, but rebellious never. This much she knew because Father had made it clear to her from the start: boy or girl, he was determined to make a musician of his first child. It would take training, stern discipline, but he would see to it that I would attain the greatest heights in music. With that would come fame and fortune for us all. What mother could object to such a prospect? Deep down it wounded her to see me subjected to harsh language and a rigorous routine. The beatings that came later were another matter. I was never sure how much she knew about the more violent outbreaks in the living room. Maybe, too, she became resigned because I myself gave no sign of rebellion.

I remember how early in my practice years, if I yelled too loudly from a series of whacks on the cheeks, she would rush frightened into the room, crying "You'd better stop that, Josef!

What are you trying to do, kill her?" Father would turn on her furiously, "Your work is in the kitchen with the kids. Mine is with Ruth. Leave us alone!" I gradually learned to soft-pedal my howling, not to antagonize Father still more.

Mainly I was disciplined for not being serious enough. When walking out with Father, I was told I took too great an interest in the children skipping rope or shooting marbles in the street. I was warned that if I skipped rope I would fall down and break my precious hands. Other youngsters on the block had dogs. I was told not to go near a dog lest it bite off one of my fingers. I was terrified of dogs for years. A girl next door had a tricycle, on which I was invited to ride. But no, that, too, was forbidden. It would turn over and crush my hands. I was never allowed to close the door when I got into an automobile: being clumsy and stupid, I would almost certainly get my fingers caught in the door. No dolls, no skipping rope, no pets, no tricycles, no marbles, nothing except the grinding routine of nine hours a day at the keyboard and lessons in reading and writing and geography in between. How the rest of my family stood that ceaseless hammering at the piano I shall never know.

I doubt if Father ever considered what the neighbors might think till the doorbell rang one night. Around the corner from us lived a Mrs. Gorrill, whose husband, a professor at the University of California, I believe, was looked up to in the neighborhood. I was in the middle of my marathon practice work when the Gorrills paid us a formal call after supper. As usual, I had been practicing all day, since six in the morning, except for the one hour with Miss Ellinwood, two short walks around the block, and a brief nap after lunch. The shades were drawn, and Father, who was a little put out by the interruption, wondered out loud who might be coming at this late hour. Now the Gorrills were not friends of ours. Father rarely made friends; when he did, he speedily lost them. His wasn't a friendly personality at all. So he was surprised, but in a way honored, to find Mr. and Mrs. Gorrill at the door. They stepped in, sat down, and I was told to leave the room and call Mother, who acted pleased at the prospect of company. My two sisters were put to bed and I remained in the kitchen. I promptly went to the toy piano, and although it was nothing compared to what I could now do on the big piano, I tinkled at it playfully. Pretty soon I heard loud voices, Father's loudest of all. I crept into the dining room and listened at the sliding doors. Mr. and Mrs. Gorrill were telling Father that it was wrong to have so much piano playing going on all day long, every day of the week, and that he'd better do something about it because the neighbors were all steamed up about it. Now nobody could tell Father off without being told off with interest. I heard him get up and violently open the street door.

"I don't go into your house and tell you what to do!" he shouted. "Whose business is it what I do in my own home? Ruth is my daughter, not yours. I'm going to do with her what I want. She is a genius. She's going to be the greatest pianist in the world, and you and all your fine friends in the neighborhood aren't going to stop her."

Mr. Gorrill made a threatening retort, and then I heard Mrs. Gorrill say: "Aren't you afraid something is going to snap up here?" I could hear her fingers click. (Several years later, while on tour, Father met Mrs. Gorrill somewhere and he reminded her of her remark, saying, with a finger at his temple, "Nothing snapped up here.")

"Work never hurt anybody," Father shot back. "You Americans are too soft with your kids. The only trouble now is that my daughter Ruth isn't in Europe. There she would get first-class training." I should point out that his references to me were almost always as "my daughter Ruth," as if that were my complete name. My sisters were merely "Helen" and "Gloria" or just "the kids." Only I enjoyed the added distinction.

"That's the place for us, Europe," Father was saying, "where we would be left alone and where neighbors wouldn't come bursting in and telling us what to do."

The Gorrills must have seen they were dealing with an unusual person and beat a tactful retreat. Our next callers were the Wrights from across the street. Their mission was also one of neighborly protest about the incessant din pouring into the street from our living room. That visit had a friendly ending, however. Mr. Wright, a violinist himself, forgot the purpose of the call when he discovered that Father was himself a violinist. They were soon playing duets together, the closest thing to neighborliness Father ever achieved. The rest of the street set up quite a clamor, however, the effect of which was that at night, instead of having to play loudly, I was made to raise my fingers as high as I could and come down softly at the bottom of each note. I think they soon put Father down as a lunatic with a daughter who was either a freak or another lunatic like him. Father said I was a genius, and he was going to show the world how right he was. I liked it. I thought it all a lot of fun. The truth is I didn't know enough to regard it as anything else. The only objection I had was the way Father would get after me if I failed to live up to what he wanted. This occurred more and more frequently as I got new things to play. Each new composition now began with these words:

"Let's see if you can learn this without a wallop."

I am ashamed to admit that until I was fourteen years old, and had already been on the concert stage for ten years, the only new piece I ever learned without a slap was the first movement of Schumann's piano concerto. For some reason I showed immediate affinity for that music, learning it in perhaps three hours. I felt completely secure with it that very first time I played it, and Father, tough critic that he was, paid me the compliment, for once, of keeping his hands to himself.

ONE of the first principles that Father hammered into me was this: whatever I did, no matter what it was, there was only one way to do it—the right way, and the right way was perfection. And he arrogated to himself the right of deciding, in anything that concerned his daughter Ruth, when that perfection had been reached. It never once dawned on him, I feel certain, that there could be any two ways about it.

There was always one thing he insisted on. I was never to play a simplified arrangement of a piece of music by some master of the keyboard. Not that he wanted me to play difficult music right off. The best start, he thought, was the original music. and the greatest composers had written enough piano music that was simple enough for beginners. He hated music in a second and easier version of the original. Working at what the composer himself had written was the best way of educating my taste and my hands, he felt. Now among the pieces Mrs. Ball had picked out, at Father's prodding, were small things by Bach, Handel, Haydn, Mozart, Beethoven, and Grieg. By Christmas time, when I was nearly four years of age, I had learned, to Father's satisfaction, twenty-one separate compositions by these composers. When I had mastered a few of them, Father brought me back to Mrs. Ball. His idea was not so much to secure her services as teacher as to show me off. That good lady couldn't believe what she saw. Out of sheer interest she volunteered to take me on. "But do you know enough?" Father asked bluntly. "I shall tell you when I don't," said Mrs. Ball coldly. On that basis, there now began a series of visits to her studio, all without fee, bless her. Each time she seemed more impressed than ever. There was rarely anything to correct in my playing. She would shake her head in bewilderment. Not once did she suspect that the miracle was nothing but a matter of relentless daily practice imposed on his own child by a harsh taskmaster.

Among many other things I owe Mrs. Ball a method of attack that I use to this day. To get over the idea of a staccato note, she told me that staccato meant "up." My hand was supposed to come up off the keyboard at least six inches. Soon each of my little compositions bristled with arrows, those pointing down at the beginning of a phrase, others pointing up at a staccato note. I still recall a little minuet by Mozart that she had all fixed up with arrows showing which direction my hand was supposed to go.

The only time I was ever secretly angry at Mrs. Ball was during a studio recital at which several of her pupils, I the youngest of them, performed for parents and friends. I watched the others as they bowed and returned to their seats, and so, copycat that I was, I planned to follow the same procedure when my turn came. I played my piece, and when everybody applauded I spread my dress between my hands and started to bow, at which point Mrs. Ball came running over, picked me off the floor, and stood me up on the bench as if I were a little doll. She told me to bow, after which she took me down and put me back in my seat. She had taken all the pleasure out of it for me, because the thought of bowing from the floor like the others had made me feel grown up.

One of the reasons I liked music so much was that it set me apart from my sisters and all the other children around me. It gave me a curious feeling of being adult. From the way Father spoke and behaved and the way I was constantly being exhibited to others, I knew I was something special. Father kept pounding it home by scornful remarks about playthings and such. If I showed signs of wanting to be just an ordinary little girl, like wanting to cuddle my sisters' dolls or make a little noise or jump up and down and run with the neighborhood kids or—my biggest dream of all—ride Gail Wright's tricycle, Father would come down on me with his pail of ice-cold water: "That's all baby stuff! You're not a baby. You're a musician! Stay away from those kids and their stupid games. It's all a waste of time! You've got to act like a grown-up young lady."

And so I couldn't have any ice-cream cones or hear about the three bears and Cinderella in brightly colored books. Instead, Mother now read me special bedtime stories about Mozart and Beethoven and Haydn and Chopin. As far as I can recall, I never tasted ice cream till I was six years old—and that was in far-off Berlin on a Sunday afternoon at an outdoor concert on the Bayerischer Platz. Father broke down finally and bought each of his three little daughters an ice-cream cone. The joy of it was indescribable. When he saw that, he turned it into another form of torture. On another extremely hot Sunday shortly thereafter, I asked Father three times if I could have ice cream. On the promise that I could if I played well, I made an extra-special effort to please him. Later, during our walk, I reminded him of his promise. This time he refused on the ground that all afternoon I had been asking for ice cream instead of paying attention to my music.

The day arrived when Mrs. Ball agreed with Father there was nothing more she could teach me. As the next step she advised him to take me to her old teacher, a Mrs. Simpson, who also lived in Berkeley. Like Mrs. Ball, Mrs. Simpson, a sweet and kindly old lady, saw at once that she was dealing with something a little on the freakish side, technically advanced far beyond my four years. So she immediately started me on an elementary book of theory and harmony. I proceeded to learn the names of all the intervals, of the different triads. I learned to transpose, till transposing all the themes of all the pieces I studied became second nature. In studying the triads, she told me that just as every little girl had a name, so every triad had a name. So I soon knew chords as "tonic," "supertonic," "mediant," "subdominant," just as I knew my sisters as "Gloria" and "Helen." I was made to identify them in their proper order in the scales. It was all elementary harmony, but it usually comes much later in a child's training, and I knew it thoroughly at four.

From the day Father told me what a concerto was, it was my greatest ambition to play with an orchestra. It became associated in my mind with all the brightly colored places on the large map tacked on our kitchen wall. I dreamed of traveling to far-off places of blue and pink and crossing large expanses of green. Playing a concerto meant something still more precious: beautiful clothes. After I had appeared in two or three student recitals at Mrs. Ball's or Mrs. Simpson's, Mother started a new bedtime routine with me. As she bathed me before putting me to sleep, she told me how, if I played very well, I would soon be giving concerts before large audiences. And, to do that, I would have to wear beautiful white dresses and white shoes and white socks. I would come out on a big stage and lots and lots of people would be watching as I spread out my dress and curtsied. If I played well, they would shout *Bravo!* and if I played very well, I would get oodles and oodles of roses—and Mother knew how I adored roses, especially big red roses. There was nothing in "Cinderella" to equal that glorious vision, and perhaps it made up for not being able to play with my sisters.

Then there were the stories of the boy Bach and the boy

Mozart, stories which my mother read to me as if I, too, were a little Bach or Mozart and there were no reason on earth why I couldn't do what they did if I worked hard enough. I was deeply impressed by the story of how Bach as a boy stole and copied some music his brother thought too difficult for him and how he kept it all in his head, every note of it, when his copy was taken away from him. If Bach could do that wonderful thing, why couldn't I? I identified myself with the tiny boy Mozart, who beat little Marie Antoinette in a musical contest but lost to her in a footrace. They were my real friends, Bach and Mozart, and their music was my playground; at least that's how Mother and Father both taught me to look at it. The rest was "baby stuff" and "a waste of time."

My latest composition at the piano always became my favorite, though not at the start. I dreaded getting to work on anything new. That was when Father was most irritable and violent. Gradually I learned to accept it as a necessary hurdle, and once I had mastered the new piece, I loved it above all the others. During that period I ran into my most serious snarl memorizing the E-flat major sonata of Haydn. For some years that little sonata held first place in the total number of whacks and wallops I rolled up while trying to memorize it. It just refused to go down the hatch. Once I ran in to Mother screaming, "I hate that sonata! I hate that sonata!" And she said, "You say that about every new piece, and then you run in to me and rave about it." But this was special. That sonata must have hurt Mother more than it hurt me. In its blameless measures Father reached a new peak of ill temper. He swore at me in five languages. He boxed my ears, pushed me violently off the piano bench, pulled my shoes off, and if there had been a dress on me, he would have pulled that off, too, in his wild rage. During one such seizure Mother burst in and threw her arms protectively about me. Father shrieked at her, "Keep out of this! It's none of your business!" A sudden fear gripped me that if I yielded to Mother, I would be forbidden to touch the piano again. I pushed her away from me, screaming, "Daddy's right! Stay out of this! It's none of your business!"

What a bewildered little girl I was then. I didn't like being hurt, and my father's blows were far from love taps. But I didn't want to lose either the piano or his respect. On the other hand, I wanted my mother badly. I needed her protection, and yet at such times as these it was a threat to the thing that was dearest to me, my music. What a dilemma for both of us to be in. Three times she seriously thought of breaking with Father. I clearly remember the first of them—in the middle of the night in Berkeley. I was suddenly aroused from my sleep by loud, angry voices. The door opened and Mother, crying, her nose bleeding, came to my side and flung her arms about me. "We're going to get dressed and go back East to live with Aunt Becky," she said. "Wouldn't you like that, Ruthie?" I must have done some fast thinking. "Does she have a piano?" I asked, looking into Mother's startled face. "No," she said. "What do you want a piano for? You get beaten all the time anyway." I said, "I like the piano," and when Mother said, "But how can you stand all those beatings?" we both started crying in each other's arms, and she put me to bed again. That was when Mother knew there was no fighting it. I wonder whether any two parents ever had a problem child quite like me.

My ties with Mrs. Simpson soon came to an end—whether by mutual consent with Father or by Father's growing conviction that no teacher was good enough for me, I'm not sure. Our next instructor was a Mrs. Swift, who lasted two sessions, for which she was paid the six dollars that were to go for a month's lessons. I remember being fascinated by the way Mrs. Swift taught me to distinguish between *crescendo* and *diminuendo*. They were to be achieved by chanting softly to oneself,

"Up the hill we go," and, "Down the hill we go." You never know what little idea is going to stick in a child's mind. That one idea, simple, even childish as it would appear to an adult, stuck. It somehow helped me to look at my music in terms of going uphill in a *crescendo* and downhill in a *diminuendo*. The suggestion was fruitful because it made me view the musical phrase in a new light. However, Father had enough of her after two lessons. Incidentally, she was the only teacher ever to receive money from Father. With the others—Mrs. Ball, Mrs. Simpson, Mrs. Kennedy in America; Cortot, Schnabel, Boulanger, Rachmaninoff, Bachaus in Europe—it was a case either of Father pleading poverty or of their volunteering to teach me, as they expressed it to Father, "for the pure joy of watching your daughter's talent develop."

The hunt was now on for a teacher who could carry me beyond the combined abilities of Mrs. Ball, Mrs. Simpson, and Mrs. Swift. In desperation Father sought out Dr. Albert Elkus, head of the Music Department of the University of California in Berkeley. That must have been early in January of 1929, when I was barely four years old. Dr. Elkus was conducting a class in harmony when we paid him our surprise visit. On the blackboard were a great number of triads. The class was almost over, when we broke in on Dr. Elkus's lecture, with me in my little blue sweater, timidly hanging on to my father's hand. The students were still sitting there as Father presented me like a prize pumpkin to Dr. Elkus:

"This is my little daughter Ruth. She knows harmony, too."

Dr. Elkus eyed me dubiously. "Oh, yes? She's a little young for that, I should think."

"Why don't you try her out on some of the stuff you've just been teaching those youngsters, and see for yourself?"

There was absolute silence among the watching students as Dr. Elkus asked me a couple of easy questions, such as what is the dominant of B major, and what is the relative minor of E major. There was nothing to it for me, but the whole class stood there gaping. Dr. Elkus, looking impressed and a bit puzzled, turned to Father: "Well, what can I do for you?" Father replied that he wanted him to recommend a good piano teacher.

"You mean, she plays the piano, too?" asked Dr. Elkus.

So I had to play a Bach "invention" to prove Father's contention that I could. Everybody of course applauded and I felt very pleased with myself. Then Dr. Elkus said he really didn't know of anybody in Berkeley who could develop an exceptional talent like mine, that maybe the place for a "young genius" like me was Europe. Which was of course Father's cue.

"That's what I wanted to hear somebody of your standing say," he said. "But I don't know how to go about it. Maybe you can help."

"For the time being the best piano teacher in Berkeley for your daughter is a woman named Mrs. Alma Schmidt Kennedy," said Dr. Elkus. "She studied with the great Leschetizky and has a fine reputation. Meanwhile I wish you'd bring your daughter to see me from time to time. I'm very much interested in the way she develops."

Having obtained the address from Dr. Elkus, Father and I proceeded to visit Mrs. Kennedy. The first impression made by that visit on me was the fact that in the middle of this great big studio of Mrs. Kennedy's were two pianos. Two pianos in one room seemed a needless extravagance. It was explained to me that the second piano took the place of an orchestra in a concerto. Again that magic word! Immediately I was convinced that Mrs. Kennedy was an excellent teacher. The fact that concertos were played in this studio was qualification enough in my eyes. I wanted so badly to learn a concerto! Like everybody else before her, Mrs. Kennedy fell an easy victim to my keyboard charms. At once she offered to take me as pupil, which suited Father fine, especially when she generously added that she would expect no compensation other than the reward of watching me grow. I knew soon enough that I had finally come in contact with the real thing, added to which was the sincere personal liking she developed for me.

There was something else that attracted me to Mrs. Kennedy. When I played well for Mrs. Ball or Mrs. Simpson or Mrs. Swift, they rewarded me with a star of merit. Mrs. Kennedy did so by reading stories to me from books on Greek and Roman mythology. Which was how I first came into contact with the myth of Theseus and the stone. That stone came later to symbolize the crushing weight of my father, a stone that had to be lifted by me alone if I was ever to live and breathe in my own right. Mrs. Kennedy also happened to be on the staff of Mills College, a post of enormous prestige in musical and social circles of the Bay Area. Now it was clear to Mrs. Kennedy that I couldn't go very far without a sponsor. Father had quite convinced her he was penniless. This was far from the truth, of course. Even without his pupils, he derived a tidy revenue from several juicy real estate deals. By the time I was four, he had put aside a very nice little nest egg. But if he was going to risk money on my future, he wanted to be certain it was someone else's money, not his. Many would call him a shrewd businessman; he was also the closest man with money I have ever known. Mother told me he refused to buy her a dish of ice cream on their honeymoon because he said he couldn't afford it. Once he came home with what he called a terrific surprise for Mother. It was a quarter of a pound of butter! Fine clothes for himself were something else. They were always of the best and costliest material, perhaps because that lasted longer. In everything else, he was an absolute tightwad. This stinginess had a sadistic side, too. All you had to do not to get something from Father was to say you wanted it. If it came at all, it had to come of his own free will. But that happened very rarely. I couldn't win there either.

As my lessons progressed with Mrs. Kennedy, it occurred to her that in a very short time I would know enough pieces to give a concert of my own. That, she thought, would be the ideal way of attracting wealthy sponsors. And the ideal place would be the big auditorium of Mills College. With this in mind, she asked the late President Aurelia Rheinhardt and Luther Marchant of Mills College to hear me play. Gratified by their reactions, she now settled down to preparing me for a forty-five-minute program. That was in May, 1929. There was enough music to choose from of the literature I already knew. So I worked away at my program in Mrs. Kennedy's studio. Father would join Mrs. Kennedy upstairs in the little gallery. It became a little game. I would pretend the studio was a concert hall and I would walk out and play. First came a group of pieces by Bach, followed by Mozart's C major sonata. There was a regular intermission, after which I played a Haydn minuet and Beethoven's G major theme and variations. I was especially proud of the latter because of the cross-handed passages in the final variation. I just loved the idea of crossing my hands over the keyboard. Somehow it made me feel adult. Intermission time and the short intervals between groups were quite interesting. "Backstage" in our little game was a wall of paneled oak in Mrs. Kennedy's studio. I would issue from this wall to play my numbers, and, after bowing, solemnly return to it. My hands would be so moist from perspiration that I placed them palms flat on the panel, thus defacing that beautiful wood. The marks remained as plain as day. Mrs. Kennedy, bless her heart, later shellacked the spot to preserve the print of my little hands.

Father was always finding that I had outgrown somebody.

The latest victim was Miss Ellinwood, who had taken charge of my schoolwork. The bartered lessons were terminated abruptly one day, and I found myself toddling over to the Anna Head School, one of Berkeley's most exclusive seminaries for young ladies. It didn't take Father long to persuade the headmistress, a Miss Wilson, that the school would be doing itself a favor by granting his daughter Ruth a scholarship. They agreed on one hour a day for me. I was placed in a class that took care of first, second, third, and fourth-graders, and in very little time I was reading with the fourth-graders whose average age was ten or eleven. The plain truth of the matter is that I was one of those precocious kids. I'd hate to know myself today as I was then. I'm told I could be as fresh and arrogant as the worst of them. In more ways than one I was developing into quite a little replica of Father. The pictures of me show a veritable female counterpart of Tom Thumb, enveloped in a size-six or -seven school uniform. Navy-blue skirt, white cotton blouse, blue sailor bowtie, navy-blue sweater, all hung on me in ill-fitting caricature. Father used to buy extra-large clothes for the three of us with the idea that we would save him money by growing into them. It never dawned on him that by the time we did the clothes would be worn out. In general, clothes were a sorry sport for my sisters and me. For a time I used to wear the hand-me-downs of other children because Father played the poor act so often that people who didn't know the true circumstances took pity on us. Several garments so acquired started with me, passed to Helen, and in due time ended on little Gloria. Father's wardrobe psychology was at its most disastrous a few years later when it came to buying traveling dresses. For that necessity he had to lay out money himself. But the buying was always done on the same principle. I always began by getting into a dress that was several sizes too large for me.

By the time it fitted me, it was no longer fresh-looking, and even he didn't want me to go out on tour looking shabby and out of fashion. By the time any dress of mine got to Helen or Gloria it was completely passé. Helen didn't get her first brand-new coat till I was eight years old and already lining Father's pocket with fat concert fees. After a while Mother learned to take advantage of Father's absences on tour with me. Wardrobes were then freely replenished on the chance that Father wouldn't know the difference when he got back home.

Preparations for my concert went on feverishly. The date set was May 11, 1929, the time 2:30 P.M., the place Mills College. There was some publicity in the press, but not as a professional concert. The avowed purpose was to demonstrate to musicians, teachers, and newspaper people that a child of four could actually play a full program by heart. The ulterior aim was to persuade some wealthy individual that there were far less interesting ways of spending money than to finance the career of a prodigiously gifted infant. Mrs. Nixon, a friend of Mrs. Kennedy, made a lovely little concert dress for me, a white silk marquisette embroidered with clusters of flowers around the neck and hem. Weeks before the concert Father made me put it on again and again for company, not to exhibit the dress, however. "Show the lady how you're going to bow in it," Father would say. Whether the dress was pretty or not didn't matter. I would dutifully take one side of the dress in my right hand and the other in my left, spread the dress wide, put both heels together, my toes out, and bow from the waist. That was how I took my first bow, a bow endlessly rehearsed before members of the family and company in our living room.

One day, early in April, I overheard Mrs. Kennedy remark to

Father in her studio: "Except for the pedaling, she plays like an adult, and of course that can't be helped."

The remark irritated me at the moment and rankled for days, because the whole idea of playing the piano and making music made me feel grown up, set apart from "babies" like my younger sisters. A few days later I happened to play for Miss Alice Seckels in her studio at the Fairmont Hotel in San Francisco. As the manager of most of the big artists who came to San Francisco, Miss Seckels was an important person for me to impress. Moreover, she was the manager of the most famous prodigy of the day, Yehudi Menuhin. This was all thoroughly hammered home to me by Father and Mrs. Kennedy.

Miss Seckels' studio resembled a little concert hall, with a tiny stage at one end, where debut concerts were often held. On the appointed afternoon I walked out on the little stage and climbed up on the bench in front of the grand piano. Before I could bring my hands down on the first notes, I heard Miss Seckels say:

"What a pity her feet have to dangle like that! Can't we put some books underneath them?"

Crushed by her words, I fought back my tears as people scurried about for some telephone books and piled them up on the floor in front of me. I played, but I felt painfully unprofessional about the whole business. Later Miss Seckels suggested to Father that before my concert he could have a plain wooden box made to the right height and finished in shining black to match the piano. My feet could rest on that.

"It will look more proper," she said.

This time I protested. "It won't *sound* proper, because I can't use the pedals until I reach the floor."

"Maybe we can do something about that, too," said Miss Seckels. "With pegs made to fit over the pedals we might be able to rig something up. I know just the man for it."

I was overjoyed. All the way home to Berkeley my eyes were fastened on Father's foot on the gas pedal of the car. In my mind I had already begun practicing the use of the pedal. Mrs. Kennedy later insisted that I knew naturally how to pedal correctly from the moment Miss Seckels' carpenter constructed the extension device for us. I found it simple and fascinating. To me, pedaling was for the purpose of holding notes that should be held but that my hands were too small to hold, and emphasizing a beautiful harmony. Many years later I learned the subtleties of the fine art of pedaling and practiced with the pedal. But perhaps the reason for my clear playing in the early years was that I did all my practicing without the pedal and applied it only as the last step in the learning process—like the icing on a cake!

I used the pedal extension from my debut at Mills College till I made my first American tour in 1933 at the age of eight. The Baldwin Piano Company had then built two concert grands for me with special legs that were six inches shorter than the regulation size. These two pianos went everywhere with me, and everywhere they went, George Wieland, my tuner (now the head of Baldwin's West Coast reconstruction department), went too. My proudest accomplishment, when I reached the age of ten, was being able for the first time to play and pedal a regulation-size piano. The Baldwin warehouse in New York still has the short legs of the two pianos that traveled with me during those early years.

The morning of May 11 we went over to Mills College to be coached in where and how I was to walk to and from the piano. Small metal markers in the center of the stage were pointed out to me as the place where I was to bow from. I was then to walk around and seat myself from the right side of the piano. I was assured by Father, Mrs. Kennedy, and all the other adults present that by so doing the audience would see more of me. But there I rebelled. At one or two student recitals I had seen performers seat themselves from the left. That was the way I wanted it to be. I insisted so strongly that they had to give in. Playing before an audience was a triumph I felt I had earned for working hard. The least I expected after it was over was lots of red roses and candy. So Mother had assured me during my baths.

There was one thing of which I was positive. I knew I wasn't going to make a single mistake during the whole concert. And this is how I knew. A few days earlier, during practice, a sickening thought crossed my mind. "What happens," I asked Father, "if I make a mistake in the middle of my concert?" and Father very obligingly told me that people went to concerts with bags full of rotten eggs and vegetables, particularly tomatoes, and if you hit a wrong note, these rotten eggs and vegetables, particularly tomatoes, would come flying at you. Sure enough, the very next day I missed a note in going over the Beethoven variations. Without a word Father disappeared through the sliding door, strode into the kitchen, opened the refrigerator, reappeared through the sliding doors, and threw a tomato at me. I ducked and the piano got it. Mother was furious because of the mess.

Further guarantee that I would play exactly as Father wanted was this: to the left of the piano on the stage was a chair. In that chair sat Father and in his lap lay a brief case containing all my music. The omen was clear. He sat looking at me throughout the program as if to say, "You'd better do well or you'll never see any of this music or the piano again," not to mention other dire consequences. I did well; that's all there was for me to do. I took my last bows, and there were the roses and the boxes of candy and the people milling around, and for the first time I heard the mysterious word "autograph." I had to run around looking for Mother to ask what the word meant. "Oh, just sign your name when somebody asks for an autograph." And so I was a star!

Then came the hullaballoo in the newspapers, some of it front-page stuff all over the Bay Area in Berkeley and Oakland and San Jose and San Francisco. They made quite a sensation of it. One writer said nothing like this had taken place since Mozart. Others found the explanation in the size of my forehead: a large head, a large brain. Comparisons were made with other large heads and high foreheads that had meant genius in history. Papers carried pictures of the size of my hand against a ruler to show how tiny it was and yet what miracles of skill it performed. Much of it was nonsense, of course. The plain fact was that I *did* play these compositions; that they *could* be done by a child of four. The marvel, I suppose, was not how I did them, though I played with a certain security and style, however infantile, but that I did them at all. Speculation about magic and hypnosis was rife. One or two feature stories even raised the specter of reincarnation, the candidates for a previous existence being Mozart, Chopin, and Beethoven. Several newspapers referred to father as a Svengali. Only a spell of some unfathomable kind could account for the way I played Bach and Beethoven. An aura of lurid fantasy grew about me.

To the Svengali theories Father responded with names like Yehudi Menuhin, Ruggiero Ricci, Mozart. Were their fathers "Svengalis"? Menuhin and Ricci were doing fantastic things at seven and eight, at which age Mozart was already a musical veteran. The Menuhin-Ricci parallel also served Father to taunt me. If they could, why couldn't I? The difference of three or four years between them and me, at our respective debuts, he seemed to imply, was too trivial to speak of. He flung at me the names of Menuhin's sister Hepzibah as a pianist of six "who could play circles around me." In similar vein I was reminded again and again of little Mozart, traveling from royal court to royal court at the age of four or five, getting gold boxes and diamond garters from kings and queens. "And you, you, sticking in one little town giving one little concert. Why, you're a regular nothing compared to Mozart." The idea was to get me to work harder by making himself still harder to please. Anything anybody else could do, I was bound and determined to show I could do too. Besides, we couldn't let down the excited prophets of the Bay Area press. There was Roy Harrison Danforth, of the Oakland *Tribune*, for example. In reviewing the first Mills College concert, he said I showed the "relish of a connoisseur." More:

"They tell us she is four; she does not look a day over three, nor does her playing sound as if she were a day under sixteen. Her father was the *deux ex machina*, but she only needed his governance until her fingers fell upon the keys: thereafter she was that individual, Ruth Slencyznski.

"She was enjoying the music, not for the mere doing of it but for the satisfaction it bestowed upon her budding esthetic sense. This was the thing that it was necessary for us to know, to be satisfied with her. For if she were merely an automaton, however precisely and assiduously and extensively she played, the augury would not be good."

Then came a few last words of prophecy: "Music already possesses this child, and more and more it will possess her."

Whatever else the concert had done, it had proved one thing to Father's satisfaction: I could memorize and play a full-size program without mishap. With ecstatic comments pouring in from all sides, what happened in Father's mind was simple enough. If my playing could attract the attention of both the public and the press, then my playing was worth money. "If my daughter is good enough to listen to and to write about in the newspapers, then she is good enough to be paid *for my work*." The answer was a second concert, the sooner the better. This took place on October 29, 1929. The program was entirely different and so was the admission. This time people paid to see Father's prize exhibit, paid up to $3.00 a seat. The auditorium was packed to the doors and father cleared $1,100. I was called a "phenomenon of nature" by one critic the following day. Another paper proudly carried a picture spread of all the prodigies who had issued from the Bay Area. There they were: Menuhin, Ricci, Isaac Stern, Grisha Guloboff, Ruth Slenczynski. I, the caption read, was the most fantastic of all. It was then, I believe, that Alexander Fried first wrote about me in the San Francisco *Chronicle*.

"Ruth," he said, "is already able to display an amazing and expertly developed musical talent. She handles the not-inconsiderable technical difficulties of her program without any insecurity whatsoever. She has lively fingers, a flexible and sensitive touch, solid rhythm, and tact for pedaling."

And again that reassuring note of prophecy: "She seems definitely embarked on an extraordinary career, even in this day of prodigies."

There seemed no doubt about it. I had my future all cut out for me, and so had my father. His vision of Europe and limitless affluence beyond was brighter than ever.

WHILE I was mastering the new program, Mrs. Kennedy had already started me on a concerto, the "Coronation" concerto of Mozart, with the idea that I might eventually play it with the Young People's Symphony of San Francisco. Father took me to a few of their concerts. I'm afraid my reaction, as I look back, was obnoxious and arrogant. I told Father I didn't like the idea of playing with "a bunch of kids." I would play with a real symphony or none at all. I thought the programs childish because parts of symphonies instead of whole symphonies were played. I thought it was "kid stuff" when the audience was asked to join in the singing of children's songs. That wasn't music, certainly not the kind I wanted. Father had made me think of music as something sacred, like going into a church or a cathedral. You sat there in awe and respect. The audiences at the Young People's Symphony Concerts did not sit the way I expected them to. How could I know that what I felt was only a twisted and exaggerated form of childishness of my own?

Something needs stressing at this point. It is this: whatever the merit of my playing, it wasn't the result of any phenomenal or miraculous gift. I was merely doing what I was taught very rigorously to do. Neither to himself nor to me did Father make any pretense beyond that. The results, such as they were, were dearly won by a driving, incessant process of teaching and learning. I played as I had been taught to play, no more, no less.

But a major divergence from the truth of even that must be revealed here. In all the newspaper interviews Father insisted no one had taught me but himself. Now that was an out-and-out lie. Father knew that it was, and so did all the wonderful, patient, generous ladies who had given me instruction. But he claimed credit for it all, and in his own mind he was justified. You see, he felt I was what I was because of the time he spent supervising my work. The accomplishment was not Mrs. Kennedy's, not Mrs. Ball's, not Mrs. Simpson's, certainly not mine. It was *his*, the result of *his* labors, *his* energy, *his* persistence. Who knows whether he did not even believe it was *his* genius?

Think where this left Mrs. Kennedy! Thanks to her we had met influential faculty members of Mills College. Thanks largely to her my two concerts were arranged, prepared, and successful. I really learned a great deal from her, all of it absolutely free of charge—lessons twice a week, sometimes running to more than two hours. How can I forget the personal love and attention and inspiration she gave me? Naturally this fine woman resented my father's blanket statement, broadcast to the world, that he was my only piano teacher. But she refrained from making a private or public issue of it. She knew Father's vile temper, and she feared that the real victim of any clash between them would be me. I interested her too much for her to risk losing me as a pupil. So, beyond a certain coolness toward Father during the few lessons that followed, there was no open break between them. The nobility of that woman! Suppressing her rightful claims, concealing her hurt, appeasing Father's outrageous ego, all on my account. That was real devotion and loyalty. They were worlds apart, those two.

Shortly after my second concert Josef Hofmann came to play in San Francisco. Immediately Mrs. Kennedy sought means of obtaining an interview for me. Now Hofmann, ranking in the best circles as one of the most accomplished pianists of his day, was also head of the Curtis Institute of Music in Philadelphia. There he was constantly being exposed to *Wunderkinder* from every corner of the globe. Mrs. Kennedy felt the verdict of a man like Hofmann would be a valuable thing for all of us to have. Mr. Hofmann at first scoffed at the idea of anyone my age being able to perform in public and having the foggiest notion of what she was doing. He had heard many little children playing simple things at the piano. He had done so himself. There was nothing extraordinary about it, and he didn't want to take up the limited time he had in San Francisco listening to still another prodigy. Several other people must have backed up Mrs. Kennedy's story, however, for pretty soon Mr. Hofmann's interest was aroused. He remained positive, however, that no child of four could play a Bach invention. "I'll give her twenty minutes," he finally said. So Father put me in a car and took me to see Josef Hofmann in San Francisco. This was in November, 1929.

There were many other people besides Mr. Hofmann and Mrs. Kennedy in the hotel suite when we arrived. Some were musicians, some were potential sponsors. Mr. Hofmann immediately put me at my ease by telling me he had a boy named Anton who was just my age. "Does he play the piano?" I asked, and he replied, "Not yet, but I hear that you do and that you're going to play for me." I said, "Yes, I'm going to play for you and then I'm going to hear you play, because my daddy is taking me to hear your concert at the Dreamland Auditorium."

Mr. Hofmann then got down to business.

"All right, then, what can you play?"

I told him what I had just played at my second Mills College concert—stressing the Bach invention.

"Before you play any of those things, do you mind doing some scales?"

"Which one do you want me to do? I play all of them every single day with the metronome."

He asked me to play the B major scale. I did.

"Do you know any harmony?"

Mrs. Kennedy replied for me. "She does, Mr. Hofmann."

"What is the relative minor of B major?" Mr. Hofmann asked.

"G sharp minor."

"Can you play that scale, too?"

"Do you want me to play the melodic or the harmonic minor?"

So he told me and I played it. Mrs. Kennedy again spoke. "Ruth also knows how to transpose."

By this time Mr. Hofmann must have been very interested.

"Can you transpose just anything?"

Father, who was beside himself with suppressed eagerness, broke in before I could answer.

"You give her a theme and she'll transpose it for you in any key you want."

Mr. Hofmann chose the opening measures of Bach's two-part invention in F major and asked me to play it for him in E major. That was easy enough, being just a half-step away.

"This is a little harder—play it in B-flat major."

I did, and I could see he was quite impressed. The agreed-on twenty minutes went by very fast; then an hour; and at the end of two hours I was still at it, with Mr. Hofmann growing more and more aroused. Finally he uttered a word I had never yet heard.

"*Bravo!*"

Turning to the others, he pronounced me the most astonishing child prodigy he had ever heard. Father promptly asked him if he would teach me. Mr. Hofmann agreed, provided

Father took me East to live in Philadelphia. When Father pleaded lack of funds, Mr. Hofmann assured him something could be arranged if he came back to see him in a few days. All the way back home Father rubbed his hands and fairly clucked with joy. My pride at having pleased him knew no bounds. When we returned to San Francisco, we were met by Mrs. Josef Hofmann, a tall, beautiful blonde, who gave me colored pencils to play with while she and Mr. Hofmann spoke to Father. The proposal was this: free train tickets to Philadelphia and a $250-a-month scholarship to cover an apartment to be selected for us by the Curtis Institute. Father grumbled that that was scarcely enough for a family of five. But they were adamant, and no doubt more than a bit ruffled by Father's boorishness. That was the highest stipend Curtis was offering, they said. So Father announced he and I would go to Philadelphia alone, leaving Mother and my two sisters behind in Berkeley.

Of course the arrangement was a triumph for dear Mrs. Kennedy, who glowed when we brought her the news. For Mother it was a little sad, especially when it came to packing my little things together for the journey. At the station she wept and wept. I'm afraid I didn't cry at all. All I could think of was that I was finally going to see the world and meet other great musicians. The exciting prospect ahead crowded out every other emotion. Besides, Father had seen to it that everyone else had ceased to exist for me but himself. Helen and Gloria were far more my mother's daughters than I was or ever could hope to be again. I promised dutifully to write, but I never once turned my head to look back. Then came the fuss all along the route. Wherever the train stopped, there were roses and newspaper interviews with the little girl who was going East to study with the great Josef Hofmann. With each stop the memory of Berkeley and my family became dimmer and dimmer.

A large, beautiful apartment awaited us in Philadelphia, and most thrilling of all, a real, genuine Steinway grand to practice on! So far I had done all my practicing on our living-room upright. I had no sooner given a cry of delight than Father dangled the old threat over me: "If you don't practice right, they'll take away the piano." How eagerly I set to work on that piano! My eyes feasted on every part of it, and my hands touched it with awe and love. Our apartment house was tenanted only by pupils and teachers of the Curtis Institute. I began to meet people and make friends . . . Efrem Zimbalist, Lea Luboshutz, Rose Bampton, Helen Jepson. Mostly, Father gravitated toward the violinists. To me the most awesome of our neighbors was Marcella Sembrich. None ever admired her more than the little girl who thought of her in whispers. She carried herself and her beautiful diamonds with such an air of majesty, and then to be told by this woman, as I was one day, that I was a genius! There was a catch, though. Someday, she said, I must study singing. Like herself I must not stop with being a pianist. Such a spirit as I had must come out pure, from my very self.

"The piano," she said to me and my father, "is only a substitute, a medium."

"Well," said my very practical father, not wanting to offend this celebrated artist, "let her learn everything about the piano first. There will be plenty of time for her to be a singer later."

Each morning Father and I went to the nearby Curtis Institute. There we had adopted a routine that never changed from day to day: knock on the door of the executive office and ask for Mr. Hofmann. Always the same answer: Mr. Hofmann was on tour. "When is he coming back to teach my daughter Ruth?"

He was expected back soon. Father couldn't pin them down to anything more exact than that. This was shortly after Christmas, a few weeks before my fifth birthday. What on earth were we to do now? Consulting David Saperton, the assistant director, Father now had a new experience: meeting a man who did *not* believe wholly that his daughter was a little genius.

"Put her on the vaudeville stage," was Mr. Saperton's unvarnished advice, "and make all the money you can out of her while she's still young."

Father told him off in equally direct language.

Meanwhile I was having lessons with the celebrated Isabelle Vengerova. I owe her a good deal, including further study in harmony and modulation, many new compositions, and a further delving into the music of Haydn and Mozart I already knew. Vengerova had her own ideas of teaching, but even at my age I knew they were good and conscientiously worked out. Father took a dimmer view of matters. He had taken me to the Curtis Institute to study with Mr. Hofmann, "not with one of his assistants." The disappointment rankled in him. To everyone, at all times, he complained of the "raw deal" he was getting. This scarcely helped him to make friends. But making friends was never his forte. Presently another grievance was added to his indictment of the school. The Fox Movietone people came over one day to make a film of me at the piano. They had rigged up their big cameras and powerful lights in the auditorium. Then began an ordeal for me that lasted three days, playing a few compositions over and over again with the lights so strong that I developed blisters on the back of both my legs. Father was fit to be tied. Hofmann or no Hofmann, this was the last straw. He was taking me back to Berkeley. No daughter of his was going to be used to publicize a school! They had taken advantage of my ability to advertise themselves! Father, of course, felt shortchanged by the whole business. Everybody was now conspiring to exploit his daughter Ruth. What a pathetic farce the whole thing was. I can still see my penny-pinching father fumbling with a needle by the light of the lamp, trying to mend my blouses and petticoats.

Then there was the old story—complaints from our neighbors, growing in venom and frequency as Father and I returned to our nine-hour routine. This was worse than Berkeley, where we had our own house. Now the protests poured in from upstairs and downstairs, to the right of us and to the left of us. Here I was up at six in the morning and banging away, with a few short breaks, till long after dark. Finally a note came from Mrs. Hofmann, relaying our neighbors' feelings.

"If," the note concluded, "your daughter Ruth has to practice as much as she does in order to get the results she does, it is quite possible that she isn't the little genius you or anyone else may believe her to be."

Stung to the quick, Father drew up a retort that went something like this: "The Ford is a small motorcar. It doesn't require very much gas to keep it going. The Chrysler is a large motorcar. It requires more to keep it going. The Cadillac is the largest motorcar. It requires the most fuel of all. The same, Mrs. Hofmann, is true of talent. My daughter Ruth is a Cadillac."

Meanwhile Mother was writing me how much she missed us and how I should eat vegetables and drink plenty of orange juice. I used to write back and draw two lips on the letter and then put a pencil mark around them. That was supposed to be a kiss from me to her. At Eastertime she sent me little rabbits and chocolate eggs. These Father promptly distributed among the children of musicians who had not registered any complaints about my playing. Not a single one for me! I felt hurt and cheated. Earlier he had refused to buy me a chocolate egg at the store, and now when I got them from my own mother, I still couldn't have one. Father wrote back, finally, about the whole dismal business in Philadelphia. We were returning, he said, and Mother should start campaigning for new support and sympathy. This was how the Smadbeck family entered the enlarging picture of my career as a prodigy.

Mrs. Smadbeck, a wealthy New Yorker interested in welfare work, was the sister of one of our friends in San Francisco. The news must have crossed the country fast that we had run into trouble. Mrs. Smadbeck herself came to Philadelphia with another sister to talk it over, bringing with her an elegant little beaded bag for me. They agreed with Father that the best thing to do was to go back to California and find a sponsor. On our way back we visited with them in New York, and there in the Smadbeck home I had my closest view of heaven. It was a playroom used by little Jinny Smadbeck. Gorgeous playthings and dolls and games lay all over it. The few hours I spent there with Jinny were a never-to-be-forgotten dream. For many years she and her brother Louis remained my dearest friends. While on tour I used to write love letters to Louis, who had adorable red hair, ending them "with all my love," and I meant every word of it, too.

Back in Berkeley, Father was more resolved than ever to take me to Europe. Mrs. Kennedy, convinced there was still a good deal she could teach me, tried to dissuade him. Unknown to Father, she had even interested wealthy friends in providing me with a Steinway grand. No man was more surprised than Father when the piano arrived. I can still see him standing there at the door telling the truckman to take it back. Didn't he want me to have this fine piano? I whimpered. There was nothing to worry about, he said; I would have lots and lots of pianos some day. Mrs. Kennedy didn't know what to make of Father's violent rebuff. The truth is, he was after bigger stakes. Accepting the piano meant accepting a very fine gift. But he didn't want a very fine gift. What he wanted was actual support over a period of years so I could study in Europe with the best masters on someone else's money. Slowly but surely Father was building up probably the most obnoxious reputation in the whole Bay Area. He had a perfect genius for antagonizing those most eager to help me. Those who held on must have had iron nerves and superhuman patience.

There now followed a series of concerts in rich people's homes, in studios, in fancy ballrooms. One program was for a charity, though my father managed to pocket a hundred dollars from it. That program I shared with a boy violinist only a few years older than I. Father took one look at his hands and flatly told him he would never be a violinist. The boy stood there crushed and speechless. He was Isaac Stern. Father was always doing that, trampling on people's feelings, ridiculing them, cutting them down, thoughtless, crude, loud-mouthed, nursing, deep down in him, a corrosive need to inflict pain, If I hadn't been there as something to show off, nobody would have put up with him, not even Mother.

About this time I met another great pianist, Josef Lhévinne. I owe that meeting to a Mrs. De Lee, an influential San Francisco patroness of music, who for many years had been his pupil. Mrs. De Lee brought him one day to our little house on Etna Street. I recall Mr. Lhévinne as a neat, kindly, and fastidious gentleman with a warm smile and a merry twinkle. At first he asked me to play Bach, then Schubert, then Chopin. After each he would nod approvingly, his eyes lighting up jovially.

"Ruth really knows what she's doing," Father finally interposed. "She's not just playing by rote. Why don't you ask her a question in harmony?"

So Mr. Lhévinne, who seemed quietly to have sized Father up, asked me to play the dominant chord of D major. When I did, he shook his head and took my hands off the keys. "I asked you to play the dominant seventh chord—this." And he played it for me. I shook my head right back. "You didn't ask for the dominant seventh." This time I played it for him. "If you had asked for it, I would have given it to you. I played what you asked for." I forget what Mr. Lhévinne said before he went. It amounted, I'm sure, to a very clean bill of health. He volunteered to teach me if we came to New York. That proved out of the question because of the expense and the difficulty of getting a large enough scholarship at the Juilliard School of Music where he taught.

Before Father took me to his concert he told me that Mr. Lhévinne was famous for the way he played a fantastic composition called "La Campanella." I was sitting in the middle of the first row center. When Mr. Lhévinne had finished his program and returned for a second bow, I got up from my seat and, jumping up and down, shouted, "Play 'La Campanella'!" He did, and it was a truly unforgettable experience for me. That piece later became one of my own favorite show-pieces. Father then took me backstage, where, to add to my day's store of thrills, Mr. Lhévinne wrote on my program, "To my young colleague Ruth."

Next of the celebrities to visit San Francisco was the brilliant French pianist Alfred Cortot. A meeting with this august personage was also arranged for me, again by the faithful Mrs. Kennedy. Mr. Cortot was far from eager to hear me, having been plagued, no doubt, by similar assaults on his precious time many times before. The same routine of repeated testimonials finally wore down his resistance. He heard me play one number, and he was a changed man. He came over to the piano and asked me to play this, that, and everything. "What does this mean?" "Are you enjoying that?" He turned to the others and said I was without question the most phenomenal child genius he had ever seen. He waxed indignant over the fact that in this great and glorious city of San Francisco not one citizen had stepped forward to finance my career. Being a Frenchman, he expressed himself in flambuoyant terms. He was due to play in the White House on his way back to Europe. "I give you my word, I shall speak to President Hoover about you." What was of more interest to Father was that he also solemnly promised to teach me—without fee, *naturellement*—if I ever came to Paris.

That was all fine and dandy, but still I had no sponsor. If the call for help was heard in the right circles, it surely was stifled by my father's savage insults and oafish behavior. Actually he could have taken me to Europe at his own expense. His property holdings warranted it. There was no real need to go everywhere, hat in hand, as if we were on the verge of starvation.

The celebrities who prophesied great things for me had come and gone. Father was at his wits' end when suddenly another luminary crossed our skies, to Father the greatest of them all. This was none other than Mischa Elman, his cherished idol since he was a boy. Mr. Elman, it turned out, was married to a San Francisco girl. Word reached Mrs. Kennedy that the Elmans had settled in the Bay Area around San Mateo for the summer. The Elmans had a little girl about my age and a slightly younger boy. Mrs. Kennedy spoke in such glowing terms about me to Mr. Elman that he immediately invited my family to spend Sunday with him and his family. This was more than Father had dared hope. How carefully he preened himself for the occasion! He had to look perfect for his idol, and naturally I had to play the same way, only better. This was no mere pianist with whom I could get by, he warned me. This was a real musician, the world's greatest violinist, a man who knew melody line and who wasn't fooled so easily. Well, all of us got carefully into the car, and carefully—and slowly—

we drove along the highway. Father said he wanted as little dust as possible on the car when we approached the Elman home.

This was an enchanting little cottage in lovely surroundings, and I remember I felt happy at the thought that I would be playing for a great musician in his home, and not in a hotel room. As we entered, I could see the dining room, the table neatly set, the beautiful glassware. This seemed so special to me. I couldn't recall being invited out before, certainly not to a place like this. I was determined to please Mr. Elman. And I did. By this time I was playing fairly difficult things, like the Mendelssohn "Duet" and Weber's "Perpetual Motion." Mr. Elman immediately took me by the hand and said he couldn't wait to hear me play. His attitude was so warm and inspiring. We two hit it off at once. And we have ever since. Mrs. Elman once told me, "Ruth, you are the only one who ever made Mischa cry." Let me say this about Mr. Elman. He has no false modesty about him. His opinions of other violinists, particularly prodigies, are emphatic and final. There is one great violinist, himself, and the others are, well, the others. . . . I had one great advantage over the others: I was a pianist. This may sound odd, but I like Mr. Elman today because he reminds me of Father; with a difference, of course. If you know how to handle him, he is a regular dear. In his cocksureness he is Father all over again. What he says is right; *must* be right. There is no doubt or uncertainty in his nature. Yet in him it is lovable, or at least inoffensive, where in my father it was repulsive. No man adores music as he does. Time and again I have seen him stride up and down his living room blissfully playing the violin, making music for its own sweet sake. That is the Mischa Elman I know and love. That Sunday I got to know his little girl Nadia, too. I began to feel completely at home with the Elmans. The rub came later in the car on our way home. Father had been talking violins with Mr. Elman, when, out of kindness, I'm certain, Mr. Elman turned to Mother and asked what time she usually put the little ones to bed. Mother, taking this as a hint, whispered a cue to Father, and we soon took our leave of the Elmans.

Then Father's nasty inferiority complex came to the fore: what a cheap way of getting rid of us; didn't Elman think we were good enough for him? He'd show him we were his equals and better. Who needed him, anyway? The fit of rage got worse and worse as Father stepped on the gas and let the car gather all the dust it pleased. We were five wretched Slenczynskis when we pulled up in front of our house on Etna Street in Berkeley. Father, however, was smart enough to confine his spleen to the family. He happened to be completely wrong about Mr. Elman. For it was he and his wife who brought us to the attention of the family that became my sponsors.

They were the Tobins, prominent in San Francisco banking circles and high society. The actual money was laid out by Mrs. Celia Tobin Clark and her daughter Agnes, both of whom already knew a good deal about me. But it was Mr. Elman's ecstatic report that turned the trick. A contract was drawn up providing three hundred dollars a month, to go out by check the first of every month, for a period of three years, in addition to steamship fare to Europe for the entire family. It was also agreed that I was to study with a teacher of my father's choice for not less than a year at a stretch. Specific mention was made that no remuneration was expected by the Tobin family, whatever my future earnings might be. Every sixty days or so Mr. Elman, or some other expert to be designated by the Tobin family, would report on my progress. There was one very stringent condition. All this was to be done *solely* for my education. During the three-year period I *was to give no concerts*.

Whatever his secret designs about that last clause, Father

felt the contract was a great personal triumph. This was exactly what he wanted. That didn't prevent him, however, from going to the bank and trying to secure the full amount in advance, with the idea of investing it. Mrs. Tobin Clark would have yielded but for Cyril Tobin, the lawyer of the family. He was adamant. The terms were fair. If my father didn't like them, the deal was off. Father promptly pulled in his horns.

Before leaving San Francisco, I gave a farewell concert sponsored by Mrs. Meyerfelt and several other music-loving ladies, who donated both the hall and $250. Tickets were purchased at fancy prices by those who wished to contribute toward my European budget. The theater, I believe, was brand-new at the time, and my concert was a form of housewarming. Most of all I remember the flowers. Packed as the hall was, the roses must have outnumbered the listeners. Backstage later, Charles Wagner, the concert impresario, came to pay his respects. It seems he had been "dragged" to the concert by the actress Blanche Bates, who had already heard me. Then and there he offered to sign me up for a concert tour, a prospect that I'm sure made Father's mouth water. But Father wasn't taking any chances, not yet, with that three-year windfall guaranteed by the Tobins. They kept in touch, however, and Wagner became my manager when I made my New York debut in 1933.

A huge throng closed in on us when Mother, Father, and I left the theater to get into our automobile. The car couldn't move. I remember Miss Seckels, who managed the concert, dashing up to the front window to say good-by and Father shouting back at her, "Well, how much did we get?" "A little over thirty-five hundred," came the reply. "Wonderful!" said Father, turning to Mother as we drove away. "We'll use it to pay off the mortgage on the house."

BEFORE sailing for Europe, we stopped for a few days in New York, a highly profitable venture as it turned out. Visiting with the Smadbeck family, we were loaded with heaps of expensive clothes to take on our journey. For me and my sisters there were dresses and skirts and blouses belonging to Jinny Smadbeck. For Mother there was a good part of Mrs. Smadbeck's own wardrobe. A second haul awaited us at the Elmans', who had invited us over for dinner. To Mother went two gorgeous evening dresses to wear on the boat, and to me and Helen and Gloria went lots of beautiful things belonging to little Nadia Elman. Father never showed any compunction about asking for and receiving other people's clothes for his wife and children. He drew the line at himself, however. There he wanted to do his own picking, at his own leisure, and with his own money. Whatever he was inside, he was fastidious and immaculate outside. At this time the name most heard in my family was that of Menuhin. Father was heard again and again to boast that he would do as well, if not better, with me than Papa Menuhin had done with Yehudi. The parallel between himself and the older Menuhin grew closer every day, except that he was a little better than Papa Menuhin and his Ruth a little better than his son. The Menuhins had had a sponsor; we had a sponsor. Best of all, here was his daughter already bringing tidy little dividends to the whole family at a much earlier age than Yehudi. Both Yehudi and I were the oldest of three children, but I was younger than the youngest Menuhin. These calculations added up to a great triumph for Father. Our very comfortable suite on the S.S. *Hamburg* rang with his self-satisfaction throughout the crossing. I loved it all, particularly the little orchestra that played during dinner.

"This," Father would say, gazing raptly about, "is the genteel way of living; not like in America. Europe is cultured, civilized. They have music with their meals. They look up to musicians."

The teacher Father had in mind for me when we reached Europe was the widely acclaimed German-Dutch pianist Egon Petri. Petri's father, Henri, had been one of Father's favorite violin teachers in Berlin after he left Poland. Henri's son Egon was the man to get me on the right track in the great adventure that lay ahead.

Berlin impressed me as no other city I had even seen. The look and sound of the city, its buildings, its automobiles, its people were different. Its language fascinated me at once. Mr. Petri, who then lived in the same house on the Victoria Luise Platz with old Frau Busoni, helped us to secure an apartment along that street with a German family by the name of Adloff. The day we met Mr. Petri, we were introduced to the widow of the fabulous Ferruccio Busoni, who had been one of the great teachers and pianists of his time. Frau Busoni was a sweet and dainty little lady. I remember her hospitality, the gentle manners, the dainty platter of cookies she put before me. "Would you have a cooky, no?" And I, not quite knowing what to make of the "no" and not daring to provoke Father's wrath, never did get to taste Frau Busoni's cookies. Then I was ushered into Mr. Petri's studio. Two great big beautiful pianos stood in the middle of it. Mr. Petri, a warm-natured man with a lively sense of fun, spoke fluent English with a British accent. I liked him at once. "So the little lady thinks she has perfect pitch?" he said, half teasingly, half skeptically. "Turn your back, please."

I did so, and he struck G in the middle of the keyboard. I got it, of course. Then he hit a high note in the treble, and I got that, too; as well as the next one, which was deep down in the bass. Mr. Petri next struck two notes together, with the same result; then three notes, which were just as easy for me, and finally he brought both hands down together, and I named the chord. He seemed flabbergasted. But he hadn't given up yet. He now began to combine notes at random, discordant, mismated clusters of up to ten tones. I got all of them right off the bat. Finally he gave a gasp and stopped.

"It's unbelievable!" he cried.

Why it was I could never understand. To me there was nothing strange in my being able to call them off so easily. Mr. Petri wasn't the only one who tried to trip me up; others had tried before and were to later. I merely took it for granted. It was something I knew that involved about as much effort, if not less, as naming a color. Arthur Fiedler of the Boston "Pops" Orchestra always shows amazement over this knack of mine, if knack it be. I have transposed themes he gave me into any requested key without practice or notes. "I don't understand how on earth you do it?" I don't either. I just do it, like breathing or reading words. Maybe those of us who have it are born with it, or get it so early they never know how it got there. I suppose Mr. Petri couldn't get over it because I was barely six. Yet I had been drilled at the piano since I was three. I had learned harmony as I had learned to talk. Some of it may have happened even sooner by absorption as an infant. All I know is this: reading music, playing the piano, harmony, feeling a phrase, and identifying single tones or handfuls of tones have always seemed perfectly natural and normal to me. My earliest recollection in life is a recollection of music. There is complete blankness before it, and after it, for better or for worse, everything I recall is associated, one way or another, with the piano. This is no exaggeration. Even in my family, the piano and I became one individual, indivisible. The very first time I met my three-year-old nephew, his mother said, "Josef, this is your Aunt Ruthie," and little Josef's first words were, "Where is the piano?" He thought I came equipped with, or perhaps that I came with, the piano. I wasn't a person; I was "Ruth with the piano," the same way another girl might be "Becky with the big blue hat."

As a teacher Mr. Petri endeared himself to me by not treating me as a child. He seemed really and truly to take me as an adult musician from the start. He saw that my scale training and harmony were solid and secure. He trusted me to do whatever technical work Father thought necessary. Right off he gave me difficult compositions to work on. Imagine assigning a child things like preludes and fugues from Bach's "Well-Tempered Clavichord"; Bach's "Italian" concerto; both the G minor sonata, Opus 49, and the G major sonata, following it, of Beethoven; Mozart's early A major concerto, and two Schubert impromptus! That's hardly a snap for any piano student, much less one of six. How I worked for Mr. Petri! As for Father, a somber new note had entered our home sessions at the keyboard.

Before I reveal the change, I must go back to the day we were packing in Berkeley to leave for Europe. Helen had been in the habit of puttering playfully about the garden in the back of our house with a rake-and-shovel set someone had given her. That set was her choice when she was told she could take only one toy with her to Europe. Now in Berlin we had no garden, and Helen's little rake-and-shovel set lay neglected, but not for long. The shovel had a wooden handle about eighteen inches long, which Father one day removed from the little steel appliance attached to it. Thus detached, the object became, in Father's words "the magic stick." That, I was told, would serve when everything else had failed to make me respond properly. I was also constantly being reminded that we were now in Germany, where nobody at all interfered with a man's rule in his own home, and where everything short of murder was permitted to make an untractable child see the light. The Americans, so Father said, were sissies with their kids. They spoiled and softened them. There were graphic stories, too, about a famous gadget that was like Father's "magic stick" except that it had nine leather thongs attached to it. Father spared me none of the gruesome details of how this cat-o'-nine-tails had been used on him as a child. I had several night-mares as a result. By this time I was used to Father's boxing my ears and hurling strong epithets at me when I made a mis-take. I put it down to anger and ill temper and perhaps a kind of rough justice, too. I know I always tried harder the next time. Actually, I suffered more when I saw my sisters being punished. So the bleak stories of Father's own beatings as a boy hurt and haunted me more than my daily cuffings. I never once thought I too might get the cat-o'-nine-tails treatment. But here was Father resolved to rule his family with an iron hand. What I had had up to now was coddling to what I was to get. Never for a moment did he make me forget the great *sacrifice* he was making for me. Five or six times a day I heard the same story. It ran something like this:

"From morning to night, every hour of every day, every minute of every hour, I do nothing but devote my life to you. I do nothing but try to make something out of you. They say it's impossible to make a silk purse out of a sow's ear. I'm going to do the impossible. I'm going to make an artist out of you—even if it kills us both."

Whether it killed us both or not, Father had no intention of shelling out a solitary cent of his own to make me an artist. This was immediately clear in Berlin, as it had been in Berkeley. Take the question of a piano as a small instance. In America we had at least owned an upright on which the whole weird business had begun. Here in Berlin we didn't have even that. So Father went to the Steinway people, armed with a letter of introduction. They were quite affable and only asked when he wanted it delivered and where. Father told them. Then, as a minor detail, they named the cost. Whereupon Father exploded. This piano, he blustered, was for his genius of a daughter to practice on. Wasn't that payment enough? And he walked out in a rage.

Next we went to the Bechstein people. Father wasn't going to risk seeing my hands get rusty from prolonged idleness. A child's hands need constant, daily activity to keep them agile and flexible. This time Father adopted another tactic. Once inside the big Bechstein showroom, he dragged me to the nearest piano, lifted me up on the piano bench, and ordered me to play. A crowd formed around us almost immediately. At the first chorus of "*Bravos*," Father asked to speak to the manager, who was forthwith given another demonstration. From being prepared to throw us both out, this man fairly burst with enthusiasm and sent for Mr. Carl Bechstein himself. A tall, distinguished-looking man with a cane, he, too, was conquered in short order. "What can we do for you?" he asked Father. When Father told him our story, complete with financial woe, Mr. Bechstein said:

"I shall see to it that you and your family have everything you need. I shall provide your fantastic daughter with a piano on which to practice."

The Bechstein Company not only provided the piano but arranged for a private tutor to come to our home for language and other instruction. This continued for the entire year and a half that we remained in Berlin. Father's clever little improvisation in the showroom had done the trick. All these efforts on my behalf only sharpened his demand for blind obedience. In his eyes this entitled him to apply a little extra pressure. Now Mr. Petri's first assignments were no cinch by a long shot. I loved every one of the pieces, but I had to learn them like anyone else. Whatever Father or anyone might think, I was no genius. I had to buckle down and plug away and memorize. And sometimes I didn't get these things as fast as Father thought I should. There was one piece in particular: the F minor variations of Haydn. The score lay closed on the piano rack. I was told that if I didn't go through the piece by heart without a single mistake and without so much as looking up at the score, he would have no choice but to resort to "the magic stick." Now the score was closed, so looking at it wouldn't help me in a pinch. But Father's use of psychology went as follows: if I so much as stole a glance at the closed score, it meant that at that point I was not quite sure of myself. All he needed was to catch me raising my eyes unconsciously to the closed book. I was doing all right, when my memory, perhaps shaky from the threat, grew weak in one place. Instinctively my eyes raced to where the music would usually aid me. That did it. Before I knew it, I was on my feet screaming blue murder, my father at my heels, "magic stick" in hand. There was no escape. Catching me by one arm, he hauled off and let me have it all over my body with the wooden handle of my sister's shovel. Father had muscles like iron. There wasn't a soft spot in his whole body. I never knew a man so proud of his sheer physical strength. And all of it seemed to come down on me that day for having dared betray a moment of insecurity. Finally I broke away. I fled shrieking out of the room, into the hall, into the bathroom. We were the only two at home. Run as I did, he seized me again and again, bringing the stick down on almost every part of me but one. Wrathful and bestial as he had become, he spared my hands. As if by a weird counterspell, the "magic stick" never touched them once.

Mother didn't find out till she bathed me the following evening. At first she thought the long black and blue streaks over my shoulders, legs, back, and arms were dirt. "How did you get so dirty, Ruth?" she said. "Those marks won't come off." Then she saw what they were and she looked horrified. "What in God's name happened to you? Did you fall down the stairs?"

"I didn't fall down," I said calmly. "Daddy beat me with a stick."

Hugging me tightly to herself, she kissed me, whispered a few loving words, and went in to see Father. What was said and what happened I don't know, but in the weeks that followed little had changed. When next Father laced into me with the stick, Mother ran into the room wringing her hands. "You've got to stop this! You've got to stop this right away or I'll call the police!"

Father gave a funny hard little smile. "We are no longer in America. Now you go and mind your own business. I'm going to do what I want in my own home with my own child. This is what I came to Europe for."

My heart went out to Mother at that moment. She stood there looking so helpless and lost. There was something going on that turned her stomach as a mother and a human being. Yet she could do nothing. And here was her husband assuring her that it was for the ultimate good of her daughter. What a horrible dilemma for Mother! She was as much a victim of my father as I was.

MEANWHILE, on January 15, 1931, I had my sixth birthday. For all its moments of agony, my life had become full of music. Along with my hard but challenging work with Mr. Petri, there were the concerts at which I heard pianists like Emil Sauer, one of the last pupils of Liszt; Ignaz Friedmann, the distinguished editor of Chopin's music. At the Beethovensaal one day I was so deeply stirred by a young man named Vladimir Horowitz that during the encores I sat on the steps leading just out to the stage a few feet away from him. I watched him, fascinated, as he kept wiping his forehead with a handkerchief. Once, catching sight of me as he returned from bowing, he leaned down and even wiped my forehead. I wanted so much to tell him that I, too, was a pianist. When I reported the incident to Mr. Petri the next day, he said he had predicted a fine future for Horowitz when he first heard him play at nineteen. Many years later Mr. Petri told my sponsors in San Francisco that in his time he had heard two great talents, Vladimir Horowitz at the age of nineteen and Ruth Slenczynski at the age of six, adding that because of my youth he had prophesied even greater things for me than for Horowitz.

Another name that comes back from this period is that of the celebrated virtuoso Leopold Godowsky. I played for him and a large group of people one entire afternoon at his home. There were loads of questions he kept flinging at me, roaring with delight at my replies. Then there were questions to which he himself supplied the answers. I recall one that stuck in my mind ever after: "What is the difference between technic and mechanics?" Technic, he said, was the entire art of expressing oneself. Mechanics was the ability to play quickly and cleanly. To Godowsky technic was the whole apparatus of playing the piano. Producing tone, transcribing ideas, expressing one's personality, all that was technic. The other was fingerwork, the acquired knack of playing fast. This was a lot easier to attain, he said, than real piano technic, which was of the nature of art.

Music in Berlin seemed part of everyday living, not something reserved for evenings out. Even when at home, we had music with our meals. Outside in the street, musicians seemed to be playing all the time. Often strains from an accordion would ascend from the courtyard, and a voice rose with them. Sometimes Mother would wrap up sandwiches and drop them out the window to the minstrels below. Thereupon, I would be told how the young Bach, on his 150-mile walk to Luebeck to hear the great organist Buxtehude, one day bit into a coin, while munching greedily on a herring head that someone had thrown to him from a window. I'm afraid Mother had no spare coins from Father's allowance to enrich her sandwiches with.

In the meantime Father was slowly evolving his own ideas about how I was to be fed. For almost three years now, breakfast was something I earned by practicing to Father's satisfaction. Lunch was soon another reward to achieve by further good work. Finally I was playing for my supper. One morning, for some infraction or other, Father drove me back to bed without breakfast. I couldn't imagine what I had done wrong. I concluded that Father was merely teasing me this time. Hearing everybody eating in the next room, I suddenly burst into tears. Presently Mother came into the bedroom. "What are you crying about? You know you're being punished for not practicing well." I protested that I had practiced well. "I'm crying," I said, "because God didn't give me breakfast." You see, Mother had been reading the twenty-third psalm to me the night before, explaining that the Lord would see to it that I never went hungry. "I was a good girl, Mommy," I sobbed. "Daddy was wrong and God forgot all about me." To which Mother said, "God only helps those who helps themselves"—a lesson that has stuck. I don't recall whether I ever got breakfast that morning. Being denied a meal for wrongs committed became standard practice, and many was the time that Mother sneaked a few snacks into my bedroom after a lost supper. Going hungry was a fixed part of my ritual of penance.

When Mr. Petri announced that he was leaving for a long concert tour, Father was again faced with the problem of finding a teacher for me. He disliked allowing too much time to elapse between teachers. On the recommendation of Mr. Petri, I studied for a time with his assistant, Sascha Liebermann—a good musician and excellent instructor. We had a few sessions at which he played second piano parts for the A major and "Coronation" concertos of Mozart. Meanwhile Father feverishly maneuvered to snare another great name for my roster. One of the most formidable at that time in Berlin was Artur Schnabel. The problem, however, was how to get within hailing distance. What time remained to Mr. Schnabel from a crowded concert schedule he gave to master classes. Father was told he did no private tutoring. Mr. Bechstein, with whom Father discussed the matter, held out some hope. He was confident that, once Mr. Schnabel heard me, he would leap at the chance of becoming my teacher. The question was how to bring the two of us together without any hint of prearrangement. I should add that, besides being a busy man, Mr. Schnabel was notoriously allergic to child prodigies. Mr. Bechstein resorted to a ruse. The double-keyboard Bechstein-Moore was then being exhibited in Berlin. Mr. Bechstein wrote to Schnabel inviting him to his place to pronounce judgment on the new instrument. Father and I were also invited, but told to sit in an adjoining room.

Now, on the appointed day, while Mr. Schnabel was admiring the new piano in the main Bechstein showroom, there suddenly reached him from the adjoining room the sound of another piano. His interest aroused, Mr. Schnabel asked who it might be. "Oh, somebody trying out the pianos, I guess," said Mr. Bechstein. "Whoever it is," commented Mr. Schnabel, "it's somebody with a great deal of talent." Mr. Bechstein told us that Mr. Schnabel stuck around a little longer, making remarks about the Bechstein-Moore. No further reference was made by either of them to the piano in the other room till Mr. Schnabel said, "Do you mind if I go in there? I don't want to hurt a sale. I just want to see who's playing." There was I industriously immersed in the G minor sonata, Opus 49, of Beethoven when the two entered. Mr. Schnabel came over. "Was that you, you tiny little thing, playing?" I said it was, and he asked what else I could play. Slowly, in my halting German, but very precisely and proudly, I told him. He asked me where I came from, and I said America, adding for good measure that I had been studying with Egon Petri.

"But you can't be studying with him now," he said. "He's on tour."

Father joined in. "The fact is I've been teaching her myself now, but she needs a real master."

"Play something more," said Mr. Schnabel.

I played the E-flat major impromptu of Schubert.

"Come to my house next Friday," he said, "I want Mrs. Schnabel to meet you."

From that point on we were good friends. I played often at his house after that, and soon he was giving me lessons that lasted as long as three hours at a stretch. They were ordeals. A Schnabel lesson would go something like this: I would play the composition through for him from beginning to end without the slightest comment or interruption from him. Hand on chin, he would give a few grunts, reflect for a moment, and say, "That was very nice, but . . ."

There followed a minute analysis of every note, every phrase, from start to finish. That would take about a half-hour. Not a single note would be played. He would hum little bits, make up words to other little bits, gradually building up a picture of what the composition represented to him. I've never met anyone who could be so graphic and articulate about a piece of music without actually sitting at the piano to illustrate. If you were to ask me, for example, to "explain" a certain Beethoven sonata, I would say, "There are nuances that cannot be put into words, things so personal, so deep they can be felt and understood and explained only through the piano." Mr. Schnabel evidently believed in the power of the spoken word to convey anything. There was no groping for the pictures and images he made of the music. After this verbal exposition, Mr. Schnabel would sit at the second piano and start playing the piece from the very first phrase.

When possible, he would make up words to fit the phrase, words, naturally, to appeal to the child in me. I remember somehow getting the whole feeling of a passage in the little F major sonata of Mozart from the words "Eine Blume, eine Blume," which he sang to them. His voice was far from beautiful, but the idea got over. To another passage in that sonata he affixed the words "Der Vogel hat einen Schnabel"; that it, "the bird has a beak." When I went over the music with Father later in the day, he turned the sentence around into something far from complimentary to Mr. Schnabel: "Der Schnabel hat einen Vogel," roughly equivalent to having bats in one's belfry.

In Mr. Schnabel's method, at least with me, there were little words and sentences to go with almost all the musical phrases.

That man had infinite patience. I recall the great care he gave to teaching me to play syncopated parts—that is, two notes against three. The same Mozart sonata contains passages in which the left hand plays a succession of three notes against a succession of two in the right. In a word, syncopation. Patiently, clearly, he taught it to me as a person is taught fractions. The lowest common denominator, he said, was six, over which stood a two as opposed to a three. It was arithmetic, pure and simple, and I actually came to feel it that way. He made me begin by accenting the count out loud: "*One*, two, *three*, four, *five*, six," and, "*One*, two, three, *four*, five, six." When he thought I had the sound and feel of it, he substituted the slow metronome beat for the oral counting. It was like enlarging a tiny area of rhythm under a microscope. Gradually we built up the speed till I had the passage completely under control in the indicated tempo. I took it all in like a sponge. I could see Mr. Schnabel was having a good time, standing there, his eyes atwinkle as I struggled on from hurdle to hurdle, goading me with comments like, "That's right; try it again now; you're getting it. Good!" Finally he turned to Father:

"How did you start her? I took my own son as a little boy and locked him in a room for eight hours a day and I made him study all by himself. That boy is sixteen and he is a young man now, but he can't do what this little child of yours is doing. What did you do with her?"

Father, all puffed up with pride, replied: "I did it all myself. It is the early training that counts, Herr Schnabel."

Poor Mr. Petri, poor Mrs. Kennedy, poor everybody else who had taught me without charge and without claim of any kind, none of them counted or even existed any more. Mr. Schnabel,

I'm certain, had his own doubts about that, but he was too polite to voice them.

The wonderful lessons with Mr. Schnabel came to an end. Like Mr. Petri, he, too, had touring commitments to meet, the result being that this time I remained without a teacher for a long period. Father grew restless and worried. Here was a nice fat repertory of pieces I had learned at such effort, going completely to waste. Maybe the Bechstein people also began to itch for some returns on the piano and the tutor they were still furnishing free of charge. In any case, it was decided that I should give a concert. Now the German critics were regarded as far more difficult to please than the Americans. They frowned on sensationalism and beheld prodigies with a jaundiced eye. Nobody could tell how they would take to the idea of a six-year-old child playing Bach, Mozart, and Beethoven on a concert stage reserved for the greatest artists of the day. Mr. Bechstein hit on the perfect compromise. The concert would be held in the Bechstein Hall exclusively for the press. This would serve as trial balloon for a later concert in the big hall.

Some time before the concert, however, I fell sick. Till then I had never had a single day of ill health, that is to say nothing my father would call ill health. I used to have colds and practice at the piano with a fever of 101. Mother's protests would be met with the remark "So long as she's warm with a blanket around her, she's all right. What's the difference, in bed or on the piano bench. She's warm." Once, when the doctor whom Mother had called departed, Father said: "What does he mean, put her to bed? He doesn't know what he's talking about. I don't want any of my kids to be softies." One thing I certainly learned at the piano: how to endure physical pain; it isn't exactly a joy ride to speed through octave passages on a piano with a hard action. This time I was really confined to bed. Whatever my mother's and father's worries about me, I had only one. All the time I was in bed I was worried to death that I would lose my ability to play the E-flat major impromptu of Schubert. I had put such effort into it, and I loved it so.

Every ten minutes I would call out to Mother, "Do you think when I get up I'll still be able to play my Schubert piece?" Mother assured me I would. I had a nightmare in which I tried to play the piece only to discover to my horror that my fingers were paralyzed. Mostly it was the right hand that worried me, the left-hand writing of the piece being less troublesome. Sure enough, when I returned to the piano I discovered, that clear and secure as the impromptu was in my mind to the smallest detail, my fingers had grown too stiff for the right-hand passages. This little episode went a long way toward persuading me that only Father's word was to be trusted in these matters. I even had the feeling, during the beatings that were soon resumed, that, much as Mother tried to protect me, she had possibly been wrong and Father right all along.

During my illness I had given some thought to this whole question of fathers and mothers and children. Looking back, I decided that the smartest thing in life was to be a father. That way, nobody could dominate you or beat you or order you around. Shortly after my illness I walked into the kitchen where Mother was ironing, and began, "When I grow up and become a daddy . . ." I was stopped cold. "You're going to become a mamma when you grow up, not a daddy." That was most frustrating. I knew now I would never be able to do all the things I wanted to do. Only being a father entitled one to that. As a child, I was immensely pleased when critics said I had the strength of a man. It may sound like a dubious compliment to one very proud of being a woman like myself. The fact is that Father had made life's problems seem so much harder for a woman.

Take his behavior toward Mother when my Berlin concert drew near. Both Mr. Petri and Mr. Schnabel being out of town, the field was clear for Father to flaunt himself as the great wizard who had taught me everything I knew. Having eliminated them, he next wondered why he should share me with Mother in public. So he politely told her she wasn't coming to the concert in the Bechsteinsaal. Mother said nothing till she learned by chance that a certain elderly Frau Schultze, who sometimes baby-sat for us, had been provided with a ticket by my father. When he explained that he was afraid she might cause some confusion with all those newspaper people around, she shot back:

"That's not it! You want all the credit for yourself! You can't bear having anyone sharing the limelight with you!"

Which was perfectly true, I'm sure. Father knew what would follow the concert, and he wanted all the adulation as teacher and parent to be his.

The concert fulfilled his fondest hopes. The critics were overwhelmed. They almost seemed not to believe that a child of six could get up on a chair and play the piano like a grownup. Herr Diesterweg, Berlin's most respected critic, telephoned for an appointment the following day. *He wanted to see me play close up!* What had happened was this. He and his colleagues had reached the conclusion that Mr. Bechstein had played some clever trick on them. It was incredible that such big music should come out of such a little creature. Only some sort of concealed mechanical contraption could account for such a feat. Herr Diesterweg came to our house accompanied by a fellow critic. Before I played for them, they asked permission to examine the piano. A diligent search was made on all fours for wires and secret outlets. No part of our Bechstein was ignored. Herr Diesterweg next subjected me to a similar inspection, to determine, I suppose, if I was a perfectly normal little girl of six and not an electrical contrivance of some kind. Replying in what was not fluent German, I think I persuaded him. Then I played and played for them and they were absolutely delighted. Mother served cookies and tea, and always they asked me to play some other composition. They were all very apologetic for their scepticism, of course. All in all, it was a nice little triumph. The next day Herr Diesterweg wrote beautifully of me. He said that to watch me was not to watch a *Wunderkind*—that is, a "wonder child"—but to watch a *Wunder* and a *Kind*—that is, a "wonder" and a "child."

About that time Berlin was undergoing a siege of prodigies. Both Yehudi Menuhin and Ruggiero Ricci had come, played, and conquered, and I recall feeling quite superior when I heard a little French girl named Nicole Henriot. I made the mistake of communicating my feeling to Father, who retorted: "If I had her as a pupil, she would play circles around you because she's much more talented." The press, however, was on my side. I was named the most phenomenal of them all in point of age and because of the fact that little as I was I played a full-size concert piano. The violin prodigies, remarkable as they were, all used half-size or three-quarter-size violins.

No sooner had the clamor died down after the Bechsteinsaal recital than Father's thoughts were on a second. This one was to be in the big Bachsaal, however. The date set was November 25, 1931. The announcement of the concert brought a swift and spectacular response. Tickets were set at twice the standard price in Berlin. Almost overnight the concert was sold out.

It should be obvious by this time that, whatever his original pledge, Father had no further intention of abiding by at least two main clauses of the contract he had signed with the Tobin family. He may have also overlooked the fact that Mischa Elman was supposed to make a periodic report on my progress. Well, one result of the announcement of my forthcoming concert in the Bachsaal was a visit from Mr. Elman, who was in Berlin for a few days. Of course we were delighted to see him, and so was he, with my development. However, he soon came to the point. He had two bones to pick with my father. The first was the lesser of the two. Father had violated the provision about my studying at least one year with each teacher he chose. This the Tobin family had emphatically insisted upon. The other violation was worse. Father had given his written word, backed by repeated assurances to Mr. Elman himself, that I would not be brought out in a public concert during the entire three-year period of the sponsorship. What explanation had Father to offer for this nice, juicy concert at the Bachsaal? What was he to report to the Tobins and the Clarks? Father had one answer for him: the same one he gave Mother. Mr. Elman should mind his own business. He, Josef Slenczynski, knew what was best for his own child, and even he, Mischa Elman, must agree I was making great progress. So what cause did anybody have for a complaint? Nobody, but nobody, he summarized, could tell him what to do!

Mr. Elman naturally didn't like any part of this. He threatened to advise my sponsors to discontinue making us the $300 monthly payments. Both Father and I knew Mr. Elman would never do that. He was only trying to bluff Father into submission for what he honestly felt was my own good. Father flung the threat right back at him: "Go ahead and tell them if you want to. They won't stop sending the money! I've got a genius on my hands and they know it!"

Father went so far as to coach me in a wicked little speech I was to deliver to Mr. Elman the next time I saw him. I was to tell him that I didn't like the idea of his interfering in

Father's affairs, that Father was the greatest teacher in the world, and that nobody had a right to tell him what to do with his own daughter. I just prayed I wouldn't meet Mr. Elman too soon. . . .

On November 25, the neighborhood of the Bachsaal was without doubt the most congested area in Berlin. The mob was such that a police cordon had been placed around it. The traffic jam, I understand, was awful. Inside, the hall was packed tight from top to bottom. Accommodation had been made for an additional 150 people on the stage. So congested, in fact, was the stage that I had to squeeze my way through to the piano. And what a demonstrative audience!

"An audience aroused to a frenzied pitch of excitement by the sensational aspects of the case," cabled the Berlin correspondent of the New York *Times*. "An audience—by turns, amused, delighted, incredulous, dumbfounded by the unbelieveable performances of a child in some respects the most astounding of all prodigies heard in recent years on either side of the ocean."

At the end of the concert I could see the crowd surging toward the stage in one large wave. People leaned with their elbows on the stage, eyes upturned, hands beating away wildly. Those on stage leaped out of their seats, crowding around the piano, bending far over it to say things to me. From somewhere in this heaving, clamorous mass a hand reached out with a great big beautiful French doll. Suddenly oblivious of everything else, my eyes fastened on this gorgeous, elegant, dazzling object. Now it lay in my arms. But not for long. Out of the wings stormed my father, pushing a slow path through the crowd. Like a maniac, he tore the doll out of my arms and flung it back into the audience.

Weg mit die Puppe!" he yelled at the top of his voice. "Away with the doll!"

With that he yanked me back to the piano, and as the crowd recoiled, stunned into a strained hush by Father's behavior, I sat down and played the three Chopin ecossaises as encores. Swept back into the music, I forgot all about that pretty little doll that had vanished into the darkness as swiftly as it had appeared.

A fresh tumult broke out after the encores. Taking a last bow, I zigzagged my way through the throng and finally reached backstage. There, beaming and leaning down to kiss me, stood Mischa Elman! Elated as I was, my heart sank. How could I deliver that mean little speech which this perfect dear of a man would know wasn't mine in any case? I only thanked him for his words of praise and kissed him back warmly. You'd suppose, in all that frenzy of jubilation, Father would have been sport enough to be nice to me for a change. Not he. No sooner were we home than he asked me in a vicious tone why I didn't tell Mr. Elman off. I told him I forgot to, and my reward for a good day's work was one stiff whack across the cheek.

ELMAN or no Elman, the concert fulfilled Father's wildest dreams. Bids now poured in from all over Europe for my services. A Dutch manager stressed the importance of an immediate tour all over Europe. Father, however, said no to the tempting offers. That such a prospect was forbidden by the contract of sponsorship never bothered him for a moment. What gave him pause was something else. Strong as my repertory was for a single concert in Berlin, he knew it wasn't quite of touring caliber. There was still a serious gap: concertos for public display with an orchestra. These shortcomings he now threw into my face daily. If only I weren't so slow and stupid. What opportunities for fame and fortune we were missing, all on account of my being such a "dumbbell." My sisters now became my superiors in all respects. At an age when I scarcely knew the alphabet, Helen was already reading and writing. That was a real brain, not a lazy, backward one like mine. A few times Father even took Helen to the piano to show how much further she could go in much less time. But Helen rebelled. Much as Father howled at her, it simply wasn't in her. At the slightest provocation she would be in tears. Even the "magic stick" got Father nowhere. Helen learned to resist that gentle reminder with a weapon of her own. She simply passed out. How often I wished I had this secret of fainting! Still, I recall feeling mighty self-satisfied that I could take it and Helen couldn't. Even that helped separate me in my mind from my sisters. It was my being stronger—an adult—that helped me absorb punishment. Only a "kid" would faint away at the first threat of a beating.

How great a teacher Father thought himself may be gathered from his state of panic each time I lost a teacher. Launched brilliantly with a Berlin concert, here I was again, rudderless. Father first tried a gentleman named Meyer Mahr. After a few lessons he was replaced by another named Georg Bertram. Both were fine pedagogues, but neither quite fine enough to suit Father. Next came a Pole, Iso Elinson. After a few visits to our house, where he played Chopin for us, he, too, vanished.

Meanwhile a whole new paradise of music was opening to me at the concert halls. I attended the Berlin Philharmonic Concerts, especially the morning series. I watched Karl Flesch and Wilhelm Furtwängler and Bruno Walter conduct. These were just moments of heaven. One day I heard Rachmaninoff play his own third piano concerto. I sat on the side away from his hands and remember being awed by the long, spare, figure, with the lined ascetic face that never smiled. I heard Menuhin and Heifetz and Erica Morini, and dear Mr. Elman. Finally an old friend from San Francisco came to Berlin, Alfred Cortot. I was in fairyland while he played the F minor concerto of Chopin. Backstage, afterwards, I was delighted that he remembered me from California. "When are you coming to Paris to study with me?" he asked, and Father said, "Soon, soon." Later I asked Father whether he had really meant it. "Well," he said, "don't be surprised. One of these days you're going to study with Mr. Cortot. We may be leaving Berlin very soon."

Father wasn't thinking only of a new teacher at that moment. What was in the back of his mind was something else. Only a few weeks after my concert in the Bachsaal a street brawl broke out in the Victoria Luise Platz. Mother had taken my two sisters to play in the little park off the square. When Father and I walked there later to pick them up, we came upon two men grappling violently on the ground. A crowd had collected. To Father's inquiry what was going on, an onlooker said, "Oh, one of them is a Jew. He deserves what he's getting." Father got angry. "What's wrong with being a Jew?" The other fellow said, "Oh, he ought to go back where he came from!" When Father asked, "Where's that?" the other replied, "Palestine; we don't want him here."

What shocked me most at the time was the sight of two grown men grimly pummeling each other on the ground. But I grew more and more puzzled by the man's remarks. Why should a grown man want to punch another simply for being a Jew? What was wrong with being a Jew? Here was Mother teaching me stories from the Old Testament, speaking with the greatest reverence of the Jewish prophets, telling me that King Solomon was the wisest man who ever lived, that King David wrote beautiful songs and played the harp. Why would anyone beat up a man for being a Jew like them? I began to think maybe the man had committed some wrong. Maybe he was being beaten for some misbehavior . . . the way I was. Maybe, like me, he didn't quite understand just what he had done that was wrong.

Father's reaction was a good deal less speculative. He rushed us all home, and we were hardly there when he announced very solemnly, "We're making immediate arrangements to go to Paris. I don't want my family to stay here any more." The Germany he had so long vaunted as the land where fathers were bosses in their own homes and brought up their children with an iron fist was going just a little too far. The next day he communicated his decision to the Bechstein people, who tried their best to talk him out of it, how sincerely it is hard to say. They had derived loads of publicity from my two concerts, and they were drawing up large plans for me. Whatever Carl Bechstein's politics, he saw a good thing in me and wasn't going to let ideology spoil it if he could help it. I must say they were gracious enough to provide us with a letter of introduction to their representative in Paris.

Early in February, 1932, shortly after my seventh birthday, Father, Mother, Helen, Gloria, and I took a last look at this friendly, music-loving city that had almost overnight become a sinister place of dark hatreds, and mounted the train for Paris.

To the end Father always had a soft spot in his heart for the old prewar Germany. That was where he grew up and received his musical education. The Germans were clean, orderly, cultured, and he even stashed away thousands of German marks, certain that someday they would be worth something again. Poor man, he just couldn't understand how the German people accepted Hitler. There was something in it of personal affront to him, as if his own family had let him down.

On one of our European tours, after Hitler seized power, we were obliged to pass through Munich and wait for our plane at the airport. The wait was only twenty minutes, but they were twenty minutes of pure agony for Father. When soldiers passed and gave the nazi salute, Father muttered under his breath. I was not to open my mouth, he said, until we were safely on the next plane. However, an official, hearing Father's fluent German and noticing that I was looking about curiously, started a conversation with us. Not to arouse any suspicions, Father kept up a pretense of affable traveler's talk. I knew how he felt inside because he hated what he called the "greedy streak" in Mr. Cortot that made him give concerts in nazi Germany. When the plane arrived, we boarded it, settled back in our seats, and while the door was being sealed and the motors were going, Father looked out the window and caught sight of the genial official he had been conversing with. The gentleman was beaming and waving to us. Suddenly Father stuck out his tongue, thumbed his nose, and made faces—a personal one-man revolt against the people who had shattered one of his most cherished illusions.

Father had a great admiration for Mussolini that ended only when he came to terms with Hitler. That was the unpardonable sin. In my father's eyes the Italian dictator represented strength, the ability to get things done. All through the Ethiopian campaign he antagonized people by siding openly with Mussolini. "What's wrong with taking a savage country and making it a fit place for civilized people to live in?" he asked belligerently. "Isn't that how America was settled?"

When sanctions were imposed and Mussolini asked the women of Italy to donate their wedding rings for much-needed gold, Father even suggested that mother send in hers. Naturally she refused indignantly. Mother wasn't sold on Mussolini in the least, and besides she had never removed her wedding band and was superstitious about it. Some time later, on our return from a particularly lucrative American tour, we were enjoying a festive homecoming dinner, complete with embroidered tablecloth and flowers. Suddenly Father said:

"Mamma, take off your wedding ring!"

"I won't!" cried Mother, terrified. "I can't!"

"You must!"

Mother began to sob.

"Do as I say! Take it off!"

As he said this, he drew from his pocket a glittering little circle of perfect diamonds. Mother's tears dissolved in happiness, and all of us laughed and cried with her. To this day Mother wears the diamond band on her wedding finger. While still in Berlin I had been modestly coached in French by the German tutor assigned to me by the Bechstein Company, a certain Frau Danziger. What a knack that father of mine had for getting something for nothing wherever we went! The first thing we discovered about our hotel suite in Paris was that we didn't know how to open the windows. The rooms being a little warm for Father, he rang for the service. When the maid arrived, Father said to me, "All right, show off your French." I told the lady to open the window and she smiled and opened it and I just swelled all over with pride. I knew I was going to like Paris.

The following day Father and I trooped down to the Bechstein office, where we were most cordially received by a Mme. Balleron, the company's French representative. Arrangements were promptly made for delivery of a piano. For an apartment Mme. Balleron suggested a spot where I could practice without fear of complaint or reprisal. That was 4 Rue Faraday. "The proprietor," explained Mme. Balleron "has a musical family."

There, in a furnished flat, the five Slenczynskis resided till the Second World War broke out in 1939. Our apartment was on the sixth floor. Outside the living-room window was a small balcony overlooking the street. The sun flooded the place a large part of the day. All in all, it was a good place to go home to. On my last trip to Paris I was surprised to learn that the building, like every other in the vicinity, was almost a hundred years old. We had a primitive icebox, an old black stove, instead of a modern gas or electric appliance. To cook and bake anything, you had to put wood and coal in it. As a rule, we reached our top-floor apartment on foot. The elevator served an almost strictly ornamental purpose. I say "almost," because, although it always carried a sign reading, "Please Do Not Use the Elevator. It Is Out of Order," there were exceptions. I remember watching the concierge blandly removing the sign one afternoon and ceremoniously admitting a dignified-looking old lady into the lift. Thus emboldened, my sister Helen and I tried to sneak a ride on it later that day, only to hear the concierge screaming like fury at us. The "*minuterie*" also fascinated us. The hallway lighting was controlled by a button on each floor. You pressed it and the light stayed on for just one minute, till you got to the next floor. If you didn't make it in time, you fumbled in the dark for your next button.

In no time at all I became a little French girl. Indeed, when I went back to America a year later to play, I was speaking English with a French accent and French idioms. Till 1939 Paris was my home; the place we lived in for months on end, the place we came back to after long tours. I used to wear a little beret and adored going shopping. I love to recall the clop-clop of horses' hoofs as the milk wagons rolled by; the long loaves of bread with tiny pieces of wrapping paper around the middle where your hand held them; the live fish one bought (you just pointed and the victim was "caught" for your dinner). What fun it was when Father took us all on shopping tours! In Paris I found myself drawing closer to Helen and Gloria, almost as if we were discovering each other as sisters. Soon we became a little private unit of our own strengthened by our common fluency in French. Mother and Father never quite got the hang of the language. Things we didn't want Father to understand we uttered in double-quick French. That made him so furious he issued orders that only English was to be spoken at table. "You should be proud that your kids speak French so beautifully," Mother protested. That fact alone, of a new language mastered and shared, helped me to feel a little bit more like the normal children my sisters were. Another new link was the French game of "à la marelle," which is our hopscotch. While Father was having his daily beer in some bistro, we would draw a big "marelle," or hopscotch design, on the sidewalk and sneak in some fun. We also played "cache-cache," which is hide-and-seek with French variations. Sometimes Father's beer lasted ten minutes, ten minutes of heaven for the three of us. If he caught us, I was the only one reviled for being a baby and a moron. Those stolen moments on the sidewalk were my escape. My sisters could do so many things that were forbidden me. For instance, I was not allowed to touch the tempting little French storybooks that Helen pored over raptly. If I so much as stole a glance in the direction of one, I got my ears boxed for not being a "serious young lady."

My eyes were supposed to be only for the beautiful seven-foot Bechstein piano that Mme. Balleron had placed at my disposal. It left precious little room for anything else in our living room, or in me. The cries of laughter of my sisters and their friends would reach me through the open window from the sunny street below. They would yell up to me in French, teasing, inviting things. I didn't even dare flick an eyelash toward the window, in dread of Father poised over me like a watchful dragon. Once a little laugh burst from me at one of Helen's sallies. Father gave me such a pounding I never flickered after that.

Shortly after the Bechstein arrived, Father took me to see Mr. Cortot at the Ecole Normale on the Boulevard Malesherbes. Mr. Cortot was conducting a master class when we arrived one morning. Toward the end of the session he turned to me, introduced me to the class, and then asked me to play. Now the room was filled with thirty or forty adults, all fully trained pianists. Each of them had played and received Mr. Cortot's comments. Many seemed amused, and some snickered when Father perched me in front of the piano and bade me play Bach's "Italian" concerto. At the end there were loud salvos of applause, and Mr. Cortot crowned my triumph by declaring to the class: "I couldn't play it any better myself." Privately, he told us the place to teach me was not in class but at his home. He said he felt that to sit and listen to a lot of other pupils, however advanced, was a waste of time for a talent as "quick" as mine. And so began an association with this French master that was to last seven years.

Alfred Cortot's home was on the Avenue Henri Martin. There I spent some of the most precious and illuminating days of my life. In very little time the place became a second home to me. There were no fixed hours or days for my visits with Mr. Cortot, weekdays, Sundays, even holidays. He seemed to prefer teaching me to enjoying the proverbial day of rest. The attractive and spacious apartment was on the top floor. In Paris when you buy an apartment, you get with it a small room for the maid in the Mansard roof. If you buy a large suite, you acquire two such rooms. If it happens to be a very large apartment house, you do still better. You get one large maid's room and a smaller bedchamber in a Mansard still higher up. Mr. Cortot's apartment was in the last category. In his case, however, the rooms formed a single unit connected by staircases which he had built when he moved in. One of these led from the main apartment to the larger maid's room; the other led from there to the smaller chamber above it. There was a large piano on the main level which Mr. Cortot used only on special occasions. The real studio was the large Mansard room to which one climbed up a winding staircase. In the middle of it stood a grand piano. Books and music were everywhere, on shelves, tables, chairs. On the floor were beautiful Persian rugs, and on an easel the unfinished picture of a violin. I assume that Mr. Cortot had given up working on this picture because seven years later when I saw it for the last time it was in exactly the same state of incompletion. To reach the smaller Mansard room on the third level, you climbed up a straight ladderlike stairway. This formed a sort of gallery over the first. Its walls were lined with books all the way up to the ceiling. Most of the windows in Mr. Cortot's triplex dwelling were hung with orange curtains. Paris is gray and foggy much of the year. Yet even on the grayest day I remember how the curtains gave a cheerful illusion of sunlight. It was a pleasant place in which to be.

I always found Mr. Cortot an easy man to talk to, and a modest one. Nothing was indisputable. There was always a "maybe," "I suppose," "don't you think?" in what he said. He was constantly searching, experimenting. A little accent or nuance might be altered the next time we met, always tentatively, as if he were consulting me. "Try a little *crescendo* here, a little *ritenuto* there," he might say. "Let's see if you like it." I would bring it back exactly that way. He would shake his head. "It sounds too set the way you do it. It has no air of improvisation. Try it this way. . . . What do you think?"

Cortot taught me how plastic the art of interpretation can be. No two persons, no two pianists, no two pianos are alike, he said. How then can any two interpretations be alike? Moreover, just as no person ever felt exactly the same way twice, so no pianist ever felt exactly the same way twice about the same piece of music. A composition was absolutely fixed only in print, he said. Beyond that, little remained static but the general outline.

"There are lots of little doors left open by the composer," he explained one day. "Through these doors you search for the composer's secret little wishes. There are always a few treasures for everyone to find."

Cortot it was who really put fascination into playing the piano for me. Mr. Schnabel had made me think of these same patterns as immutable. Detailed instructions had gone with every phrase. There was only one way to play a piece of music. Any other was infidelity to the composer. Mr. Cortot's teachings seemed wholly opposed to this. But a strange thing happened. Instead of being rattled by the two methods, I found they gave meaning to each other. Things I hadn't quite grasped in Mr. Schnabel's studio I now saw clearly for the first time in the new light shed by Mr. Cortot. Mr. Schnabel had said of the second movement of Mozart's F major sonata:

"Start *pianissimo*, make a very gradual *crescendo* with the right hand till you reach F. Round out the phrase on the C very, very softly. Make it ask a question. Meanwhile keep the left hand absolutely smooth and even."

Mr. Cortot, hearing me do the passage to the best of my childish ability, would say:

"Think of the spring. There are butterflies in the air. Birds are singing. Isn't it a beautiful day? Let's hear you sing, because you are happy and it is spring! If you make a little *crescendo* because you feel you would like to, that's fine. . . . Relax!"

I found out that if I started *pianissimo* and made the gentle *crescendo* up to F and rounded out the question on C—the way Mr. Schnabel showed me how—and if at the same time I could think of green trees and children playing in the sunlight and smile in my innermost soul, I was obeying both Mr. Schnabel and Mr. Cortot.

In so much that he said and did as a musician Mr. Cortot was dominated by a twin sense of drama and expression. When it came to building a program, he was like a playwright planning a three-act play, studying the effect of every scene in relation to the next.

"Never give the show away at the very beginning," he once said to me. "Tease and excite the audience little by little. Save your best effects for the end. Tantalize them at first, arouse their sense of anticipation."

He cautioned me against placing side by side two compositions in the same key or in related keys.

"Give each piece a fresh start with a new key," he said. "Moreover, don't play two slow pieces or two dramatic pieces one right after the other. Alternate them."

The worst mistake of all was to place compositions of exactly the same type together, unless one was playing a special program in some series or other.

"One waltz," he used to say, kissing his fingers, "charming. Two waltzes, quite nice; three waltzes, eh, a little tiring. Four waltzes, impossible. The audience walks out."

I remember entering Mr. Cortot's studio one day while an audition was going on. The pianist was a boy of fifteen or sixteen. In the corner of the room sat a sweet-faced woman who every now and then gave Mr. Cortot an eager, hopeful look. This was the boy's mother. They had come all the way from Algeria to play for Mr. Cortot. The boy had given a few small concerts at home and both were persuaded a glowing career lay ahead. Mr. Cortot was expected to confirm their hopes. He sat there smoking cigarette after cigarette as the boy played. The mother's eyes traveled from one to the other. Father and I sat near by. The boy played some Bach, a movement from a Mozart sonata, and some Chopin. After each piece, Mr. Cortot would say, "Very nice, very nice," and other encouraging things. Finally the boy stopped. The mother looked at Mr. Cortot: "Well, master, what do you think of him?"

"I have been telling you compliments all along," said Mr. Cortot slowly. "I think your boy needs and deserves good training. My advice is to enroll him at the Ecole Normale. He should do very nicely in our classes there."

"But, Monsieur Cortot, I want him to have private lessons with you," said the mother in an aggrieved tone.

"I'm sorry, Madame," said Mr. Cortot, "I am very busy. My concert tours take me constantly out of Paris. If you desire private lessons for your son, you must go elsewhere. I don't teach privately."

"But we came all the way from Algeria because we heard that you were teaching a little girl and getting astonishing results from her."

Mr. Cortot said: "Ah, but there is a difference. . . . Would you like to hear that little girl play?"

"Oh yes! Oh yes!" cried the mother, and turned to look at me in frank amazement when Mr. Cortot introduced me.

"Ruth," he said, "will you oblige by playing the same music that our handsome young visitor from Algeria has just played for us?"

I was child enough to relish the situation without sensing its cruel side. I played each of the boy's numbers, and when I turned around, the mother was crying. She thanked Mr. Cortot for the interview, then kissed both my hands, and gathering her son to her, left the studio. I don't dare guess what the boy's feelings were. I know what mine would have been had the roles been reversed.

I wince to think of the number of times my name must have come up in parental sermons addressed to laggard would-be prodigies. Hopeful fathers and mothers looked on me as a shining example of infant achievement. I was a model of obedience and hard work. The child pianists and fiddlers who suffered on my account must run into the hundreds. If any of them read this book, they have my deepest apologies. They also have the satisfaction of knowing that my career was far from the bed of roses their parents pictured it to be. I would not wish its black years on my worst enemy. I only hope they will spare me any further rancor. I was a prize exhibit and merely did what I was told. I had not been taught to worry about other people's feelings.

Mr. Cortot soon became quite proud of his little protégé. I

was paraded before all his friends, made to play for anyone who had the slightest wish to hear me. Father reacted to all this with mixed feelings. He resented deeply the fact that for the first time I was officially and conspicuously the pupil of someone other than himself. At the same time he saw the advantages of my being thus exhibited in the best Parisian circles. For it was through Mr. Cortot that I met the Baroness Edouard de Rothschild, who immediately arranged a reception in my honor. There I gave a little concert and Artur Rubinstein came over to congratulate me. He took my hand in his after I finished playing Weber's "Perpetual Motion," and said "You're going to make a fine pianist. You see, your hand is square-shaped, like mine; just as broad as it is long. And your fingers are good and solid." I have always worshiped this princely artist. At that time he was still far from being fully appreciated by the public and press. This sad state of affairs even got into one of Father's warnings to me:

"Ruth, if you don't work hard, you're going to wind up some-day like poor Mr. Rubinstein." At the reception he and Father exchanged a few words in Polish. Our little chat was in English. The Baroness overwhelmed me with gifts that night. There was a sterling-silver fountain pen, which wound up as a wedding present for one of Father's nephews. There was a solid-gold pencil with calendar attached, which Father sold. There was a gor-geous little evening bag with money in it. Heaven only knows where that went. If the Baroness thought that by the simple act of giving them to me they became mine, Father knew better.

Nor was the loot all that Father acquired from the reception at the Baroness de Rothschild's. That good lady asked Father what she could do for me during our stay in Paris. Father promptly suggested she might provide me with a French tutor. So, twice a week thereafter, a Mlle. Jeanne Knoertzer, who had been her daughter's governess, came to converse in French and teach me French poetry and literature. Together we read plays by Molière, Racine, and Beaumarchais; novels by Balzac; stories by De Maupassant. Some weren't exactly the sort of thing mother approved of, and some of the more shocking I scarcely understood. But Mlle. Knoertzer said they were good literature. That sufficed to make them acceptable to Father. The truth is that this was all out of his line, completely alien to him, like everything else outside of music. Yet he knew its value as part of a prodigy's stock in trade. Twice a week Mlle. Knoertzer and I talked French history, French drama, French fiction, always in French, and twice a week I was out of Father's reach. These sessions occurred on Tuesdays and Thursdays. Meanwhile a Mrs. Webb, soon replaced by a Miss Graves, came on Mondays, Wednesdays, and Fridays to tutor me in English and English literature. My day was now something like this:

Promptly at six o'clock Father would sweep the covers off me, pull at my leg till I was in a sitting position, growl a "Time to get up," and go back to bed. I was up, washed and doing my English or French homework till 7:30, with Mother helping me. By that time Father was ready for me at the Bechstein. That continued till 9:30. Then came breakfast. By that time my sisters were off to kindergarten or school and Mother was tidying up the back of the apartment. Breakfast over, back to piano till 11:30 or 12, followed by a half-hour walk with Father, during which we met my sisters on the way home for lunch. This was often our playtime together for the brief, stolen games of tag, hopscotch, and hide-and-seek, while Father quaffed his beer. Then came the family lunch, after which my sisters would hustle back to school, Father would take his nap, and one of my tutors would come for an hour's instruction. At 2:30 I rejoined Father at the piano till 5:30 or 6. Another half-hour walk with Father and my sisters was followed by supper, topped off by more practice till 9:30 or 10. The practicing would have begun at 6:30 A.M. instead of 7:30 except for a neighbor's complaint, followed by a visit from the concierge. Even so, we still managed to get in our nine hours a day at the keyboard.

This schedule was only varied on Sundays, when instead of practicing till 5:30, I stopped at 4:30, at which time the family donned their Sunday best and might be seen strolling down the Champs Elyséss. Sometimes the parade ended at Louis Sherry's for an ice cream; sometimes at Flambaum's to indulge Mother's craving for *kreplach*; and once in a long while at a Chinese restaurant. Once or twice, en route, I pestered Father into telling us stories. I had hoped for the strange tales of lions and dragons and wizards I had heard Mr. Smadbeck tell his daughter Jinny as she sat in his lap. There were no lions in Father's stories, only poor boys who through hard work and study one day became famous and wealthy as great musicians. The stories never varied; they never had suspense, they were never funny. The result was that while Father and Mother went in somewhere to have coffee, Helen and Gloria would grab hold of me and beg for real stories, and I made up all sorts of yarns about fairies and princesses and ballerinas, and we three just sailed off into dreamland together. There wasn't a musician in any of my stories. Sometimes on the Place Wagram we watched the song vendors hawking their wares to the strains of an accordion till Father and Mother emerged from the café. If you lingered long enough, as I did, you could learn the song by heart without buying it. I acquired dozens and dozens of them that way. Father would have paddled me to within an inch of my life if I had dared play any of them at home. Years later, while at college, I sometimes entertained students at parties with tunes I had picked up on the sidewalks of Paris.

Soon after introducing me around to French society, Mr. Cortot decided the time had come for me to give a recital in Paris.

And the place for it was the Salle Pleyel. However, there was one small hitch. The French public might not take kindly to a Bechstein piano in the Salle Pleyel. The feeling against rival German products was too strong, he said. Since he himself used the French piano, he proposed that we talk to the Pleyel officials. When Mme. Balleron got wind of this, a bitter fight was fought over me between the Bechstein and Pleyel factions. Thanks largely to Mr. Cortot, Pleyel won. Mme. Balleron was deeply hurt by our ingratitude, and her house lost whatever sales they were hoping to promote from my use of the Bechstein piano in Paris. Father himself really preferred the Bechstein at home to the Pleyel that came now to replace it. He was quite put out when the truckmen showed up to remove it. He had no choice, however, but to side with Mr. Cortot.

I believe it was sometime in May of 1932 when, at Mr. Cortot's advice, I gave a special concert for the press in the little Salle Chopin. The critics were absolutely wild about me. Immediately a grand concert, with orchestra, was announced for the great Salle Pleyel, which is the Carnegie Hall of Paris. Actually it was a combination concert and recital. Between two groups of solo numbers I was to play the A major concerto of Mozart, with Alfred Cortot conducting the Orchestre Symphonique de Paris. This was, in short, my debut as a concert soloist, the fulfillment of a dream that began that evening outside Miss Ellinwood's house when Father first told me what a concerto was. This was also one of the very few times in my life when I was nervous at the prospect of playing the piano in public. I was just plain scared. I had gotten to know orchestral music pretty well. I loved going to concerts and watching other pianists and violinists playing in front of a hundred musicians. That was what Rachmaninoff and Heifetz and Elman and Mr. Cortot were always doing. The fact that I was now going to do the same thing, with a real genuine orchestra to accompany me, completely overawed me. I dreaded telling Father about my sudden qualms. Instead, I told Mother, and she told Father, and Father went to work on me. Was I going to let Menuhin and Ricci do things at my age that I couldn't do? Was I trying to show what a sissy I was? What was there to worry about anyway?

"You've been playing this concerto long enough on two pianos, haven't you?"

"Yes, but that's different."

"It's not different! You watch and see. After you rehearse it with Mr. Cortot and the orchestra, everything will be fine."

So I turned up for rehearsal at the Salle Pleyel looking like a frightened little rabbit. Mr. Cortot was going over the *tuttis* with the men when I entered the hall. There, to one side, ominously black, stood the piano waiting for me. Before I took my place, Mr. Cortot gave a little speech to the orchestra. They were going to play, he said, with a very young lady, but please to ignore her size, for she was really a fine little artist. There was some polite applause when I climbed up the piano bench, and I thought I caught a few snickers. At a wave from Mr. Cortot's baton we started to play. Midway in the first movement Mr. Cortot signaled a halt. Someone had misunderstood his beat. Mr. Cortot turned to me and said in French, for everyone to hear:

"Something went wrong, mademoiselle. Was it you? Was it me? Was it the orchestra?"

I replied in French: "It was not I. It was not you. It was the flutist. He came in a little late."

The orchestra gave one big cheer, and from that moment on we were the best of friends. I think there then began for me that warm feeling of *camaraderie* I have whenever I play with an orchestra. I knew then there was no fun in the world like making music together. . . . My fright had vanished.

I had a little pink georgette dress made for me for my concert. This was done on the initiative and at the expense of the Baroness de Rothschild's daughter Jacqueline, who is now Mrs. Gregor Piatigorsky. Jacqueline was taking master classes with Mr. Cortot at the time—unlike privileged me, who was being coached privately. Her interest in me was touching and practical. One day she came with her beautiful, chauffeured car to take Father and me to her dressmaker's. There she had this dress made for me, and I simply went wild over it. I called it "my ice-cream dress." In time, it became a favorite of my sisters, too, first Helen, then Gloria. When it finally descended to Gloria, I was working on Liszt's arrangement of Paganini's "La Campanella." I was practicing the piece one Sunday when little Gloria marched out in the pink dress, ready for the family stroll. Thereafter it was known as "the ice-cream Campanella dress."

The concert, which took place in June, 1932, was everything we hoped for. I had the crowd in the palms of my two tiny hands, and the uproar that followed the Mozart concerto equaled, if it didn't exceed, the upheaval at the Bachsaal in Berlin. I felt a deep glow of triumph as I walked out after the concerto between two throngs of applauding admirers, the orchestra to the right of me and the audience to the left. Backstage I was greeted by several French relatives, bearing flowers. They had come distances of five and six hours from Paris to hear me. A scout for Columbia Artists must have sent urgent word about me to New York, for their Mr. Coppicus immediately cabled Father that he was leaving for Paris to discuss an American tour for me. This coincided with a brisk exchange of telegrams and letters between Father and Columbia's rival, Charles Wagner. Arriving in Paris, Mr. Coppicus sought out Father for a quick decision. He was turned down in favor of Mr. Wagner for two reasons: Mr. Wagner did not require a contract; and

Mr. Wagner sent us boat tickets to America prepaid. This appealed to Father's shrewd business sense, soothed his instinct for thrift, and left him a free agent.

The following night it was my turn to sit and listen as another pianist played. The pianist was Ignace Paderewski. At the Champs Elysées Theater, where he played, Father and I occupied the same box with the singer Ganna Walska. Electrified as I was by the playing, I couldn't take my eyes off a fabulous-looking woman in a lower box. To me she was a figure out of fairyland, white hat, white furs, dazzling white dress. Only such splendor could lure my gaze away from the romantic Pole who was playing the piano like a god. At intermission time someone knocked on Mme. Walska's box. The gentleman bowed and delivered a message: "Her Majesty Queen Astrid of Belgium would like the honor of meeting the little lady if she would be so kind as to accompany me to her box." Eyes popping, I followed the gentleman downstairs and when the door of the box opened, I saw that it was my lady in white. I stood there speechless with adoration. Smiling, she asked me to sit beside her, and as in a trance I heard her say she had heard me the night before and would have come backstage but feared she might keep me from getting to bed as quickly as possible. She told me her mother-in-law had been a pupil of the Belgian violinist Eugène Ysaÿe, that she herself took a great interest in music and musicians, and that I had a standing invitation to the palace if ever I came to Brussels. "I wish you a happy life," were her last words to me.

Before the second half of the program started, an even more picturesque figure made his appearance in Mme. Walska's box. When the door opened, I was convinced the man was a pirate. He wore a big turban, had diamonds in his ears and another diamond encrusted on each side of his nose. I was pretty sure I had guessed right because I was then reading *Treasure Island*.

I was wrong, of course, and perhaps a little disappointed, too. The exotic-looking gentleman was the Prince of Morocco. He stooped to kiss my hand and said in a very British accent:

"I have been told that you are a stupendous pianist."

I said proudly, "Yes, I just played last night with orchestra in the Salle Pleyel."

"Oh, I must hear you sometime. I adore music."

He took my hand and studied it awhile.

"How little, and still you play."

And I said, "That doesn't mean a thing. I played when I was four years old and my hand was still smaller then."

I was dying to ask him if he was or had ever been a pirate. Something restrained me. Instead I asked: "What do you do?"

"Oh, I'm the Prince of Morocco."

"Gee," I said, remembering Mother's geography lessons, "aren't there lots of oranges growing there?"

And then the lights were lowered and he left.

The music critics all said flattering things about me the following morning. A few reviewed my concert and Mr. Paderewski's together. One of them remarked that in the space of twenty-four hours he had heard both the youngest and the oldest pianists of the concert world. I thought that cute. What Mr. Paderewski thought I never found out. I can imagine what Mr. Schnabel's thoughts were, however, on a somewhat similar occasion. I was about ten when he and I happened to be giving recitals the same afternoon in New York, he at Carnegie Hall, I at Town Hall. Whether by chance or design, both of us also played the same Mozart sonata that afternoon. Since the sonata came at different times on our programs, the critic Samuel Chotzinoff reviewed us together. Comparing both interpretations, Mr. Chotzinoff said that in all honesty he had to prefer mine because mine was so fresh.

In the fall of 1932 I made a second appearance in Paris with orchestra, this time under the baton of Pierre Monteux. Like Mr. Rubinstein, Mr. Monteux was not quite yet the world-renowned figure in music he was to become in a few years. The program attracted considerable attention on two counts: it bracketed the music of Bach and Debussy, and in the F minor concerto of Bach it had as soloist a seven-year-old pianist. The event was a triumph for both me and Mr. Monteux. We were to make many appearances together in years to come, both in France and in America. Yet Father never quite hit it off with Mr. Monteux. "A viola player," he would say sniffing, "who became a ballet conductor." I myself worshiped him.

By this time Father was talking turkey with Mr. Wagner about a debut in New York. In his eyes I was already established. If the people of Berlin and Paris flocked to hear me play, why not the people of New York? If Europe's toughest critics hailed me, why shouldn't New York's? However he might beat and belittle me, he knew he could count on me to play three full solo programs well. I had mastered two concertos by Mozart, one by Bach, and was now working on Beethoven's first. There was also Mr. Saperton's advice about making all the money he could out of me in vaudeville while I was still young. Those words never stopped rankling in Father's mind. One of his latest jibes at me was this: "Mr. Saperton was right. You don't belong on the concert stage; you belong in vaudeville."

Under Mr. Cortot's care, I had mastered Beethoven's "Pathétique" sonata, Bach's "Chromatic" fantasy and fugue, and an immense amount of Chopin and Schubert. I had ready three completely different programs of such music, each running seventy minutes, none of it children's music, none of it simplified, and I wasn't eight yet! Perhaps as a freak I did belong in vaudeville. I worked like a fiend on the Beethoven concerto, my biggest accomplishment before returning to America. I had always had a healthy respect for Beethoven. But some teachers had warned me to stay away from his music till I grew up. Neither Mr. Schnabel nor Mr. Cortot was of that school. Mr. Schnabel always called it the most mature music ever written, but that I should learn it young so that I could mature with it. Mr. Cortot's idea was that, too: I should grow up with music rather than grow up first and then meet the music on more even ground.

While working on the Beethoven concerto, I asked Mr. Cortot what I should do about a cadenza in the first movement.

"Why don't you write one?" he said.

Well, a week later I announced to Mr. Cortot that I had completed my cadenza. "Where is it?" he asked, and I told him I had it all worked out in my head. "Play it," he said, and when I did he was delighted. "Is there any key you have overlooked?" he said, laughing. He wouldn't let me change a single note, however. When I first played it in America the following year, everyone urged me to publish it. Of course it was still only in my head. So Mr. Carl Deis of Schirmer's came over to the Ansonia Hotel to write it down while I dictated from the piano. Mr. Deis later had me play the cadenza for Ossip Gabrilowitsch at the Beethoven Association. After listening gravely, Mr. Gabrilowitsch took me in his lap and told me to call him "Uncle Ossip." Some time later I met him again in the same place. "Come," he said, " I will play for *you* today." And "Uncle Ossip" sat down and played my cadenza!

During the summer of 1933 Charles Wagner wrote Father that he had booked Town Hall for me for the evening of November 13. Now that the step was taken, we were all in a state of confusion and excitement. Who was to go with me? Father or the whole family? Father decided a precedent had been set with our trip to Philadelphia. Mother should remain behind with Helen and Gloria. That didn't please Mother one bit. She insisted I would need a mother's care in the nervous and uncertain ordeal ahead. Father asked her if anything bad had happened to Mozart and his sister when their father took them away on tour. There was nothing to worry about. He was perfectly capable of taking care of me. Hadn't he done all right by me so far? In the end I suppose Mother was more resigned than persuaded. She knitted a white scarf and beret for me, and did so thereafter every single time I went on tour. I'm afraid it didn't quite sink in that I was leaving Mother and my two sisters till we boarded the boat train. We talked and talked about it, and I still recalled that earlier leave-taking in Berkeley. Now, as the train pulled out, I burst into tears. I cried as if the world had come to an end. For once Father did not scold me. He understood. Gently he said:

"Come now, Ruth, you've got work ahead, lots and lots of concerts to give. You're going to play beautifully. You're going to wear pretty dresses and bow to thousands of people. You're going to America where they speak English all year round."

He took out some American dollar bills.

"Look at this money, so solid and green, not like those big dog-eared floppy French bills."

I must say he did his level best to get me in the mood. I took out a little chocolate bar Mother had given me and nibbled on it thoughtfully.

DURING the crossing I could feel from Father's behavior that he was rehearsing the many things he planned to tell the press once we were settled in New York. This was the great moment of his life. He would shine in all his glory as the maker of a genius. Imagine his chagrin when Mr. Wagner insisted on granting no interviews till after my debut. Father ranted in protest. Mr. Wagner let him rant on. When the storm subsided, he quietly warned Father that a preconcert hullabaloo might prejudice the critics. Also, it might give rise to extravagant expectation. The less the event was publicized the better: there would be no letdown if something went wrong. Grudgingly Father gave in. Mr. Wagner then proceeded to put the damper on me. I had raved to him about the gorgeous long formal gowns a French designer had made for me. They were part of Father's free-loading, a promise of free advertising in the Town Hall program having been made to the gullible lady earlier that year in Paris. I had already worn one of these gowns with great pride at my concert with Mr. Monteux. And now here was Mr. Wagner telling me that I couldn't wear them on the Town Hall stage. They might be all right for Paris, he said, but they were far too fancy on a child for America. In my own way, I felt just as deflated as Father. Instead, I wore a short white dress with red velvet bows, white shoes, and white socks, all bought for me at Saks Fifth Avenue by Mrs. Smadbeck.

It took some persuading to make me feel I was still a concert pianist in that short dress.

Even without the long formal, I guess I just took the Town Hall by storm. The cheering crowd rushed to the stage, shouting for encores. The *Tribune* put me on the front page the following day, as "The Amazing Ruth Slenczynski." A headline in another paper read, "Not Since Mozart."

To the critic of the New York *Times* I was an "electrifying experience"—something "nature had produced in one of her most bounteous moods." I showed the "temperament, the brilliance and the confidence of the born virtuoso." My tone was "big and clean and refreshingly musical." My phrasing had "breadth and spaciousness." My musical instinct was "innate" and: "What fire!"

The writer ("H.T.") admitted being prepared, when he entered the hall, "to get wrathful with management and parents for causing so young a child to face a big piano and a bigger audience." He was won by my "unaffected stage presence, adorable smile and marvelous pianism." I had not, he summed up, been "wasting my youth."

Jerome D. Bohm, of the New York *Herald Tribune*, also entered Town Hall a skeptic and came away "astounded" by what he termed a "musical phenomenon." These secrets "of touch and technic which many pianists strive futilely for years to unravel," had been imparted to me "through some inexplicable source."

"This sturdy girl of eight" he went on, "was in some ways even more amazing than was Yehudi Menuhin when he first appeared in New York as a boy of eight." It was one thing, Mr. Bohm said, "to manipulate a half-size violin, as Menuhin and Ricci did, and quite another to place a girl of eight before a huge concert grand and await anything more than the weak tones one would naturally expect. But sitting on the edge of the stool, with her feet barely able to reach the pedals, this child drew from her instrument incredible volumes of sound."

In the *Daily Mirror* Julian Seaman detected "immaturities of course" in Bach's "Chromatic" fantasy and Beethoven's "Pathétique," but found my technic, my "fluent singing tone," my "instinctive feel" for balanced phrasing "almost incredible."

W. J. Henderson pronounced the only strong note of doubt. My "valuable gifts," he said in the New York *Sun*, were obvious, but my "interpretative intelligence" could not be determined at so early an age. I was playing notes as I had been taught, even "carefully taught to distort phrases." Despite my gifts, I should have been kept at studies till she is about twice my age.

That review by the then dean of New York critics positively infuriated Father. He felt personally maligned by the remark about distorted phrases and the clear innuendos about child exploitation.

For days reporters and photographers crowded into our room at the Hotel Ansonia to view and interview "the red-cheeked girl of eight who wanted to be the best pianist in the world." To one and all Father solemnly announced he had "willed" my genius into being. When someone addressed me as "Ruthie," I protested with great dignity that my name was "Ruth." To a photographer who asked me to pose holding a doll, I said: "It wouldn't be natural." To a *Daily Mirror* man who asked me what I thought of my own talent I replied:

"I have a great deal to learn yet. I hope in the next five years I can learn a little of the great deal I don't know."

The public and the New York press, or at least most of it, seemed to be of one mind: I was something extraordinary.

Less than two weeks later, on November 25, 1933, I played an entirely new program at the Brooklyn Academy of Music. That, too, was a spectacular success. A significant second review appeared in the New York *Times* the following day. This one was signed by Olin Downes, the paper's first-string critic at the time. It said I "confirmed the impression" I had made a few days previous. I was not, of course, "and could not be, a matured musician," but I was phenomenally precocious in a way that "connoted exceptionally great gifts and incipient virtuosity of a remarkable order." A year later Mr. Downes wrote I should return to my studies before making any further public appearances. That statement was to start Father on a rampage of hate and slander against the distinguished critic of the New York *Times*. Of that, more later. . . .

The point of all this is that, reservations and warnings to the contrary, I was launched in grand style. Prodigy, phenomenon, parrot, freak, automaton, circus performer, whatever it was they labeled me—even genius—I was on my way. Three months later when Josef Slenczynski went back to Paris he had stashed away something better than $35,000. The business instinct in Father was now in full flower. My fees went up by the hour. A single five-minute broadcast brought us $3000, when $3000 was what it says. A few times Father overshot his mark. Leopold Stokowski wanted me to do three concertos at three separate concerts. Father coaxed the offer up to $3000, held out for $4000, and lost the deal. He blamed the mishap on me, reasoning thus: "I would have let you play with Stokowski at that measly price; but I didn't trust you to play right." When the Metropolitan Opera Company wanted me to play at one of their Sunday-night concerts, Mr. Wagner asked Father how much he should demand. "How much do you think?" asked Father. Mr. Wagner said, "Oh, five hundred, maybe seven hundred and fifty ——" Father stopped him cold: "My daughter Ruth won't play a note for less than fifteen hundred dollars." Father had now established that figure as my "rock-bottom" fee.

During this time a whole new world had opened to me at the Ansonia Hotel, where we were stopping. This was a kind of Mecca for musicians from all over the globe. Here they congregated to talk, practice, teach, eat, and breathe music. The building is solid, the walls between rooms are soundproof, and everybody bellowed scales and banged out octaves to his heart's content. Outside on the street it sounded like a menagerie. One day I ran into my old friend Leopold Godowsky; the next I met Mr. and Mrs. Feodor Chaliapin and their son Boris; then old Alexander Siloti, one of the last surviving pupils of Liszt. There I came to know Tullio Serafin, then conducting at the Metropolitan; the whole Menuhin family, and the Riccis.

I remember Chaliapin, a huge, bright, and lavish personality. From his great height he would ask me to play something, and as I did he would go marching up and down the living room, conducting, humming, singing, dancing. If I played anything at all spectacular, he would turn to his accompanist and, in a voice that made me tremble for the poor fellow, say:

"Listen to this child! Why can't you do something like that?"

Mrs. Chaliapin hovered about the apartment, always in an apron, always cleaning house, always, it seemed to me, a little afraid of Mr. Chaliapin. There was something overwhelming about this restless giant whose love of life and music was limitless. The man was music in action. Almost as awesome as Mr. Chaliapin was a great big painting that hung in the living room. It was a portrait by his son Boris of Mr. Rachmaninoff seated at the piano in his shirtsleeves. It looked so like Mr. Rachmaninoff that the first time I saw it I wanted to go up and talk to it.

The Chaliapins were always worrying about my health, what I ate and where I ate. Mr. Chaliapin used to tell Father about a little Jewish restaurant on Seventy-third Street and Broadway, just a short distance from the Ansonia Hotel.

"Take her there and order some chicken soup and nice boiled

beef," he would say. "Very simple food; that's for her. She's putting on the wrong kind of flesh."

Which was all Father needed to berate me later for my big stomach and bad posture. I was a fat and lazy good-for-nothing, and it was all because I ate too much and worked too little. I had disgraced him before the great Feodor Chaliapin. Yet Father was the one who was gorging me with rich foods and bragging about my fat rosy cheeks!

Every time we stopped at the Ansonia, Father and I used to walk over to the Automat around the corner on West Seventy-second Street for breakfast. On the way back one day we noticed a couple of ladies with baby carriages and little children sunning themselves in a bright patch of sidewalk outside the door of the hotel. One of the little girls was particularly adorable. It was a fine day and Father must have been feeling in a good mood. He struck up a conversation with the girl, and, turning to the mother, who had no idea who we were, said:

"Such a beautiful child! What would you like her to be when she grows up?"

Without a moment's hesitation, the mother replied:

"Ruth Slenczynski."

And my father said: "Why is that?"

"Oh, it must be wonderful to be so famous, to have such a gift, to give so many concerts, and make so much money."

"Hmm. What do you think of my little girl? Do you think she looks unusual at all?"

The woman gave me a polite look of appraisal.

"She's a mighty cute little girl. You keep her nice and chubby, don't you?"

"Well," said Father coldly, "you're looking at Ruth Slenczynski."

The mother gaped at the two of us as Father took my hand and pulled me into the lobby.

My favorite spot in the lobby was the newsstand. It was there I discovered the bright-colored funny papers that fascinated me more than anything in America. I never bought them, of course. They were strictly forbidden fruit. I filched precious moments devouring them while Father stood talking to someone in the lobby or went for the mail. Once he caught me and fairly screamed:

"Why must you act like a baby and disgrace yourself?"

That winter I went all over America, stopping off for a highly triumphant return to San Francisco. Out of this first tour Father paid back to the Tobin family half of the money already advanced, or well over six thousand dollars. This he had resolved to do to free himself of any sense of obligation to anyone. Meanwhile terse, to-the-point cables were reaching Mother periodically. The first of them, following the Town Hall debut, ran, "Dearest Mamma: Great success"; the next one, "Dearest Mamma: Still greater success." I recall one that read, "Dearest Mamma: Great Success—financially too."

Father's new-found affluence brought on a buying splurge at one of the best tailors in New York, Rolnick's. The recommendation was made by a friend of Mr. Smadbeck's, a certain Mr. Marx who was rated "one of the ten best-dressed men" of the time. At one crack Father bought six suits costing $250 each. At no cost at all, on the other hand, he wangled from Saks Fifth Avenue a handsome wardrobe for me, including a squirrel coat made to measure, a designer's hat, and several dresses. I was widely photographed in these garments, so I assume there was adequate publicity for all parties concerned. The photographs certainly came in handy. Articles, with art displays, appeared in many of the big magazines. The very first issue of *Life* carried a picture of me. *Time, Town and Country, The American* wrote Me up. *Etude* ran a piece about how I practiced.

I was even called "Girl of the Month" in an article in *Good Housekeeping*.

That same "Girl of the Month" had soon acquired another unique distinction. It was announced that the following year's contract would gross me over $75,000 for thirty concerts. Much was made of the fact, then and in the years to come, that it was possible for an eight-year-old girl to earn more money with her own two hands than the President of the United States.

Then there were the presents. This was quite natural considering how young I was and how people like to shower performing children with little tokens of their appreciation. Father had early learned how to turn this to his advantage. My private teachers were urged to make out lists of books I should read. When people asked me what I should like to have, I was to name these books. Father's idea was that it would prevent my getting such useless trifles as candy or flowers. Books were far more useful, as were petticoats, which came after books on my request list of presents. My sister Helen had been pestering Father for roller skates. Father had the answer to that. On my very next tour the first time someone asked me what I wanted as a gift, I answered without a moment's hesitation, "Roller skates." The gentleman who provided them, a newspaper man, may be pleased to know that my sister put them to very good use, and Gloria after her. I didn't get on them once. You see, I might fall and damage the little gold mine Father had discovered in my hands.

A woman once stepped out of a crowd backstage at the Metropolitan and coming up to me, tense with emotion and crying, took a diamond pin off her dress and pinned it on me, with the words: "I want you to have this." I accepted it gratefully, knowing full well what would become of it. Sure enough, Father found a very practical use for it. Noticing that the diamond perfectly matched the one in a ring he wore, he had it removed from the pin and set in the ring. Not to waste the pin, he had a cheaper stone set in it and gave it to my sister Gloria as a birthday present. Mother acquired a diamond watch that way.

As for books—oh, the beautiful, costly, leather-bound volumes that people brought me backstage! Father would promptly take possession of them, return them to the bookshops where they were purchased or otherwise dispose of them at a good price, secure cheap copies, and pocket the difference. Once I didn't even get the cheaper edition. I was given a gorgeous copy of Lamb's *Tales from Shakespeare*, printed on extra-fine paper and bound in red morocco, a luscious book! Father took one look at it, said, "Who needs this?" and went out and sold it. There was a very simple theory behind all this confiscation. Whatever came to me was really being given to him. Wasn't I wholly the product of *his* genius? "You wouldn't be playing the way you are if it weren't for me," he said time and again. That, of course, applied to the fees, too. The money was his the moment I was paid. He had earned it, you see, not I. All that survives from my years as a child prodigy is a pin that I now wear everywhere. It is a little gold antique inlaid with seven tiny diamonds. I received it on my twelfth birthday . . . from my father. He had actually paid for it out of his own pocket.

IN the rich harvest of comments following my first series of appearances in America were testimonials of the most flattering kind from many celebrities in and outside music. John McCormack was quoted as calling me "unquestionably a rare genius." John Charles Thomas said I possessed "a gift that could not be explained by any reasonable solution." Wilfred Pelletier dubbed me "the wonder of the century." And Louis Bromfield, the novelist and one-time music critic, confessed that I made the hair stand up on his head. It wasn't wholly a chorus of praise, however.

This brings me to the subject of Sergei Rachmaninoff. This man represented something supernatural to me. When I heard him play his own third piano concerto in Berlin at the age of six, it was the same as if Beethoven had come out on the stage to play his own "Pathétique" sonata. I had retained a haunting image of this sad-looking giant of the keyboard. It was this same Rachmaninoff who, in a press interview after my Town Hall debut, was asked, "What do you think of Ruth Slencynzski?" His reply was:

"People should not be encouraged to applaud little children who play wrong notes."

Mind you, he had not heard me play. So my manager, Mr. Wagner, possessing a rash sense of humor, made the following comment in print:

"People should not be encouraged to applaud people in their second childhood who play wrong notes."

Father roared over this crushing retort. I was appalled. The following year I played in several concert series in America in which Mr. Rachmaninoff was also one of the artists. Once, whether because he was ill or for some other reason, I was even called upon to pinch-hit for him at a recital in Philharmonic Auditorium in Los Angeles. An infant of nine replacing a god! But still we had never met. . . .

In the spring of 1934, after I was back in Paris from that tour, I was just starting to get back in harness for the following season. Mother was in the hospital for some minor surgery, and Father was busy at home taking care of his three daughters. One day the telephone rang. Father answered it.

"This is Sergei Rachmaninoff," said the voice. "I want to speak to Mr. Slenczynski."

Father nearly dropped the phone.

"I want you to bring your daughter Ruth who plays the piano to my apartment next Tuesday morning at eleven. You will find me at the Villa Majestique."

After spluttering some sort of reply, Father hung up and returned to me and the piano in an excited state. I didn't know whether he was kidding, teasing, leading me on. I simply wouldn't believe it.

"Anyway, we can't go on Tuesday," I said. "Mama will still be in the hospital."

So Father picked up the phone, and when I heard him ask for Mr. Rachmaninoff, I knew this wasn't a practical joke of some kind. The appointment was changed for the following week, and I was glad. It would give me that much more time to prepare. The next eight or nine days I worked as I never did in my life. I prepared an entire program for Mr. Rachmaninoff. I intended to warm up with some preludes and fugues of Bach.

After that would come four Beethoven sonatas—the "Pathé-tique," the sonata "*ala Tedesca*," in G major, and the two Opus 49's. Next I would play a few "Songs without Words" by Mendelssohn, and finally two groups by Schubert and Chopin. I had not learned any of Mr. Rachmaninoff's music. Maybe it was just as well.

I just worked like a horse. This one time I exceeded even my father's demands. For the first time I heard him plead exhaustion. I was up before he was and had to be forced to bed at night. Our average during those eight or nine days must have been eleven hours of grueling practice. I think it wore Father out more than it did me. I was too keyed up to think of being fatigued. Bright and early on the fateful morning I was all decked out in my best concert dress, complete with white shoes and white socks. Father took me by the hand, marched me down the six flights, hailed a taxi, and off we went to the Villa Majestique. I still remember the curious ringing in my ears, the pounding of my heart. Father must have been giving me some last minute pep-talk in the cab; I saw his lips moving, but I couldn't hear a single word. Finally we were in the lobby of the Villa Majestique. Word was sent upstairs, and the message came back that we were to be taken right up. At length we stood before the door, my hand still in Father's. I was nine years old, so short I didn't look half my age. I stood there trembling with awe. Every split tenth of a second was like an hour till that door opened. The hush was so thick you could cut it with a knife. When I thought I couldn't stand it any longer, the door opened. Towering there was a dark, gloomy-looking figure, so high above me that I had to throw my head far back to see the face peering down at me and Father. First he looked at me, said nothing, turned his gaze to Father, and stamped his foot angrily.

"You are Mr. Slenczynski?" he asked abruptly in English.

Father stammered that he was.

"I asked you to bring your daughter *who plays the piano*," said Mr. Rachmaninoff sharply.

Father quickly assured him he had done so. "*This* is my daughter," he said, pointing down at me.

By this time I was practically in tears. Mr. Rachmaninoff looked me over again, stretched out an enormous hand, and pointed a long finger at me.

"You mean *that* plays the piano?"

I just shriveled up. The thought crossed my mind that it was only now dawning on Mr. Rachmaninoff *what* had filled his place at the piano in Los Ángeles a few months before. I felt so little and so insignificant. It was one of those things.

Finally he straightened up, opened the door wide, and said, "Come in. Come in." Whereupon, thinking to put the three of us at ease, Father said something to Mr. Rachmaninoff in Russian. They chatted in that language while I removed my coat and beret. Mr. Rachmaninoff then motioned me to the piano and, as if dismissing Father, turned to me and started speaking in Russian.

"Please," I said, "will you speak to me in French, or German or English, because I don't speak Russian or Polish."

He replied in French: "I hope you speak music, though."

That broke the ice, as far as I was concerned.

It was a simple hotel room. Where I sat the windows were at my back. The piano and piano stool were obviously a make-shift arrangement provided by the manufacturers. The rest was hotel furniture. Over the piano were photographs of Mr. Rachmaninoff's wife and daughter, and beside them mounds of piano music and a metronome. Father sat off in a corner. Mr. Rachmaninoff simply ignored him.

"What are you going to play for me?"

I carefully enumerated all the things I had prepared, beginning with the Bach pieces. But he went on asking me little questions and making occasional comments, "What else? What else?" and pretty soon I had given him my entire repertory. This went on for about fifteen minutes. Finally he asked me if I knew theory.

"Oh, yes," I began proudly. "I know figured bass and chords and ——"

"Do you know how to transpose?"

"Yes."

"Do you have perfect pitch?"

"Yes."

Then for some reason, out of that whole program I had prepared for him, he picked on a very trivial composition, the "Rondo Brilliante" of Weber. The other things were so much more important. Maybe he just picked it out of the bag, so to speak.

"In what key is that?" he asked.

"E-flat major."

Leaning back and smiling, he said: "Play it for me in E major."

I played it slowly at first, working it into the new key, and as I kept building it to the right speed, Mr. Rachmaninoff came closer and closer to the piano. By the time I finished he was leaning on the piano with one arm on my back and chuckling like a little boy. He took my hands off the keys and said:

"Enough of that. Now play me anything you want."

I was used to him by now, and I sensed that he liked me. Again I itemized my list of prepared music, Bach, Beethoven, Mendelssohn . . .

"Well, let's hear some Bach."

I played the C minor prelude and fugue from "The Well-tempered Clavichord."

About the fugue he asked, "Which is the second subject?"

I told him.

"You have had very good training. How about your Beethoven?"

I played the "Pathétique" for him. While playing, I could see him out of the corner of my eye, sometimes sad and frowning, sometimes laughing out loud. I think we were enjoying each other. This went on for about two hours. "With whom did you study these?" he asked about several compositions, and I, using the pat answer which Father always gave, said, "My father was my only teacher."

Which was the cue for Father to come out of his corner.

"Well, what do you think of her?" he asked, speaking English, because his French was never too good.

And Mr. Rachmaninoff replied, "She needs a better teacher."

Father was forced to admit the truth. "The fact is, Mr. Rachmaninoff, I've been taking her to Alfred Cortot for the past two years."

To which Mr. Rachmaninoff replied: "Why did you pick on Cortot? He's no pianist. He's always playing wrong notes."

"Well," rejoined Father, "he's the best teacher in Paris."

And now Mr. Rachmaninoff gave it to us.

"If you take this child to a teacher who has no technic, how can you expect her to acquire any? She has no idea how to practice. She has no technical foundation. She is all talent. She is probably the greatest talent I have ever heard. If she gets first-class training, by the time she is fifteen she will play so well that other pianists hearing her will give up the piano in despair."

I took this to mean I hadn't made much of an impression on Mr. Rachmaninoff. Father looked dumfounded, having been told by everyone else how wonderful I already was. To be told that I could be wonderful some day in the indefinite future wasn't very consoling. Pleased as he was with me, Mr. Rachmaninoff wasn't pulling any punches about the great deal that was still needed to make me an artist. Again turning his back to Father, he said to me:

"Do you know what I was doing when I was not your age, but twice your age, and first really learning to play? I was practicing exercises with the metronome every single day. I made exercises out of the compositions I played, transposing them into every key."

He went over to the piano. "I used to raise my fingers very high, like this."

He showed me and I said, "Oh, I once had a teacher who made me do that?"

"Who was that?"

"Egon Petri in Berlin."

"Hmm. Well, let me see you do this passage in the 'Pathétique' that way."

Suddenly, as he watched my hands coming down on the keys, he said: "You have fingers like overcooked spaghetti."

I let that pass and tried to remember what Mr. Petri had told me about raising my fingers, and Mr. Rachmaninoff was fairly jumping with glee.

"You know exactly how to do it! This is fantastic! What you must do now is work over all your technic that way. In six months you will be a different pianist. In one year you will be magnificent. In two years you will be unbelievable. . . . Would you like some cookies?"

Would I! Mr. Rachmaninoff summoned his daughter from the next room and she soon had tea and cookies for us.

"Would you teach her?" Father asked.

"I?" he replied. "I hate teaching. I taught once many years ago in a girls' school. That was the last time. Take her to a teacher who will make her work. Of course there is nobody here, but do the best you can."

This seemed to end it. Mr. Rachmaninoff had satisfied his curiosity, and now I was being dismissed. As Father thanked him for the interview, I dawdled with my hat in front of a mirror. Actually my hat was on all right. I just wanted to remain in that man's presence as long as I could. Mr. Rachmaninoff studied me a moment and said to Father:

"She is vain already. She will never be an artist. She is like all other women, a peacock."

Turning his eyes back to me, he said: "Little girl, when are you coming to see me again?" I was speechless with joy.

Thus began a succession of visits over the next four months at intervals of ten days, followed by a similar series the following year spread out over the same period. Each time Mr. Rachmaninoff insisted he wasn't interested in teaching me, and each time he gave me things to prepare for the next visit. At first I had to play very very slowly and staccato, raising my fingers high, and working with the metronome. One day, in amusement, he studied my hands closely and said:

"Your fingers are a brush for putting posters on walls."

Gradually, patiently, never coddling or puffing me up, Mr. Rachmaninoff put new strength into my fingers. Almost always he gave me pieces of his own to study at home, and very often he sat down to play for me. The coloring of his tones was an ever-increasing marvel to me. He seemed to have an infinite variety of touch. And what a perfectionist! This was one pianist who could not allow himself a single mistake. If he so much as flubbed the tiniest note, he suddenly became solemn and distant, saying to me:

"I'm tired. You'd better go back home and practice. Come and see me next week."

My happiest memories are of the times he would unexpectedly draw closer to the piano as I played, till he practically hung over it, a broad grin on his long, deeply furrowed face. I think he relished me as a little girl, and perhaps as a sort of plaything, too. But there was serious work to do and he never spared me. I owe a great deal to Mr. Rachmaninoff for the faith and confidence I have in my fingers today. The way I was going I might never have achieved real technical security. I knew what Mr. Rachmaninoff meant about Mr. Cortot's not having any technic. The truth is Mr. Cortot had no idea of how to make the hand work to its best advantage. Cortot's whole theory of teaching was this:

"Improvise! Lose yourself in the music! Say something new each time you play. Find the best parts of the piano and magnify them. Never play the same thing twice the same way."

This was terribly important, to be sure. But how is one to do all those fine things without having an absolutely firm basis to work from? The practice method I learned from Mr. Rachmaninoff has stayed with me to this day. I am never in doubt about my technic. He showed me how to build up a reserve fund of finger power which has never failed me.

As it happened, Mr. Cortot had as little respect for Mr. Rachmaninoff as Mr. Rachmaninoff had for him. Mr. Cortot thought him "decadent" and "passé." He said so many times to me. This became an odd situation. Since both cordially disapproved of each other, I was constantly preparing one set of pieces for Mr. Cortot and another for Mr. Rachmaninoff, and neither ever knew of my work with the other! I was literally caught between two piano stools. Oddly enough, it worked out beautifully. I found myself playing Mr. Cortot's pieces with better fingering and Mr. Rachmaninoff's with greater expression. The happy result was that each thought I was making marvelous progress, without ever suspecting that I so much as saw the other! We kept quiet about that, Father and I. Without realizing it, those two men, who professed to have no use for one another as pianists, were praising each other's work in me! The whole situation was ironic. Here was Father telling the world he was my only teacher. Here was Mr. Cortot proudly calling himself my teacher. Here was Mr. Rachmaninoff denying that he was teaching me. My visits were social calls, he said, with a few suggestions on how to improve my playing thrown in. At the end of one such "social call" he said:

"I've told you before, I hate to teach. If you were an ordinary pupil, of course I would never see you, but then you would not be giving concerts in the first place."

Mr. Rachmaninoff completely disapproved of my giving concerts. He was very sharp with Father about it, urging him to withdraw me from public view and have me concentrate on real study till I was fifteen. This must have been the magic year in his eyes, fifteen. It came up again and again in conversation. He said I was wasting precious time in concertizing that should be going into earnest work at home and in the studio. My father's answer, no matter how vehement Mr. Rachmaninoff became on the subject, was always the same: we needed the money; the concerts had to go on. Mr. Rachmaninoff went on objecting to the end, sometimes only to me. We had our own little musical level in French from which Father was excluded. Mr. Rachmaninoff was the only teacher I ever had with whom I could effect an escape in Father's presence. Mr. Cortot always conversed with me in English so that Father could supervise my practicing.

I remarked before that I was a kind of plaything to Mr. Rachmaninoff. He was forever amusing me with little stories and quaint expressions, and he enjoyed playing little games with me, mostly about his own music. One time he was put in a very gay mood by what must have been an exceptional performance of mine.

"What do you do when you don't play the piano?" he asked in French, as if meaning to keep Father out.

"Oh, I have my tutors. I do my homework."

"Don't you ever run in the streets? Don't you play?"

"Well, I go on walks. My sisters run much better than I do because I'm so fat."

"Oh, fat! It's quite all right for a little girl to be fat. You'll lose that later. . . . But tell me, do you ever read fairy tales?"

"Oh, I love fairy tales, but Father doesn't like me to read them because he says they're not serious."

I told him I thought of my music as a sort of fairyland.

"Good!" he said. "Do you know the story of Little Red Riding Hood?"

I told him I did.

"I put it to music once," he said, and he went over to the piano and played me the etude tableau in A minor. I could see Little Red Riding Hood racing through the woods, the wolf at her heels. I felt all her fright and all her relief. It was all in the music. I always feel I am telling a story when I play that etude tableau.

Those were precious sessions with Mr. Rachmaninoff when he showed me how he liked his preludes and etudes to be played. Nothing was overlooked in the fingering, coloring of tone, rhythm and phrasing. Father, who liked practically no music after Brahms, used to say after leaving the Villa Majestique:

"When is he going to give you anything but Rachmaninoff to learn? It's only publicity for his own compositions." Honored as he was by Mr. Rachmaninoff's interest, he never let me put any of his music on my programs.

While I was playing for Mr. Rachmaninoff one day, I caught a glimpse of his huge figure in the middle of the room, thoughtfully regarding a rubberband stretched between his huge hands. When I finished the piece I was playing, he drew up, his eyes still on the rubberband.

"Ruth," he said, "I want to show you something."

He slipped the rubber band over three fingers, stretched it a little, and let it snap back to normal.

"That is the true essence of a rubber band," he said. "You pull it a little, then you let go and it settles back, complete, whole, undamaged. It has proved its value as a rubber band, its beauty, its use.

"Now if you strain it too much, pull it too hard, like this"— and he snapped the rubber band in two—"it breaks and is lost. The same thing is true of a musical phrase. A little stretching is sometimes good, to point up the beauty of a line or modulation.

"But stretch the phrase too far and it begins to gasp for breath and lose shape and continuity."

That was how Mr. Rachmaninoff explained the use and abuse of *tempo rubato*.

Which reminds me of the way Pablo Casals explained a *ritardando* to me—that is, the gradual slackening of speed in a composition. "Imagine yourself in a train coming into the Gare St. Lazare," he said. "If the train were to stop abruptly, your head would hit the back of the seat in front of you. Instead, the train loses speed so gradually that when it finally stops you are not even aware of it. That is a true *ritardando*."

Developing a sense of detachment about one's own playing was another cardinal point of Mr. Rachmaninoff's teaching. "In your mind," he said, "place yourself in another room and listen to your playing. Does it sound like Beethoven?" It was an ideal, a mental exercise, that perhaps he came closer to achieving than anyone else. The nearest he came to a real explosion was once when I was playing a composition of his:

"You are a child! You played that for yourself, like a child! However, *I* am not a child. You're playing *my* music. Make it sound like mine!"

Another point he stressed was the importance of bringing out the less salient ideas of a piece of music, the almost half-hidden thoughts of the composer. He showed me all the little subtleties of counterthemes in Bach's fugues that were often slurred over. It was a kind of subworld teeming with tiny forms of pulsing life.

Music, he once said, was not just a picture to look at but a panorama in motion. Things were happening every split second, not only in the most obvious places but in deep, shadowy areas.

Even a rest was a living moment of music crowded with meaning. Childlike, I aped him, not knowing exactly what I was doing or how I was doing it, yet somehow achieving the very effect he sought, and he would burst out laughing.

"You see! That's what I mean! Bring out the countertheme even more. Pedal this. See if you can get more strength with the thumb."

Mr. Rachmaninoff didn't care whether I used the thumb on a black key or not. He would have allowed me to use my elbow or my nose, if that brought the effect closer. He was happiest when I did well in his own music. He would stoop down and kiss my forehead, summon refreshments, and we would have a regular little feast. His daughter would bring in a great big silver samovar and large glasses with silver handles for the tea. There were slices of lemon and sometimes pieces of cinnamon. I never once let on that the hot glass almost burned my lips. I just sat there sipping tea with father, Mr. Rachmaninoff, and his daughter, and tasted paradise.

That started me on my tea-drinking career. It made me hate even more the diluted, gluey, and tasteless fluid that passed for milk and had to be boiled before Mother served it to us. I was too old for such kid stuff, anyway, and would beg Mother to give me a cup of tea, "just as I had it at Mr. Rachmaninoff's." I adore tea any time of the day or night and usually drink three or four cups with a piece of lemon, at a sitting. This habit I owe to those sessions at the Villa Majestique when Mr. Rachmaninoff liked the way I played his music.

On one point he remained firm to the end, however: that I should stop appearing in public, give all my time to study, and not come back to the concert stage till I had passed my fifteenth birthday. He warned me and he warned Father of the hazards ahead, if I didn't. But Father knew better. Nobody was going to tell him how to run his business, not even Sergei Rachmaninoff.

WITH nothing and no one to apply the brakes, my concert career now moved on at a more feverish pace. Fabulous years followed my debut of November 13, 1933, in Town Hall; years of travel, of wild public acclaim; years of practice and study . . . and castigation. There were years, too, of acute sieges of loneliness when I longed for any other kind of life but my own. But these were rare. I had been swept into the strong current of public life and there was no sweeping me back but a change in Father or the jolt of disaster. And Father wasn't going to change. . . .

Often I wondered whether it was all real and such things could be happening to a child my age. There was the time in Boston when I couldn't leave Symphony Hall for three hours after a final encore. The crowd had piled thick outside the stage door. Police officers warned Father it wasn't safe to attempt to break through. And there was I an ordinary little girl with one thought on her mind—food. I was practically starved when someone finally lifted me high above the heads of the crowd. While two huge policemen broke a wedge through that mass, I was borne to a waiting cab. It brought back the time in Berkeley when Father tossed me up in the air. I was three then and terrified, and kept yelling, "'Fraid of my life! 'Fraid of my life!" This time I wasn't scared in the least; only happy at the prospect of a long-deferred supper. . . .

There was the time in Copenhagen during the first European

tour that followed my American debut when a delegation of critics came to our hotel, accompanied by a doctor. Like their Berlin colleagues of three years before, they suspected a hoax of some sort. It wasn't the piano they wanted to inspect this time; it was me. One or two papers had openly accused our concert manager, Mr. Hansen, of misrepresentation. And what was their accusation? I was a midget! No child of nine could play as I did. So here were these grave gentlemen sitting with Father in one room while the doctor followed me into the bedroom. The first thing he did was to look at my teeth. Finally he muttered some words of apology, returned with me to the next room, and solemnly announced:

"Gentlemen of the press, this is a genuine child."

This episode only served to whip up more sensationalism in the press. I think for a while I must have had all Denmark in the palm of my hand. I remember that at my third concert a tall, handsome young man with blond hair, who is now King Frederik, occupied the royal box. In Copenhagen I first met Nathan Milstein, who used our hotel room to practice in and brought me all the flowers of his own concert. Reporters were always amazed at how much I knew about their countries. It was simple. Mother always boned me up on the industries, products, and landmarks of all the places on my touring itinerary. Special geography books would be borrowed from the Paris libraries, and special tutors would supplement her lectures. I made a dreadful *faux pas* in London at the time of King Edward VIII's abdication. I was glibly reeling off replies on English history, when a strained silence fell on the gathering. Before I could catch myself, I had said:

"Oh, yes, I know all about the six wives of Edward VIII."

In Budapest I first crossed paths with Jascha Heifetz and was introduced to the brilliant composer-pianist Ernst von Dohnanyi. For the first two or three seasons tempting bids even came from Germany. These Father brushed violently aside. That was forbidden territory for me, even though I noticed that Alfred Cortot went on playing there. I find from a New York *Daily Mirror* interview of November 19, 1933, that I was quite the little prophet on the subject of the Third Reich. "I despise Hitler," David K. Gross quoted me as saying. "He is a beast. I am sure he is going to fail. You cannot persecute people like he is doing and be successful. I hope he is soon put down."

One year I played as many as five concerts in New York alone. I was told—though who could prove or disprove this—that I broke the record for number of encores played in Town Hall. I also broke something else, the no-encore rule at the Metropolitan Opera House. At that Sunday night concert the conductor Wilfred Pelletier requested me to play three extra numbers. I would have needed little encouragement to make it six. I made the headlines once for asking Herbert Hoover a conundrum. Dining with him at Palo Alto, I asked the ex-President, "What is every President of the United States?"

Mr. Hoover's reply was quick: "Why, a darned fool, I suppose." Which wasn't the answer I was seeking—that being, "A cabinetmaker," uttered with all the proud superiority of the true conundrum-collector. About that time I was entertained in Hollywood by Robert Montgomery, who took me to visit a movie studio, which I'm afraid was wasted on me because I hadn't the faintest idea who Robert Montgomery was, other than a polite and handsome young gentleman. I had never even seen a movie! What time was there for such frivolity, practicing nine hours a day!

Rachmaninoff wasn't the only musical celebrity for whom I was called upon to substitute in time of emergency. In Hartford, Connecticut, I once replaced Lily Pons, who was to have been paid $2500 for the appearance. Father insisted on the same fee for me, and got it. That was still $500 less than the fee

I received as a "substitute" for Mr. Rachmaninoff in Los Angeles. A particularly thrilling experience of the kind was the time I replaced Ignace Paderewski in Carnegie Hall. The concert was to be the climax of the Polish master's farewell tour of America. A few days before the concert Mr. Paderewski suffered a heart attack, and I took his place and played his exact program! I remember the date, January 27, because it was Mozart's birthday. As my first encore I played the entire sonata in F major, K. 332. As my second encore I played Chopin's "Chromatic" etude in A minor. Years later I learned that Ossip Gabrilowitsch, who was in the hall, turned to the pianist José Echaniz seated next to him and said, after my Chopin encore: "I worked on that piece twenty-five years before I dared to play it in public. I'm sure she hasn't put quite that much time on it." I was all of ten years old!

To musicians everywhere I must have been some sort of freak. I can imagine what many of them secretly felt to see the crowds jamming the concert halls of two continents to hear a pudgy little pianist who could scarcely climb up a stool unaided. Yet they were kind and flattering in the extreme. They treated me as a colleague, bowed to me gallantly, and seemed generally to be having a good time with me. Many were like Mr. Rachmaninoff, treating me as a combined toy and pet. Others looked on me as a circus performer or prize exhibit at a fair. I was a diversion, a stunt. It was all in fun and I loved every minute of it. On the boat returning to America once, I found myself part of a hearty holiday group that included the Conductor Sir Hamilton Harty, the pianist Harriet Cohen, the tenor John McCormack, and the actor George Arliss. The day was usually given over to shop talk, managers, backstage incidents, far-off places, and people of interest. At night, after dinner, when the rest of the ship was watching movies, the five of us, and Father, would troop into the private dining room for a jam session. All had to donate a bit of fun. Mr. McCormack would open up in heroic style. Sir Hamilton would direct him with mock ferver; Miss Cohen would mingle wild Cockney tunes with Bach at the keyboard, and I would be put through my usual paces. Sir Hamilton would say:

"Let's hear you transpose a fugue from 'The Well-tempered Clavichord.'"

Miss Cohen would take the treble, and I the bass, and together we would struggle through the fugue as the others stood around making scathing gibes or shouting loud *"bravos!"* The men would have their whiskies and then George Arliss would go up to the piano with his back to it, hands stretched out behind him, and come down anywhere on the keyboard with all ten fingers.

"Go ahead, Ruth, name every single one of them!"

And Miss Cohen would stand at his side to see that I called them out correctly. Mr. McCormack would shout out, "Oh, no! You left one out! What's the third note from the bottom?" I would start all over again and of course get them all. They would all express amazement and say teasingly, "You'll get by." On Captain's night we put on a show for the benefit of the Seamen's Fund. The sum raised was something over $6000. Naturally the whole boat came. Each of the Big Four performed and the small Fifth came last. After innumerable encores, Harold Holt, who got up the program, took me by the hand, and as we stood side by side facing the assemblage of passengers, he said:

"I'm sure we both look very small to you from down there, but Miss Slenczynski at least is a very great person."

I suppose the word "exploitation" is in the minds of many people as they read these pages. I cannot truthfully say I looked at it then the way I see it now, that Josef Slenczynski was in every sense abusing his claim to me as a father. I accepted his word as law, looked up to him as an infallible source of wisdom, and took the periodic beatings as my due. There were these fat returns in money and fame to prove he was right, no matter what anyone else might say. That he was anything less than a god and a King Solomon only dawned on me later in a slow series of steps.

So far only Mother had sought to restrain Father, and then only to spare me the trouncings. A few well-meaning neighbors had registered warnings about what this excess of practice might do to me. But they were less interested in my welfare than in their own. Father had it his way . . . till we ran afoul of the child-labor laws. And of course he was furious. There was only withering scorn for the cities that refused me a booking till I was twelve. I remember a sweet little lady from the Child Labor Board used to call at the Ansonia Hotel to inquire if I got to bed early enough. Fine people wrote letters to newspapers and stirred up small controversies about man's inhumanity to precocious children. Ominous reminders were bruited about of how arduous touring as an infant had brought Mozart to an early grave. A twenty-five-dollar fine was levied on the manager after a Philadelphia concert because I was underage. A similar fine was imposed in Washington, D. C.

In London, when I was ten or eleven, I was scheduled to appear as soloist with Sir Hamilton Harty at a Sunday concert and later in the week in a recital at Queen's Hall. The London County Council ruled that I could appear at the second but not at the first. The law was that no child under fourteen could work on Sundays. So my appearance with Sir Hamilton was canceled. For the weekday concert I had to submit to a physical examination in the Council chambers. I remember feeling a certain glow of adventure as I stood on line to get my permit. The others before and behind me were newsboys and bootblacks.

It was my aunt Dottie who signed the paper for the S.P.C.C. as my tutor while on tour. Actually she said I was so far ahead scholastically of the average child my age that the three months spent playing hookie while on tour were a deserved vacation from tutoring. Once, while passing through New York, Father phoned and insisted that Aunt Evvy and Aunt Dottie come over to the hotel that evening. He knew their father was dying and they tried to beg off on that account. But Father insisted so hard that Aunt Dottie took the subway and came alone.

I was a little fat thing practicing in my slip and not allowed to stop or say anything when Aunt Dottie came in. I gave her an almost imperceptible nod as she withdrew to a corner and sat down. Again and again Father had me repeat a slow passage, never failing to make some cutting remark or other. I said nothing, but merely breathed more heavily to show I heard and understood. Finally, in exasperation, he pointed a finger to Aunt Dottie:

"Do you love your aunt?"

I nodded vigorously.

"Do you know that her father is very ill—that he may die?"

I gave another nod.

"Well, play that passage again and *pray for him with your music*. Ask God with your whole heart that he may get well."

I played as I had never played before, and the tears just streamed down Aunt Dottie's cheeks.

Father just couldn't stand any talk of child labor or child welfare in his presence. Anything along that line seemed to reflect on the way he was bringing me up. He strongly resented the slightest hint that he was exploiting me. It was all for my own good, you see. But then he bristled at any kind of criticism. Where his judgment was questioned, he could become quite arrogant and mean. Often he antagonized the very people who could be most helpful to me. His ego was such that he once referred to Artur Schnabel as "the teaching assistant I liked best while I was training my daughter Ruth." We saw how he could pitch into an idol like Mischa Elman. Once, after Wilfred Pelletier and I had gone over a concerto together at the home of Ernest Hutcheson, Father said to him: "Don't you pay any attention to that fellow Hutcheson. Just follow Ruth and you won't go wrong." Imagine saying that to the man who was going to conduct my performance! Mr. Pelletier took it like a sport; maybe he thought Father meant it as a joke.

A somewhat different customer was Bernardino Molinari, the famous Italian conductor. The collision between Father and this volatile Latin deserves a few words if only to show how vindictive Father could be when his vanity was bruised. I was nine years old at the time, making my second tour of America. Mr. Molinari was then conducting the San Francisco Orchestra. The orchestra had to raise some money, and Richard Tobin, as president of the San Francisco Symphony Association, asked me to play at a benefit concert—asked Father, that is. This was the least we could do for any member of the family that had financed my early years in Europe. Father agreed, one of the very few times he ever let me play in public for nothing. Now Mr. Molinari, benefit or no benefit, may have been just a little dubious about accompanying a nine-year-old child in Beethoven's first piano concerto. Whatever it was, he made what struck Father as an insulting request to hear me play in private before the rehearsal with orchestra. Father flew into one of his rages. Nobody could do this to him! Who did Molinari think he was? Stokowski?

Toscanini? Naturally I disliked poor Mr. Molinari before we met. Well, the private rehearsal took place, and Mr. Molinari was pleased. Father, perhaps fishing for still warmer compliments, then asked him: "Have you any suggestion to make as to how my daughter Ruth might improve her playing?" Mr. Molinari thought a moment. "Well," he said, "I see no specific place for improvement in this concerto. However, since you ask me I will say this: If you take her to a really fine teacher, *other than yourself*, she could in time become a remarkable pianist."

Father didn't like that one bit. To begin with, in his mind I was not only a remarkable pianist already, but an extraordinary one. Even worse was Mr. Molinari's temerity to suggest that anyone could do a better job than himself as my teacher. Father was ready for him. As rehearsal time approached, he coached me in a little scene the memory of which makes me blush today. Keep in mind that I had never disobeyed him. I had no will of my own. I was too carefully trained to question or dispute. It almost never occurred to me not to do something that he specifically asked. I had played hookie on that little speech aimed at Mr. Elman, and paid for it. What Father wanted was simply this: during the *presto finale* I was suddenly to raise my hands from the keyboard, turn to Mr. Molinari, and say in a loud voice, so everybody could hear: "Faster, faster, I'm not sick! The tempo is all wrong!"

Thus coached, I went to the rehearsal. Seated in the auditorium were a great number of musicians and patrons, among them Mr. Tobin and members of the orchestra board. Everything went smoothly till we reached the middle of the *presto finale* and up spoke the little parrot:

"Faster, faster! I'm not sick. The tempo is all wrong!"

The effect was wholly unexpected. Mr. Molinari proved a perfect gentleman. Bowing gallantly to me, he turned back to the orchestra and said:

"Of course she is right. We must take it a little faster. Miss Slenczynski is younger than we are."

Far from mollifying Father, this annoyed him still more. He had wanted to precipitate a temperamental outburst. He wanted to see Mr. Molinari disgrace himself in a quarrel with a nine-year-old girl. Father had heard stories about Mr. Molinari's temper. Well, he had badgered him and been outsmarted. He would make him pay for it yet. And this was how Father went about it. The Beethoven concerto was to be followed on the program by Respighi's "Pines of Rome." There Mr. Molinari would have the spotlight to himself for a rousing finale. Father's plan was to keep Mr. Molinari offstage as long as possible before the last number. Now the only way to do that was *to keep me on* as long as possible, and the only way to do that was to have me play a long list of encores after I finished the concerto and took my first bow. I wasn't to leave the stage at all. I did exactly this. I bowed to the ovation that followed the Beethoven performance—bowed, returned to my seat at the piano, and began a recital. I played preludes and fugues of Bach, Chopin etudes and ballades, Schubert impromptus. Mr. Molinari, in the meantime, was having fits backstage. I was told he broke his baton in two, threw his coat on the floor, jumped up and down on it; in short, was fit to be tied. Mr. Tobin tried desperately but fruitlessly to signal me offstage. At length Father walked out, took me by the hand, and marched me into the wings, where a coatless maniac, gesticulating wildly, screaming vitriolic oaths at both of us. The poor man still had "The Pines of Rome" to conduct! He refused flatly and vociferously and had to be physically detained from leaving the hall. When he returned to the podium, a final humiliation awaited him. Half the audience had left!

Father exulted in his revenge. His nine-year-old daughter had stolen the show from a world-renowned conductor who had dared to imply that he wasn't the best teacher for her. I feel sick at the memory of my part in that degrading conspiracy. I will say this for myself: I hadn't the faintest idea, as I came offstage, why Mr. Molinari shouted all those horrible things at me. I only understood it later when I understood Father and the grotesque pattern of abuse and exploitation I was trapped in. For that there was no child-labor law.

To drive home the point that I belonged wholly to him, Father never tired of reminding me of the two occasions on which he saved my life. The first time was in the bay at Alameda, California, when I was three years old. I would have drowned if Father hadn't pulled me out of the water by the hair. Seven years later I had another close call in the little river at Glendelles, where we used to vacation while in France. I got caught in some weeds, and in my panic screamed out to Father to save me. Fully clothed, he jumped in, disentangled me, and carried me to shore. There he sat me on a bench and said:

"Ruth, I just saved your life. Your life belongs to me and me alone. When I tell you to do something, you must do it without question, because I tell you to."

He whispered this fiercely while drying me, and right there, while I shivered with the fear of having almost gone under, with my hair clammy and prickling, he exacted a ritual of bondage which I had to repeat ten times:

"My life is yours. I must do as you say. . . . My life is yours. I must do as you say. . . ."

To this day I have a horror of water. In spite of swimming instruction, the best I can do is to paddle helplessly across the shallow part of a pool.

IT hurts me to think that Father got his fancy name for the handle of my sister Helen's toy shovel from my favorite fairy tale, *Aladdin and His Magic Lamp*. When Father gave us a choice of one plaything to take with us to Europe, I chose my illustrated copy of *The Arabian Nights*, Helen having picked her rake-and-shovel set. This is how Father's mind must have worked: if the magic lamp could perform such wonders for Aladdin, he was going to show me what a "magic stick" could do for him. That grim joke became a terrifying reality.

After several thrashings in Berlin, I tried in desperation to hide the stick when Father wasn't looking. I was never quite clever enough to elude his searching eyes. Wherever I concealed the hateful thing he found it. It was not till we got to Paris that I found an ideal hiding-place for it. This was the dainty shuttered little fireplace that is found in so many French homes. The shutters could be turned up and down. One day, as one of Father's seizures was coming on, I hid the stick in the bottom shutter while his back was turned. The tantrum that followed his inability to find it was worse than anything I can recall. I hastened to retrieve the stick myself. In his frenzy he let me have twice my usual quota. One day the wretched thing broke, and for the first time Father finished the job with his belt.

This is what I did to earn the extra attention:

After three or four successful tours, I got used to the fact that I was an accepted concert artist with a nice following in many parts of the world. I knew the fees Father collected were high, and I knew that Mr. Cortot himself would have been happy to give concerts in America at half the fee I was getting. All this brought on a slight attack of swelled head, I'm afraid. Father had given me an exaggerated idea of my own worth. Beatings to the contrary, I was—and he never tired of repeating it to everyone in the world but me—"the greatest pianist the world has ever seen." There was one thing I knew, however, that he didn't. I had one very serious musical weakness. I was unable to sight-read beyond the medium-difficult stage. I could do a Haydn sonata, a Mozart sonata, a Bach prelude at sight. Put a Beethoven sonata or a Bach fugue before me and my sight-reading simply did not function. . . . Brahms was altogether beyond my capacity.

Well, one Sunday morning Father and I arrived at Mr. Cortot's home for my usual lesson. I could never get over the way he kissed Father on both cheeks by way of greeting. Immediately he took us up the winding staircase to his studio. Seated there were the Spanish cellist Pablo Casals and the French violinist Jacques Thibaud. They had been rehearsing Brahms's trio in E-flat major. After introducing us, Mr. Cortot said:

"You know what, Ruth, this is so difficult and I'm so tired, suppose you sit here at the piano and play with these gentlemen. I'll turn the pages."

I was completely nonplused. I had played concerts everywhere, alone and with orchestra, but never chamber music. I just could not sight-read this music of Brahms. I could not even play it in tempo. All I could do was fake. I was never so embarrassed in my life. Shame mounted up in little waves and came out of my eyes in tears. I must have been as red as a beet. My hands simply refused to operate. I knew what Father would do to me when we got home. I would be punished for both having this weakness and for making such a sorry spectacle of myself before three artists of the first caliber. I must say I got through with it, when I started, but it was bad. The compliments of Mr. Cortot, Mr. Thibaud, and Mr. Casals were gallant little lies that only made me feel worse. I suspect Mr. Cortot, who knew this failing of mine, was secretly glad of the harsh lesson I had learned. I became a good sight-reader after that, though it is not one of my strong points. The fact is I played miserably. I knew it, and Father knew it. As for the others, I think I redeemed myself somewhat by playing a few solos exceptionally well. By the time I had my lesson with Mr. Cortot, the episode was forgotten. By everybody but Father, that is.

Since Father didn't like the French subway, we usually walked home or took a taxi. This time we walked. I could see he was boiling inside. His lips were tight and cruel and white, and gradually I became terrified. The compliments, the solo playing, the wonderful lesson with Mr. Cortot all vanished in the memory of the horrible mess I had made of the Brahms trio. Father never said a word. To my horror no one was home when we arrived. There was no restraining him now. First he went at the things that he knew were dearest to me. Like a madman, he strode over to the piano, which was heaped high with music books, and shoved everything off, till the floor was strewn with hundreds of scores. Then he screamed at me:

"You idiot, you imbecile, you dumbbell, you've disgraced me!" He started kicking the music around and jumping up and down on it. "I was too easy with you. I let you get away with it. But not any more!" And he pointed a scornful finger at me. "*That* wants to be a musician! Why, you're a thing, not a person. A person has brains. You're not even a lump of clay. You're a failure and I've wasted my life on you. You're no damn good for anything!"

And then he came at me with the stick. I tried to run and I slipped on the music. There was no escaping him. He wasn't my father any more, but some black monster out to get me. I screamed and screamed as the stick came down on me. Suddenly I heard it crack, and I had a moment of hope till I heard the sound of a buckle and the swish of a leather belt coming at me. It was horrible, but the worst was still to come. The lashing had stopped. Through a blur of tears and sobs and aches, I could see Father pushing the piano. In a sickening flash I saw what he was up to. He was turning the piano keyboard to the wall. I knew what that meant. I gave one big long howl of torment. The physical pain was gone in this final torture.

"You will never play again," he shrieked. "Not if I can help it. I'll never teach you! You've disgraced yourself, me, your whole family! We're all going back to California."

With that he stalked out of the room, slamming the door after him.

I was alone, a whimpering, shivering mess, red, sore, and bleeding; nose, arms, legs, everything bruised, *even my hands*; this was one time Father didn't spare them. I was black and blue and wet, looking worse than the "lump of clay" Father had called me, when Mother opened the door and gave a shriek. She folded me in her arms and turned furiously on Father. Had he gone out of his mind doing this to his own daughter? And what was the meaning of this mess all over the room? What was going on?

"*This, this,*" retorted Father, "isn't going to play the piano any more. I'm through with her. I can't make anything out of her. She's a nothing, an absolute nothing. The piano is going back, and we're packing for California."

Finally, after exchanging all sorts of threats and counter-threats with Father, Mother bathed and soothed and combed me, and left on some errand with Father. Because I was in disgrace with Father, my sisters went into their bedroom without saying a word to me. By myself in the living room, I suddenly felt cold and lonely and unwanted. Even my piano had turned its back to me. As a kind of escape I read a book for five minutes and gradually calmed down. I looked at the mess at my feet, and began picking up the scores one by one. Slowly I put all my Bach together, then my Beethoven, then my Schubert, then my Schumann. Much of the music was torn and covered with footprints. Very neatly I stacked it all up on the piano that was facing the wall.

That done, I tackled the piano. I crawled between its legs and shoved and shoved with my shoulders until I got it moving. It was slow, hard, panting work. The Pleyel was a seven-footer and I wasn't much bigger than one of its legs. After what seemed hours of labor, I moved it away from the wall, turned it around, and brought it to the position it had had before Father's convulsion. I never saw anyone so surprised as Mother when she walked in and saw everything set to rights again. She insisted I had called in the janitor to help me. I had thought of doing that but hadn't dared go down looking the way I did. Even my sisters wouldn't believe I had done it alone. Like Mother, Father couldn't get over it. When he saw the trouble I had gone to for the sake of my music, he relented.

"I'll go on teaching you," he said, *"but don't let me down again."*

That was it, you see; I was letting *him* down when I failed to come up to his fondest hopes. And it was shame compounded when it happened before musicians whose good opinion he craved. What praise I got was praise of him, the mastermind behind the miracle. Anything short of praise was my fault; good reviews were his doing; bad reviews mine. There were times when, even as a child, I pitied him. I would say to myself, "Think how his father must have thrashed *him*, if he does this to me." I believed him when he said I had it easy compared to the poverty he was brought up in. And the harangue would go on. I didn't appreciate the advantages I had. Here I was living in the lap of luxury: private tutors, travel, good food, and my own father, not a stranger, to coach me. And what was he doing it for? To keep me from making mistakes now and in later life when he wouldn't be there to correct me. He could have been an ordinary father, an ordinary man making an ordinary living. He had given up his own life to help me to become a great artist. Was this how I showed my appreciation, by shaming him before others? What was my sacrifice compared to his? If I was a success, I knew it was only because of him. My effort was nothing beside his. Didn't I know that I was nothing without him, that if he suddenly died I would never be able to play the piano again? This was his main theme, in fact; the thing he held over my head and Mother's, and over his own, too, because he was thoroughly convinced that I could function only at his will. This being so, I was flouting his will in some malign or perverse way when I hit a wrong note, got a bad notice, or botched a sight-reading job in a trio by Brahms. Because pleasing him meant having my music, I wanted very much to please him. Nothing else mattered to me. The fear of a thrashing was nothing beside the dread of his displeasure. He exploited even this simple yearning for Father's approval.

In June of 1936 I played in Portugal and Spain. For weeks before we left Paris for the short tour, Mother, who always read the newspapers out loud to us at breakfast, warned us about the growing ferment in Spain. Father and I were uneasy all during the trip to Madrid. "A pity there is so much unrest," Mr. Cortez, the manager, said to us, "or I'd ask you to play for our President." A big government dignitary was on board the plane when we flew to Barcelona. As the plane landed we passed over rows of neat little airplanes lined up for inspection like so many shining toys. "American planes," said Father. "The only kind that are any good." Barcelona was strangely quiet and sultry for a large city. The day after we left all the windows of the Ritz Hotel, where we had stopped, were broken in a political riot.

In Lisbon, Father and I hired a cart with a mule and driver that took us slowly jogging up narrow streets until we were high above the city. There we rested near a tiny chapel dating from the twelfth century. I was impressed until the driver said that the ancient but still green tree against which I was leaning was even older. It was thrilling to think that the blue ocean was the same ocean that Columbus had sailed. . . .

The hours that people kept on the Iberian Peninsula were odd to our way of thinking. A matinee concert started at 6 P.M., an evening concert at 10 P.M. No one, as far as we could see, thought of getting out of bed before 10 A.M. On our first morning Father and I rose at eight, which was late for us. Outside, the streets were empty. Breakfast was out of the question. I couldn't practice because the Pleyel offices did not open till noon, and the Museum was closed till 2 P.M. What a waste of beautiful morning! I remember Father pointing out some grass growing between cobblestones in the street.

"Such a country where the day is wasted and the grass grows on the street will never get ahead."

Schedule and punctuality were Father's philosophy. I don't think he was ever late a half-minute in his life. His days were governed by rigid timing. His gods were system and method. He hardly ever wavered or let me waver from the rigorous time schedule he adopted for my training. There was a time for scales, a time for other exercises, a time for working on a composition. This timetable was a religious observance. Father so organized my work that it was always well in advance of my lessons. My technical studies were timed to prepare me to do far more than the music required, a principle he once enunciated as follows:

"If you want a horse to win a mile race, train him to run a mile and a half."

Later that year, while touring America, Father became a diabetic. I remember he went to take out an insurance policy and was refused because of his condition. So, for a time at least, our roles were reversed. I became the trainer and he the trainee. It was my job to memorize his diet and see that he stuck to it. On the restaurant menus and at the homes of people where we were invited I would pick the foods he could eat. How he sulked when I forbade him to eat something he craved. "If I hadn't devoted my whole life to training you," he growled, "I wouldn't have diabetes now." For once I didn't mind. I was his nurse. I recall how acutely I felt his suffering when he had several teeth removed. I learned to take his tantrums and to give him the special warmth he needed away from the rest of the family. Mother had often told me how Father had jealously watched over my feeding as an infant, supervised the formula, seen to it that I was put to sleep at exactly the same time each day, fed at the precise minute no matter how loudly I yelled. I was *his* child, you see; never Mother's. Now it was my turn. It was I who tucked him into bed with tea and soft milk toast of gluten bread, I who dictated his diet and watched over him. That was probably the closest we ever came as father and daughter, the closest he ever allowed. When the barrier fell again, it remained for good.

Nobody ever became Father's real friend, certainly not for long. He was argumentative and positive, vengeful when he was crossed, and revolting in his manners. What polish there was to Father was all in the way he dressed. People's sensitivities were an open target to him. He spared no one; if they were great and influential, he might do it behind their backs; if they weren't, he did it to their faces. How he avoided being thrashed by one of his victims I shall never know. There must have been explanation for all this, rooted in his childhood and youth. Over the years I gradually pieced together a partial picture of what he was like before I knew him as my father. . . .

To begin with, he came of a large family living on an impoverished farm outside of Warsaw. His mother died when he was still a boy. My grandfather remarried and in time the family grew still larger. There was friction; Father was beaten almost daily; and there were too many mouths for any of them to eat too well. Father had one friend, a small violin that my grandfather, who was himself a violinist of sorts, had given him. Who taught him as a child I don't know, but when he left home, never to return, he was talented enough to be taken as a scholarship pupil in Vienna by Professor Grün. Later he moved on to Berlin, where he enrolled at the famous Hochschule für Musik, studying with Willy Burmeister. He must have been a good student. When he graduated in 1913, Burmeister gave him a letter of introduction to Josef Stransky, then conducting the New York Philharmonic Orchestra. Armed with this letter, Father came to America late in 1913.

Two things which Father brought with him to America were a methodic thoroughness instilled in him in Berlin and an abnormal sense of thrift. You see, during all these years Father had maintained himself by all sorts of menial jobs. He shined shoes in Warsaw, washed dishes in Vienna, swept out stores in Berlin. Every *pfennig* was stretched to go a long way. The specter of want was always at his shoulder. The job with the philharmonic never materialized. Instead, he was forced to accept work in a small dance band in Providence, Rhode Island. This job infuriated him. The band leader, according to Father, couldn't even hold his violin properly, yet he made money and bossed everyone around. One day he thought:

"What does this ignoramus have that I haven't got?"

Surely it wasn't education, he reflected; certainly it wasn't looks or charm. The answer was business ability, money. That did the trick in America. Nothing else. So Father developed a strong respect for money. First he set himself up as a teacher, trying to attract the more affluent pupils. Then he found a side line: he began to tour the pawnshops in New York, picking up inexpensive violins for ten or fifteen dollars apiece and selling them to the families of his upper-bracket pupils for perhaps several hundred dollars apiece. The violins were always worth it, he insisted. The pawnbroker just didn't know their true value, and he saw no reason to enlighten him. The profit was coming to him, he felt, for three excellent reasons: his superior knowledge of violins, the trouble and time he spent hunting for them, and because the violins served a more useful purpose in his studio that in a pawn shop window. In this way, plus odd jobs playing in dance bands at weddings and church affairs, he managed to put by quite a bank roll. Next he settled in Paterson, New Jersey, where he set himself up as "Professor Josef Slenczynski." Because of its Old World connotations, that title meant everything to him. The pupils always addressed him as "Professor." The studio was in the house of a German woman named Elisabeth Spangenmacher. The atmosphere reminded Father of his Berlin days, and he loved it. He must have had a small genius for making money. The profits from his violin trade he now invested in buying and selling mortgages. This developed into real estate deals of a larger kind. By the time he was thirty, he had twenty thousand dollars in the bank. Meanwhile, he mingled mostly with Europeans. They, and not the older-stock Americans, he felt, spoke his language of music and tradition. Germans, Poles, Russians, Viennese, they understood "Professor Slenczynski."

An occasional haunt of Father's was the back of a millinery trimmings store owned by a Morris Goldkind. There, after closing time, Father and a few cronies gathered around a stove. Over a glass of beer and roast-beef sandwiches they discussed politics, mortgages, and music. Often he brought his violin and played. Father was only five feet four inches tall, but a dandy, fussy and meticulous in the style of a European gentleman. His suits, tailor-made of the finest material, were always a perfect fit. He changed his shirt every day, sometimes twice a day, no small extravagance for a man as tight as my father in a time of high laundry bills. He wore white gloves and carried a silver-knobbed cane. Dapper and vain, he thought himself the epitome of good taste. He even went so far as to purse his lips to make a small mouth, an effect that he thought gave him added tone. Before he knew much English he used to say to Mrs. Spangenmacher, while he was adjusting his tie in front of the hall mirror: "Me pretty boy?" And he was ready to go out. Mother's family used to roar with laughter when they first beheld this paragon of fashion coming down the street to call upon the lucky lady of his choice.

There had been other attractions in Father's life before Mother but none that lasted. Usually they were pianists. Father would rip their playing to pieces, ridicule their schooling, laugh at their clothes, mock their habits of speech. Finally he gave up: American girls were not for him. The story goes that Mr. Goldkind took the bull by the horns during one of the beer-and-music sessions in the back of his millinery store and asked pointedly how it happened that such a personable and steady young man hadn't yet found himself a wife.

Father evidently got furious. Who is there in America? he wanted to know. The girls have no taste for music. Look at them: they paint themselves up; they cut their hair; they have no morals; they let their fingernails grow long; they spend every last nickel on movies and Broadway shows. That wasn't the sort of wife he wanted. If Mr. Goldkind or any of the others could dig up a nice girl with a good figure and education; a girl with a good business head who didn't use lipstick or rouge; who wore her hair long and lived at home with her family; a girl who didn't squander money on nonsense like high-heeled shoes, earrings, or bracelets . . .

"I would be very happy to meet such a girl and marry her," Father concluded.

While the others munched roast-beef sandwiches and Father doodled on the fiddle, Mr. Goldkind began singing the praises of his niece Dora. Here was the girl for him: a fine Jewish family, no extravagant tastes, not badly educated. She would have gone on to college if her mother hadn't died while she was in high school. Now she was making a nice salary as secretary, had no bad habits, had never been on a date in her life, and as for a figure, "Professor Slenczynski" could see for himself. If he wanted to meet Dora, he would ask her to come down to the store the following Saturday. That was how the two met. Mother liked him, his aura of foreign polish; his elegant clothes, the way he played the violin, and the twenty thousand dollars in the bank—a fact the whole neighborhood knew because Father went around bragging about it. The poverty routine began much later. Mother didn't find him too easy to be with, however. Nothing pleased him. Her clothes were scandalous. Saturday evenings were spent before shopwindows observing more suitable shoes and dresses for her. For the first and last time in her life she found herself spending lavishly. Fifteen-dollar shoes; eighty-dollar coats. Father's theory was sound enough: the costlier brands would wear longer and be cheaper in the long run. He completely remade her as far as taste went. His standards became hers. Already he was imposing his will on her. As Mother tells the story, the proposal and acceptance were a grammatical accident. During a walk in Paterson one Sunday, Father suddenly turned to her.

"Would you marry me?"

Now Mother took this to be a hypothetical question: would a girl like her consider marrying a man like him? In that spirit she answered him: "Why, yes, I think so, I'm sure you'd make an excellent husband."

Nothing more was said. The next time they met, Father gave Mother a ring set with three little pearls and two diamonds in the shape of a flower. The ring had been his mother's, he said, adding that he now considered themselves engaged. Mother didn't know what to say or do. He was obviously a good catch, but she wasn't at ease with him. His stinginess in matters that pleased girls was incredible. Once he bought Mother a box of chocolates, only to reprimand her for sharing them with her family. Flowers he regarded as useless and extravagant fripperies. Since she was secretary in a theatrical agency, Mother often got excellent tickets to Broadway shows. These she paid for out of her own earnings, however. Father would say, "Get two seats for any play you want for Saturday night and we'll go." Not once did he volunteer to repay her. Yet she married him. After the episode of the ring, she shed many bitter tears over it. Her family were just as divided on the subject as she was. They didn't relish his snobbish attitude toward them. In his eyes they were never his equals. It was a tough decision, but Mother made it. Nobody seems to understand how I grew up taking what I did from my father. But Mother took it in another form long before I was born. Father's was a fearful and imposing personality. If you were the sort to submit, you learned to live with it. Josef Slenczynski wasn't going to change. You were the one that was going to change.

Father was superstitious. A black cat crossing his path could mean anything from a bad notice to a canceled tour. He would have made a five-mile detour to avoid walking under a ladder. Thirteen he considered a lucky number. My sister Helen was born on the thirteenth of February and I made my big New York debut in Town Hall on the thirteenth of November. In these matters, as in all others, I never as a child once doubted that Father was infallible. Just before my first concert in Queen's Hall, London, Father ordered tea with milk for me. I had never tasted the combination and hated it with the first sip.

"Come on, drink it!"

I tried and grimaced pitifully.

"I'm going to make a wish," he said solemnly. "Drink it and your concert will be a great success."

I tried to get the stuff down, but gagged and began to whimper. It was getting late and Father grew more and more impatient. "All right, leave it then—and see what happens!"

Remembering how Father's past "wishes" had worked, I made

another heroic effort to gulp the concoction down and failed. And of course when the reviews proved far from ecstatic, Father didn't have to tell me the unswallowed tea and milk had done it. It was not until many years after I ran away from home that the sinister weight of his prophecies lifted from my mind. By then I had ceased to believe in either bad luck or good luck. I had learned to play without him and his threats.

There you have my father, a bitter, ruthless, superstitious, arrogant man, constantly deprived, in his own mind, of life's highest prizes, a violinist who never quite made the concert grade, a man who thought himself too good for his wife, a father who wanted a boy so he could make him the greatest fiddler in the world, and instead got a girl who wanted no part of the violin and who, when she became a world-famous pianist, disgraced him before musicians like Cortot, Casals, and Thibaud by messing up the piano part of a trio by Brahms.

EVERY year, about the time the weather was beginning to mellow into spring, Father invariably looked around Paris for another name to add to my collection of teachers and coaches. Sometimes they volunteered, sometimes they were persuaded; never were they paid. Father's spring shopping tour of 1936 brought me the friendship of Georges Enesco. When I first met him, the Rumanian composer was a striking man—long dark hair, fiery eyes; eager, youthful warmth; rich, pleasing voice. To me as a child of eleven there was a force and breadth of personality about him that made him seem taller and broader than he actually was. He lived in a simple ground-floor apartment on a courtyard. The apartment was dark, but you almost never noticed it because of the bright, generous spirit of the man. Music lay everywhere, on chairs, tables, bookcases, in the living room and the study. Violins, in and out of cases, rested on the piano; a desk burst with manuscript, and all over the place were autographed pictures of fellow musicians. In the middle of it all stood Georges Enesco, like a warm lamp, giving out light and joy. He spoke excitedly of music and musicians, of the sheer thrill of producing beautiful sound. He recalled the contrast between Debussy's voice and what he once said to him:

"*Il faut que chaque son soit beau!*"

"It was such an ugly voice," said Mr. Enesco, trying to imitate

Debussy, "that was saying every sound must be beautiful. But of course he was right. Debussy thought of music as a luxury of the ear."

Mr. Enesco warned me against studying with one teacher, saying that at best I would become a good imitation of the one teacher. He urged me to study and weigh and analyze the style and advice of many masters, never more than a few lessons from any one pianist. He spoke to me as an adult and a colleague. That made me cherish this vital and fascinating man dearly. Our friendship was interrupted by the war. I did not see him again till the spring of 1954. I was in Paris on my second European tour. At the hotel awaiting me was a note reading:

"Would you do me the honor of visiting me on Tuesday at five o'clock. Respectfully,

Georges Enesco"

The address was the same, the dark little apartment on the courtyard. When the door opened, I received one of the worst shocks in my life. I scarcely recognized the vigorous and dynamic man I had once known in the humped and stooped figure standing before me in clothes that looked as if they had been slept in for weeks. Everything about him was sad and old, except his eyes. They were like big live coals. The apartment was like an untended storeroom. The old piano, a little older, and probably a little more out of tune, stood in the same place.

Music and photographs and furniture seemed dumped about like forgotten junk. Forgotten like this bent old man with trembling hands. He was a very bitter old man. The world had passed him by. Music, he said, had gone off in the wrong direction. As he spoke his eyes bored through the half-light like fire.

"Mechanism," he said, "has replaced beauty. People worship speed, clash, dissonance, harshness. The true art of music is dead. Discord is king. Even the pianos have changed. The mellow old quality of sound has been replaced by a hard brilliance. The softness has gone out of music. When one thinks of the giants! . . . This is an age of pigmies."

I had the uncomfortable feeling that a ghost was speaking to me of a dead and glorious past. Maybe somewhere out of a tiny, tiny corner of that past came the pallid ghost of an eleven-year-old prodigy who had once listened avidly, and these words of his were a farewell warning and present. Then he asked me to sit down and play for him. It was five o'clock when I began. Battered as the piano was, I was determined to play as I had never played. I wanted to make this dear old man happy for a few hours. I began with Bach, first the "Italian" concerto and then a great number of preludes and fugues. Next I played the "Waldstein" sonata of Beethoven, following that with the G minor sonata and "Etudes Symphoniques" of Schumann, and ended with the four ballades and the B minor sonata of Chopin.

The effect was all I could have hoped, and more. Mr. Enesco wasn't an old man any longer. He was humming and conducting, by turns seated and standing and striding about the room. Between movements and numbers, he discoursed warmly about Debussy or Joachim or the pianos of Chopin's days. The hours sped by, the shadows deepened in the drab little *pied-à-terre*. When it got too dark to see the white keys from the black, Mr. Enesco turned on a small lamp that threw all its light on the keyboard.

"You have grown, Ruth," he said as he adjusted the lamp. "I see Cortot in a great deal of your work. Don't ever strive for brilliance. Too many of the younger pianists worship force and technic. It is a false trail that leads nowhere."

It was ten o'clock when I stopped. I had played five hours with only brief pauses. As I got up to go and looked at Mr. Enesco I felt happy and refreshed. There seemed less bitterness now. Standing there in the dimness, eyes agleam, both his hands grasping mine, he was more like the Georges Enesco of eighteen years before.

"You will play for me again, won't you?" he said.

What a small thing to ask of someone who had received so much and given so little in return. I remembered his words with a pang when I read less than two years later that Mr. Enesco was dead. Few musicians have given themselves so lavishly to both their fellow artists and the art they served.

To that same spring of 1936 that brought us Mr. Enesco belongs another of Father's trophies—Nadia Boulanger. It may be that Father's thoughts were running in the direction of composition. Not that he regarded composition as a paying proposition; merely that it might be one more feather in my cap and his. So one bright day he decided that what I needed was some rigorous training in harmony and composition. The next move was to ascertain who had the best reputation in that field. The final step was to get that individual to consent to teach me free of charge. All these conditions were met by Mme. Boulanger. At our very first meeting I was completely fascinated by the woman and by her apartment, particularly the pipe organ that ran all the way up to the ceiling.

"A lesson," she said to me right off, "has to be an affair of give and take for both parties; never all the giving on one side and all the taking on the other."

I was positive it was going to be a joy and inspiration to work with this gracious lady; that is, till Father told me at which time of day I was supposed to work on my harmony lessons. My nine-hour routine at the piano was to remain undisturbed. The only spare hour was the one that came after lunch. It was then that Father took his siesta and I had my brief respite in paradise. I read or played or walked with Mother in the park. When

Father told me I would have to give over that hour to harmony, I cried bitterly. I felt as if I had been robbed of my dearest possession. And naturally I resented everything about harmony, including Mme. Boulanger. This mood lasted only two weeks. Then a dramatic change occurred. I found the work such a snap that I could finish it in five minutes and still have fifty-five minutes of fun and freedom while Father slept. Neither he nor Mme. Boulanger ever suspected I gave it less than the prescribed hour. Moreover, I became gradually enthralled by Mme. Boulanger's bold and refreshing approach. Harmony, she would say, wasn't always a matter of obeying the rules; disobeying them was just as important, so long as you knew what you were doing. She encouraged freedom and flexibility.

"Look for the violations of theory in any composition you study," she once said. "They often tell you more about a composer than the rest. In creative art it is often necessary to break a rule to avoid a mistake." Once she asked me if I was working out my harmony lessons on the piano. I told her I was.

"That's like cheating at a game, Ruth," she said.

"But everybody else does."

"Everybody doesn't have perfect pitch," she said. "You do. Besides, I want you to develop your inner ear. You can do that best away from the piano."

Today I can look at the most complex score and "hear" it without benefit of a keyboard, a discipline I owe to Mme. Boulanger and her theory of the "inner ear."

Our sessions were interrupted by my next tour, at the end of which I returned to Paris to learn to my great sorrow that Mme. Boulanger was not in France. I continued my harmony studies with a fine French composer named Georges Dandelot. This was the typical musician to me, intense about music, carefree, and poor. I came to think of poverty as a sure sign of the really fine musician; Mr. Dandelot never had any money; Mr. Glazounoff was in the same boat; Mr. Rubinstein wasn't exactly affluent when I first knew him in Paris, and Georges Enesco looked like a beggar when I last saw him. It made me wish Father wouldn't brag about how much money my concerts were bringing in. I had the distinct feeling it was slightly disreputable for a musician to be wealthy.

It was at the same Villa Majestique where I used to visit Mr. Rachmaninoff that I learned one of the simplest but most vital lessons of the art of interpretation. The teacher this time was not Mr. Rachmaninoff but the German pianist Wilhelm Bachaus, who is rated by many critics today as the finest Beethoven interpreter of our time. I must have been about eleven when Father took me backstage to meet him after his concert at the Salle Pleyel. Mr. Bachaus, curious to hear me play after all the stories he had read and heard about me, asked me to come to his hotel room next day to play for him. The Villa Majestique is the Hotel Ansonia of Paris, a haven for musicians from everywhere. After hearing me play, Mr. Bachaus agreed to give me a few pointers once a week while he was in Paris. I learned my big lesson while working on the finale of the "Moonlight" sonata with him. That movement starts with a cascade of arpeggio runs in the right hand against staccato eighth-notes in the left. I wasn't at all satisfied with these staccato eighth-notes the way I first played them to myself. They sounded too delicate. Wanting more volume, I couldn't resist pushing them down until they were almost legato. When I played the passage that way for Mr. Bachaus, he merely remarked: "The left hand is staccato."

Without another word he took his pencil and marked extra dots over the already existing dots in my edition of the "Moonlight." Later at home, when I again tackled that passage, I was still convinced I couldn't get the necessary volume by playing the left hand staccato. I went right ahead with my heavy legato, and once again appeared before Mr. Bachaus. This time he took my hands abruptly off the keys.

"I corrected this once before."

Somewhat nettled, I said: "I know you did, Mr. Bachaus, but I don't see why you want me to do it that way. I get more power doing it my way. Why must it be the other way?"

"Because," he said very calmly, "it is written that way."

The truth of it struck me with startling suddenness. Why must things be done a certain way at the piano? Because the composer wanted them that way. The logic of it was clear and strong. When in doubt go back to the music. That is the final authority. To think that I was better known to the public at large than an artist like Mr. Bachaus! What's more, I was getting much higher fees for my concerts than he was. Yet Father never paid him anything for the lessons. What a grotesque situation, that people should flock to hear me and pass up a superlative master like Wilhelm Bachaus! But then I was a sort of female Tom Thumb of the keyboard, and Mr. Bachaus was an artist.

From Alexander Glazounoff I learned another little lesson in humility, the memory of which has served me whenever I find myself being too positive about anything. I had first known Mr. Glazounoff in Berlin, where I had played for him at Mr. Petri's. We renewed ties in Paris, and one day he asked me to come and play for him at his hotel. I was particularly pleased with myself at the time for having just completed the whole Chopin repertory. When Mr. Glazounoff asked me what I was going to play for him, I said, in my full pride of achievement, "Well, you name anything you want by Chopin. I've finished learning all of his compositions."

"Hmm," was Mr. Glazounoff's comment, stroking his chin. "Play me the Chopin 'Fugue'."

I thought he was kidding. I had never even heard of a Chopin fugue. Without a word, he dug under a pile of music and brought out the piece in question. Pointing a warning finger at me, he said: "Never say you have played everything of any composer. Nobody has, perhaps not even the composer."

Mr. Glazounoff lived in great poverty during those last years of his in Paris. After we became friends, I used to go up and play regularly for him on an old upright piano that hadn't been tuned in years. The room was bare and shabby except for a set of laurel wreaths that had been awarded to him at various times in years gone by. They were so glorious in my eyes, and yet so forlorn. Once I tried to beg off playing, pleading the wretched state of the upright.

"My dear child," he said, "you can play on a casserole."

I lost a sweet friend and wonderful listener when poor Mr. Glazounoff died in 1936. I thought sadly of all those laurel wreaths now lost and meaningless that had meant so much to both of us. A year after his death, when I was presented with a wreath of my own in Budapest, it pained me to think there would be no Mr. Glazounoff to whom I could show it proudly on my return to Paris. . . .

Budapest was an exciting and colorful city when I played there in 1937. The Danube was gray, but that only helped to point up the many-colored lights of the bridges and the bright scarves of the children walking along Budapest's main boulevard. The embroidered blouses and handiwork in the windows were fascinating, and in every restaurant an accordion player or a couple of violinists would play enchanting obbligatos to a gypsy melody. Even the friendly singsong of the language was wild and free and musical.

In the hall of the Ritz-Carlton Hotel, where Father and I

stayed, hung a large painting of a beautiful lady. The porter explained proudly that the beloved Emperor Franz Joseph used to visit that lady in this very hotel. It was romantic just to be there. When I played the "Rakoczy March" at the end of my program the public rose cheering. The following day Father and I were invited to a tea party at the home of a family on the St. Elizabeth Platz. There I was presented with a laurel wreath of silver leaves and red and white ribbon streamers. This was my very first laurel wreath, and to me it was all tied up with the old Greek custom of awarding a wreath to an Olympic champion. Receiving it was one of the proudest moments of my career. The wreath went with us everywhere, to Paris and later, when the war drove us from France, back to Berkeley, California—still silver, still beribboned. There it hung in our living room except for the few days at the end of the year when it hung on our front door as a Christmas decoration. But it was always my wreath. Somehow it survived—after all my precious autographed pictures of Eugene Ormandy, Feodor Chaliapin, Rosa Ponselle, and others were torn to bits during Father's bursts of temper.

Could it be that during those black years of loneliness and self-disgust soon to follow it was the twinkling laurel wreath that gave me courage and a feeling of pride—and perhaps a burning ember of hope that if I could earn such a wreath once there might be enough championship material deep down inside of me to earn one again?

This habit of Father's of taking me from one teacher to another had its paradoxical side. You see, I wasn't supposed to be anybody else's pupil but Father's. I knew it was a lie but I did my utmost to back Father up. I used to wonder in my own mind why, if he thought himself such a brilliant teacher, he had to shop around every spring for a new teacher. As I look back, I suspect that deep down under that blustering exterior, he wasn't very sure of himself. I remember the first time I played for Marguerite Long, she asked Father: "And who taught this girl?" When Father blandly replied, "I did," Mme. Long said, "Monsieur, you are a remarkable professor of the piano." I was always reminded of this statement whenever I felt disinclined to follow a suggestion of Father's. If Mme. Long ever learned the truth, it wasn't from me. Father would have brained me!

Isidor Philipp's reaction was a little more subtle. When Father first took me to this shrewd and scholarly dean of piano pedagogues, he was asked the usual first question: "Who taught this girl?" To Father's reply that he had been my sole teacher, Mr. Philipp raised his eyebrows.

"You are teasing me, monsieur. If this child were the daughter of a janitor, he might well be tempted to put out a sign saying, 'I am the greatest piano teacher in the world.'

"If people were to come to him and say, 'But, Monsieur, you are a concierge; how do you come to know what is a great piano teacher?' the concierge would merely shrug his shoulders and say:

" 'Well, look at my pupil.' "

The point Mr. Philipp was trying to get over to Father was that whoever professed to be my only teacher had the right to proclaim himself a great pedagogue. He was telling my father that I was indeed a phenomenal talent. But he was telling him something else. First, that he didn't believe Father had taught me exclusively, and second, that it didn't much matter who taught me, so long as I developed properly. This theme he enlarged on in a series of long letters he wrote to Father. I went repeatedly to Mr. Philipp's house to play for him and his wife. I liked him extremely, his candor, his insight, the vast music library he owned, the unfailing charm of the man. He taught me many little things about pedaling and phrasing. Some of the finer subtleties eluded me, or perhaps were absorbed without my noting them.

"Our American friend, the little great artist," was the way Mr. Philipp would introduce me to his fellow musicians and pupils.

From Lazare Lévy, another Paris acquisition of Father's spring tours, I learned ingenious ways of fingering tricky passages. Compared to most of my colleagues, who are so much taller and more largely built, I have a very small hand. Now while I never thought of my hands as a problem, it has served me well to know how to make the best of what nature gave me. Mr. Lévy showed me clever little ways of fingering Bach fugues in which two or more voices sometimes move together in one hand. Greater teachers than Mr. Lévy had taught me *which* voices to bring out. Mr. Lévy taught me *how* to bring them out. He showed me how sound fingering could simplify the most crowded passage. These fingerings were designed to help a small hand. During my teaching years I found they were just as helpful to a larger hand.

For this precious tutoring, as for so much else from so many others, Mr. Lévy never received a sou. It never occurred to him to expect payment and Father never encouraged him to expect it. It is very possible that I got more free lessons from more teachers than any other pupil in all music history.

IN looking back, I realize now that long before I fled Father, even during those first fabulous years as a child prodigy, I had already begun to play mental hooky. I must have known for certain as a small child that I would never be able to escape my father in any physical sense. There was no running away from the beatings, the tongue-lashings, the virtual imprisonment. Bound as he had made me to the piano, there wasn't even a desire to run away. But I was eluding him in ways he couldn't suspect—or if he did, could do nothing about. There were the little mental flights to my sisters' cries of glee in the street below as I practiced in our Paris flat. There were the letters I began secretly writing to Mr. Tobin always with the warning not to reply. Very early I began having terrific crushes on men I would have preferred as my father had the choice been mine. It will embarrass Eugene Ormandy to learn that he was my first candidate for the job. I thought he had just about everything a father should have. I played with him five or six times, first when I was eight years old in Pittsburgh. We took to each other instantly. After our first rehearsal he spent the afternoon kidding and teasing and amusing me; treating me like a little girl but like an equal, too. When I next played with him, in Minneapolis, he was at the train to meet us, the perfect gentleman, playful, attentive, exactly what I wanted my father to be. On my twelfth birthday Mr. Ormandy gave me two gifts. One was a book inscribed to me by "Uncle Eugene Ormandy and her orchestra," meaning the Minneapolis Symphony. The second gift was even more precious. After rehearsal Mr. Ormandy handed me the baton and said, "Now, Ruth, you conduct Sousa's 'Stars and Stripes Forever.'" I did, loving every minute of it, the glowing sense of power. The men played good-naturedly, and we had a grand time.

You can see why for three or four years I had daydreams about running away to Eugene Ormandy's house in Minneapolis. I had these imaginary flights all over America and Europe, between concerts, at night in a hotel room, during the ticking away of the metronome as Father stood watching with his "magic stick." They had their practical side, those day-dreams. I would try to figure out how I could reach my dream father without money. Sometimes I'd say to myself: "Well, I'm too fat anyway. I'll walk to Minneapolis and not eat anything on the way. By the time I get there I'll be thin and beautiful." I would picture Mr. Ormandy opening the door and joyously inviting me in to play with him. I would go to all the concerts I wanted to, play when I felt like it, and practice only an hour or two a day. At that point a slap on the cheek, a whack on the back, or a loud oath would yank me back to reality. Father was still Father.

I even found ways of taking mental excursions in the music itself. This was possible in passages requiring endless repetition for absolute ease, asking but little thought. There was one such passage in the last movement of the "Waldstein" sonata of Beethoven. This is a purely technical episode toward the very end, where the climax is being developed and both hands play contrary triplets. I worked on the triplets hours on end, with a metronome, from slow to fast, using the method Mr. Rachmaninoff had taught me. I made such an automatic process of it, that my mind was free to leave my Father and the piano and go frolicking all over the streets of Paris below.

As for dreams of romance and marriage, Father took care of

that very early. I would never marry, he said. That was only for ordinary girls. I wasn't a girl or a woman; I was a pianist. I knew as a child that if ever a Prince Charming came along, he would never get by the barrier of Father. The only time he relented a bit was when he told me that possibly, when he got too old to handle my career, he would find me a wealthy old suitor with a few million dollars who would marry me, watch over me for a few years, and then die like a gentleman and leave me his millions. I don't think he meant it, however. In his mind I was never to marry. I was not to be shared with anyone, not with Mother, not with my sisters, not with a husband. All I could do was dream.

I used to dream, for instance, of being with people, talking with them, playing games with them. One way or another Father was always in the way. If I talked to people after a concert, later he would tell me I was a chatterbox and a simpleton. If I was expected to say anything to a prospective hostess, Father would coach me in a little speech, after which I was to hold my tongue. I was forbidden to speak unless spoken to. I would sit in agony during conversations at dinner, tempted to join in, but thwarted by a glare from Father. Back home in Paris after a tour, he would tell Mother of the numerous times I had made an idiot of myself by opening my mouth. Even Mother would say, "The best thing for you to do is to be quiet. Remember, an empty barrel makes the most noise." Which made me reflect: "The safest thing to do is to say nothing to anyone at any time, at least when Daddy is around." But Daddy was always around. This inhibition remained with me till years after I broke away from Father. Even when I was married and a young hostess in my own home, I was scared to open my mouth for fear of saying the wrong thing.

It was almost as if Father had wanted to crush every human

and social instinct in me. I was isolated, cut off from the normal world of things and people. I was to think of myself only as a pianist. Everything else was irrelevant and wasteful. How ironic, when you come to think of it! Here I was appearing before thousands and thousands of people everywhere. Yet I had no real contact with them. In every true sense of the word I was alone. The physical pain of the thrashings was nothing compared to this growing sense of isolation. I felt cut off and unwanted. I had virtually no one to talk to in confidence. The long hours of practice had set up a wall between Mother and me and my two sisters. The tours had made us complete strangers. Later Helen and Gloria came to think of me more as a maiden aunt than a sister.

It was during these years of loneliness that I found a secret outlet for my thoughts and feelings. I began corresponding with my godfather, the late Richard M. Tobin, brother of the Celia Tobin Clark, who sponsored me. Nobody knows about these letters, not even Mother. It was a one-sided correspondence. I ended every letter with a plea to please destroy it the moment he read it. I hope his widow, Mrs. Tobin, will understand. You see, in this time of need I remembered Mr. Tobin as a man who had been very kind to me as a child. Each time we were in San Francisco he would take me either to the zoo or to Chinatown, and buy me costume jewelry. Once he bought me a bag of peanuts to throw to the seals at the zoo. He was a wealthy banker and an amateur violinist, at least sixty years of age to my eight or nine. Somehow we understood each other perfectly. Once, at his office, he let me dictate a letter to my mother in Paris. And so, a few years later, he began receiving monthly letters from a lonely little girl whom he had so gallantly befriended. All my innermost longings went into those letters. They were never once alluded to; they were never answered, and I'm certain they were never seen by anybody but Mr. Tobin. He was another one of my dream fathers, and the letters a way of talking to someone, even though it was only a monologue in the dark.

At the beginning I used to think that I was something of a sneak to steal off on my mental journeys away from Father. I felt like a traitor the first time I wrote a secret letter to Mr. Tobin. You see, I lived to please Father, to obey him in everything, to take for granted that whatever he said about me or anyone else was the truth. When he beat me, I assumed it was for my own good. I even sided with him against Mother. Father was Father, and he had made me what I was. He never tired of telling me that and reminding me of his great sacrifice. There was always that twinge of shame when I played hooky from him in my thoughts, at least at first. Gradually it became a habit to hide things from him. And now something else began to happen. At first I was barely aware of it. Then one day it dawned on me. *I was losing faith in Father as a musician.* It came about by degrees, one thing piling on another, as I grew older and started to see him differently. Possibly the first time I felt anything like doubt was during a visit with Mr. Godowsky at the Ansonia Hotel, when I was about ten years old. I had just learned Chopin's "Funeral March" sonata and was planning to play it in New York and everywhere else. Now this happens to be one of the most awesome monuments of piano literature, and certain people, among them my manager, Mr. Wagner, suggested to Father that it was a mistake for a child my age to perform this somber classic in a concert hall. Father scoffed at this. The more difficult the music was, he said, the more spectacular the feat, and he was one for keeping me as spectacular as ever. Secretly he was worried. I could tell because he had me play the sonata for many musicians. So that's how it was that we barged in on Mr. Godowsky early one morning at the Ansonia.

"What are you going to play for me today, Ruth?"

Before I could open my mouth, Father said: "How would you like to hear the whole 'Funeral March' sonata of Chopin?"

Mr. Godowsky looked just a little surprised, said: "Hmmm . . ." and after a pause, "Oh, nothing would surprise me about Ruth."

So I played the whole sonata for him, and for a few moments there was complete silence, till Father broke it impatiently: "Well, what do you think of it? Shall I let her play it on her programs?"

All Mr. Godowsky would say was: "Well, she's playing it, isn't she?"

That was approval enough for Father. But I knew better. In my innermost heart I sensed Mr. Godowsky's hesitancy; his lack of enthusiasm; his evasiveness. He knew it was wiser for me not to play the Chopin sonata and I wish he had said so bluntly. Mr. Godowsky was amazed, I suppose, that I could play it at all; but he didn't say a word about whether it was beautiful; he made no comment about my phrasing, my pedaling, my fingering. Usually people gushed over my playing. So a little imp of doubt rose in my mind, and went on rising. I knew I was right when I began to play the sonata in public. The controversy that followed was fierce. In the smaller towns people bought tickets just to see the feat accomplished. To them it was a *tour de force* that I could play all the notes. In the larger cities the critics denounced whoever was responsible for allowing me to play the sonata. The musical and emotional implications of the music were beyond the scope of a ten-year-old child, they said. Only an adult could bring any true maturity to this mighty lament. That was the first year that a new word began to appear in my reviews. The word was "immature." It was to haunt me like an avenging fury.

Incidentally it was during a tour of Switzerland, when I was eleven years old, that I first programmed the even more formidable B minor sonata of Chopin. Difficult as it is, I learned to play all the notes and to perform it with a certain dash. My favorite sections were the rollicking start of the *scherzo* and the *rondo finale*. The rest was an impenetrable jungle as far as understanding went. The first movement, with its subtly changing moods, was completely beyond me.

Always on tour I practiced wherever and whenever we could locate a piano. In a Lausanne hotel I labored on the first movement, trying to memorize in minute detail the scale of dynamics Father wanted me to use. In my mind it was like one of those relief maps showing the mountains, peaks, and canyons of a country. I trained myself to think geographically of the accents, *f*, *ff*, *pp*, etc. As I was not permitted to express a phrase as *I* felt it, the only way I could hope to please Father was to establish in my mind this artificial map of what he wanted. It was fiendishly hard and hopelessly frustrating. Every time I went to bed, whenever I took a walk or sat down to eat a meal, always my mind was busy rehearsing parts of the first movement of the B minor sonata. And still I couldn't master it to Father's satisfaction. He was perfectly furious at me when the first severe reviews appeared. In the hotel rooms he would scream nasty oaths at me as loudly as he dared.

Once, as we walked along Lausanne's lovely arcaded sidewalks, I trying desperately to fix a part of the relief map in my head, Father still burning from the acid reviews, he turned on me wrathfully:

"Look at you, you unnatural, artificial thing! Look at what wants to be a pianist! You don't deserve to sit in front of a keyboard, much less give concerts!" People turned around as he worked himself into a frenzy of shouting and gesticulating. Finally I could bear it no longer and screamed at the top of my lungs: "Go away from me!"

Taken aback momentarily, he eyed me with redoubled rage. "I'll cancel the rest of your concerts, you, you nothing! A piece of wood would play better than you."

He grabbed me and pushed me along as I sobbed and blubbered. Suddenly I tore away from him and ran ahead, my hands over my ears, the hot tears streaming down. Nothing mattered any more, nothing but to get away from his harsh, pounding voice. Then I felt a hand on my arm, and through the mist of tears I saw a little old lady peering anxiously into my face. "*Sind Sie die Frau?*" she asked. "Are you his wife?"

I was so astounded, and I guess she was, too, when she finally saw how wide of the mark her question was, that we both started to laugh, and all at once everything was all right again.

We took Chopin's B minor sonata off the program. I can never forget a single note of it, I drummed it so thoroughly into my subconscious. I never did and do not now memorize quickly. I must laboriously assemble every sound in my mind and train it to run at the proper speed—like film in a movie camera. Once when I was nine and about to play in Canada for the first time, the manager told us it was customary at all public performances to open the program with "God Save the King."

"Naturally you are going to play it."

Naturally Father said yes. Now this may sound unbelievable, but *I had never heard the tune before.* It took two hours of practice, tears, and beatings to get that simple composition into my head! However, when I learn something thoroughly, it is there forever. I need only a brief review for a composition that I may not have thought of in years. I learned Liszt's B minor sonata when I was thirteen and played it every morning before breakfast as an exercise but didn't put it on a program till many years later. When I play one of these big things now I am conscious of great freedom. I have absorbed the notes and technical problems of these masterpieces so completely that they are a part of me. My fingers are thus free for the greater adventures that lie on the other side of technic.

Then there was the time we had a grand reunion with Egon Petri in London, our first meeting in six years since our Berlin days together. I was practicing the G minor concerto of Saint-Saëns at the Bechstein place when Mr. Petri came in and gave me a splendid greeting. Immediately he sat down at a second piano, and *without the music*, played the orchestral part of the concerto, an incredible feat! Imagine a pianist memorizing the whole orchestral score of a concerto! Afterwards Mr. Petri praised me to the skies:

"You've fulfilled every one of my predictions!" he said.

"What would you suggest as the next thing for her to study?" Father asked.

Mr. Petri thought a moment. "Well," he replied, "I would imagine that for her musical growth a work like Beethoven's 'Les Adieux' sonata might be very valuable."

Father exploded. " 'Les Adieux!' What kind of effect would that have on the public? I want something brilliant that will knock them out of their seats!"

Mr. Petri made no further suggestions. I remember being both startled and ashamed of Father. For days I puzzled over this conflict of views between Mr. Petri and Father. I was wondering more and more about Father's musical integrity. Finally there was the curious episode with the young English nobleman. For reasons best known to himself, this wealthy and good-looking gentleman was so fascinated by my playing he followed me and Father all the way from England to America, attending all my concerts here and in Canada. He evidently had time to kill and the money to kill it with. He was also trying to prove something; what, I never quite knew. Anyway, here he was trailing us like a pet poodle. On my birthday he gave me a diamond watch. He was one of those people who adore music for its own sake, for Beethoven's sake, for art's sake. The three of us talked endlessly about music. Father must have scented something he didn't quite like. He began to grow impatient with our titled camp follower. The blowup occurred in Los Angeles, where I saw him for the last time, and considering what a musical fanatic he was, I can see why. Father had been waiting for an opening, and the esthetic young Englishman gave it to him.

"What is it about Beethoven and Ruth that is so completely sympathetic and fascinating?" he asked Father. "She seems, even though so young, to grasp the master's most profound and personal ideas almost without effort."

Father quickly retorted: "My daughter Ruth doesn't have any ideas of her own. They are all mine."

The young man persisted: "But still she must feel something; otherwise it would be impossible for her to project . . ."

Father cut him short: "Young man, there is only one thing in this world that counts and that is money, and I teach Ruth to play Beethoven because it brings in the dollars."

I was shocked. At first the Englishman thought my father was joking; but it soon was clear to him that Father had expressed his sentiments exactly. I was prepared to believe he had said that only to rid himself of this strange hanger-on. If that was his object, it worked. I never saw my English nobleman again. I had been given another revealing glimpse of what my father was really like. He had shrunken considerably. Better than ever before, I knew now that money, not music, was his controlling passion. One day I even discovered that Father had developed a profitable little offshoot to the business of exploiting a prodigy. Mothers and fathers everywhere brought their would-be *Wunderkinder* to him for a hearing. They seemed to think that here, if anywhere, was the miracle man who could detect the divine spark. They found him most hospitable, most thorough, and most candid. It was truly magnanimous of Father, I thought. Then I found out he charged fifty dollars for a consultation. My whole conception of the man was changing; I was slowly but surely losing my very feeling for him as a daughter. My attitude toward music was changing. I was beginning to think for myself.

While on tour I always shared a hotel room with Father. The reservation invariably called for twin beds and bath. Neither of us ever gave the arrangement a second thought till I appeared in London at the age of twelve. Harold Holt, the London impresario, had booked the usual accommodations at an old English hotel which for some reason failed to meet Father's standards of service. On our own, we hunted for another hotel and decided on the Regent Palace. For the first time, while registering, he met resistance.

"Twin beds and bath for me and my daughter," said Father to the clerk.

"Shouldn't you have two rooms, sir?" asked the clerk.

"Of course not," growled Father. "My daughter Ruth and I always share a room."

"How old is your daughter?"

"Twelve—but what has that got to do with it?"

"Is that the child there?"

"Why sure, and she's a real healthy specimen, not like your underfed bellhops. Are you booking the room for me or not?"

Hesitantly the clerk responded, "Well, I guess it's all right. . . ."

Suddenly I felt self-conscious. I had always thought of my

sole reason for being as giving satisfaction to Father in some way, never as a person in my own right. Here was someone, a mature and practical man at that, actually regarding me as a young lady with a private identity of her own. At first I smiled at the clerk's words; then I braced myself for the altercation I was certain Father would start; finally, like a heralding trumpet, the golden thought flashed across my mind:

"Really and truly I am an individual, not a baby any more but a young lady with a mind and a life of her very own."

I said nothing then, but when we returned to our Paris home I refused to sleep in my bed in my parents' room and was promoted to the couch in my sisters' room. I was a woman and proud of it.

From all these gathering signs of dissent and doubt, it is obvious that at this time my life was moving toward a crisis. Some such turning point arrives in the life of every child prodigy: the day when allowances cease to be made on grounds of youth; the time for reappraisal; the need for readjusting to new values. Father must have thought the career could go on indefinitely at the pace and pitch he had set for his wonder-child. If people paid to hear me at eight and nine and ten, why not at thirteen and fourteen and fifteen? Surely there were many more good years to his golden goose. But the warnings were multiplying. . . .

Take the case of Olin Downes, the late critic of the New York *Times*. When I was five, Mr. Downes was one of the experts consulted by the Tobins on whether I was worth investing money in. His verdict had been an emphatic yes. "Every day," he had said, "people put thousands of dollars on the nose of a horse; why not on the talent of a human being?" But he drew the line at bringing me out in public too soon. My early success did not change his attitude one bit. Like Rachmaninoff, he was convinced I could advance better by broadening my studies than by concertizing. This finally precipitated a head-on collision with Father at a dinner given for me by the Smadbecks on East Eighty-seventh Street. Father was still gloating over my first Town Hall triumphs and the ecstatic notices of several of Mr. Downes's colleagues. To Father this was proof conclusive that Mr. Downes didn't know what he was talking about when he insisted it would be wisest to take me out of circulation for a few years. Father quoted review after review to Mr. Downes. When Mr. Downes refused to yield, Father lost his head and shouted:

"What do you know about music? And who asked you to come to any of my daughter's concerts, anyway?"

"You needn't trouble yourself on that score," retorted Mr. Downes. "I've heard your daughter play for the last time." Whereupon he turned his back on Father and left.

Now Mr. Downes had no ax of his own to grind in this dispute. He honestly believed I could be a finer musician by abandoning my concert career till I was old enough to know what I was doing. I know now that he strongly opposed what he saw to be a glaring example of child exploitation. Like so many other critics he could applaud my musical gifts and still look ahead with misgivings to what the next few years of touring might do to me. Being told by Father that I was a genius, that I was a born musician, and that I wasn't to be judged by ordinary rules didn't impress him at all. Mr. Downes had been in the game long enough to have observed the decline and fall of many an infant meteor of music.

The question now became almost a public issue. Sides were taken by musicians and managers and concertgoers. Many attacked Father purely on grounds of exploitation. Others agreed with Mr. Downes that a great talent was being squandered prematurely. Josef Hofmann, an ex-prodigy himself, wrote an article defending Father's position. It would be a crime to take me off the public stage, he said. I was setting a marvelous example for other gifted children; my concerts helped me to grow and mature, and he was sorry he hadn't done more concertizing at my age. Besides, said Mr. Hofmann, I loved to play in public; so what possible harm could it do me? Of course Mr. Hofmann didn't know all the facts of the case. Neither did Mr. Downes. I'm sure both would have been revolted by the story of my physical mistreatment and inhuman schedule of work. So there were two strongly opposed factions on the subject, both sincere and both valid. I only came to understand the issue later as the reservations cropped up with increasing frequency in the reviews. I did enjoy my concerts; music was my dreamland; the piano my unfailing friend and savior. I knew little else, till adolescence set in and brought a rude awakening to what was happening.

Little "buts" began to creep into more and more notices. The word "immature" became almost as regular a slap as one of Father's disciplinary blows. At first Father dismissed the matter with a scoffing remark about the reviewer's ignorance. Then he began to resent it furiously. Finally he struck back by having me write letters to the critics. In them I both defended myself and questioned the critic's own maturity. Some were nasty little notes of crude spleen and malice, every word of them dictated by Father and signed by me. I'm afraid that didn't stop the gentlemen of the press from calling me immature. There being nothing else to do, Father now shifted the blame to me. Whenever that ghastly word appeared in a review, the newspaper containing it would be tightly rolled up and brought across my cheek. He would scream the word two or three times.

"Immature! Immature! If you played the way I taught you to, they'd never be calling you immature. *How could they when I am a mature musician?*"

What was I to do? I was trying my best to carry out Father's instructions exactly to the letter. At the same time I kept in mind what Mr. Rachmaninoff and Mr. Cortot and Mr. Schnabel had drilled into me. I played as well as I could, was obedient as I had been trained to be, and yet was accused of disobedience because the critics found my performances immature. It was like being beaten for carefully *not* stealing the jam. I was damned if I did and damned if I didn't. I began to feel like someone trapped in quicksand. The harder I tried to please Father, the deeper I sank. That was the irony of it. The more I did what he wanted me to, the more my playing was found immature. There seemed no escape. For weeks and months I cried into my pillow every single night. Deep down, Father must have suspected the fault was his. That's what stung him, this change toward me was in reality a change toward him. It was as if he knew they finally had his number. It got to the point where I was actually afraid to walk out on the stage of Town Hall and play. Whatever the critics said about me, I was maturing in one respect: I was becoming more and more convinced that something was wrong with my playing, something I couldn't yet put my finger on, something Father was utterly incapable of correcting. This time I wanted him to consult someone whose judgment I respected, who had befriended me as a child. This man was Howard Taubman of the New York *Times*. I wanted Mr. Taubman to say whether he thought I should go ahead with my next Town Hall recital. So Father invited Mr. and Mrs. Taubman to the Ansonia Hotel and I played, among other things, Beethoven's E major sonata, Opus 109. Mr. Taubman was gracious and complimentary. I felt relieved, till Father asked him point blank:

"Do you think we ought to put on a Town Hall concert?"

After a moment's hesitation Mr. Taubman replied in all honesty: "I don't think I would in your place. I would wait for Ruth to grow and broaden a little more and return as a mature personality in her own right."

This was sincere and helpful advice. But truth and honesty never sat well with Father. Mr. Taubman had said the same thing as Mr. Molinari, Mr. Rachmaninoff, and Mr. Downes. But it wasn't what Father wanted to hear. He knew what Mr. Taubman's advice meant if he acted on it: no more Town Hall concerts meant no more engagements in the smaller towns; no more engagements meant no more fees. What kind of business was this? So, despite Mr. Taubman and my own misgivings, the concert took place. The critics, though still kind and courteous, were even more insistent about the immaturity. And of course every one of them was right. What maturity could you expect of a thirteen- or fourteen-year-old pianist? I knew I played well technically and never missed a note. In that respect my performances were flawless. The rest—the musical ideas, the poetry, the emotional quality—simply wasn't grown up. How could it be? At the very best I could offer only my own digest of the advice of my teachers—often nullified by my father—and as filtered through a child's imagination. I say this quite frankly in self-defense. The critics were perfectly right when they found me immature, but wrong to expect me to be anything else. Wronger still was Father. To his thinking I should have been the perfect reflection of his own maturity. That, he reasoned, would have happened if I had worked harder. So he bludgeoned me with this weakness as a betrayal of himself. I became his scapegoat. I had no mental recesses to hide in, no way of breaking out of this psychological trap. I didn't know where to go, what to think, whose advice to take. Every road I might take led into a blind alley. At every juncture Father was there to revile me for disgracing him. I dreaded my concerts. On tour, at night, I would cry ever so softly into my pillow for fear of waking up Father, because that only meant another thrashing. I used to think often of Mr. Rachmaninoff. If only I had had him to confide in, to speak to in French. . . . I was blocked on all sides.

This dread of giving concerts gradually became a dread of music itself. Everything it had meant to me began looking dark and ominous. I saw myself as a normal happy girl if only I could suddenly, magically, be divested of my music. I remember we spent a short vacation in the country right outside of Paris. The family that sat next to us at the big table of the dining room had a talented daughter who was in her second or third year at the Paris Conservatory. They regarded me with a certain awe. I was a *vedette*, a young star already on her way, while their daughter, who was older than I, was lagging far behind. "Of course," said the mother, "Ginette would do lots better, but she has to be coaxed to practice." Which brought the boastful remark from Mother: "Our Ruth has to be dragged away from the piano. She adores her music."

Ginette must have had her doubts. Later, while I was playing with my sisters, she asked me: "Do you really like to practice nine hours a day? Do you love music that much?" I took her aside and said: "If you promise not to give me away, I'll tell you the truth." Ginette crossed her heart.

"I hate music," I said. "I hate practicing. Don't practice too hard. Whatever you do, the critics will say bad things about you. You're lucky you aren't advanced enough to give concerts. Do you want my advice? Don't get good enough to play in public. It's the worst thing that can happen to you."

I said that in the strictest confidence. Ginette, of course, told her mother, her mother told my mother, Mother told Father, and did I get it! The episode was not divulged to him till we got back to our apartment in Paris. Finding me sullen and lackadaisical one day, he got suspicious. "Aren't you happy to be back?" he said. "You used to speak to the piano every time you returned to it. Now you look as if you hated it." When I burst out crying, he knew something was wrong. He pumped Mother, who dreaded telling him, knowing what the consequences would be. But he dragged it out of her, and the fun started.

How could I explain to this madman who came at me that I was fed up with being blamed for the bad notices; that I couldn't get better notices while I played the way he wanted me to; that there were many things wrong with his teaching; that I was ashamed—a girl turning fourteen—of practicing nine hours a day in my slip; that other girls my age already wore lipstick, went to the movies, and were not thrashed by their fathers for missing a metronome beat. I knew it was hopeless. I just watched Father building up this new tirade that would only end in another beating. . . . Yes, I was a genius once, he began, but that was a long time ago, when I was four and five and six and even eight. But did I know why I was a genius? Because *he* was a genius; because I did exactly what *he* told me to do. Then look what happened. I got bad, lazy, disobedient. I became unmanageable. I distorted everything he taught me. That's why the critics called me immature. I would never grow up, not in a thousand years; I was rotten and corrupt inside, and the proof of that was the idiotic statements I had made to a complete stranger.

"The world must think I have a crazy daughter," he ranted. "All right; I'm going to knock that craziness out of her."

And he proceeded to do so with his belt till I was so bruised I had to be put immediately to bed, a sorry, tearful, whimpering, humiliated girl of fourteen. This time Mother came to my bedside distraught and anguished. For the second time in my life she asked me this question: "Ruth, do you really love your music? Because if you don't, we'll all leave Father in Paris and return to Berkeley. You'll go to school like ordinary American children. You'll forget all about the piano. You won't have to play concerts any more. You won't get beaten any more. You'll begin to live like a decent human being. Please, darling, tell me the truth."

I replied, as I had replied ten years before:

"Will we have a piano?"

Her face and her voice fell. "You still want a piano?"

"Yes, Mommy, I can't go on without a piano."

"Well, suppose your father weren't around, suppose you didn't have any teachers, do you know enough to go on by yourself?"

And I said, "No, I've got to have somebody to tell me what to do. I don't understand what's wrong with my playing. But I believe the critics and I believe them when they use the word 'immature' about me. But I don't understand what it means, and I've got to find out."

"Wouldn't you rather go to high school and meet boys and learn how to dance and go to the movies and do all the other things that little girls do?"

"No, I'd rather play the piano and give concerts. No matter what."

She was crying and I was crying and I was aching all over in bed.

At that moment Mother must have agreed with Father; that I was crazy. Here she was offering to take me away from all the pain and suffering and humiliation and make a normal little girl of me. She was prepared to leave her husband and go to work for Gloria and Helen and me. And there I lay wet with tears, covered with bruises, racked with pain, rejecting her sacrifice, preferring the piano and all that went with it. In her heart she must have felt I was a musician and that all musicians were just a little impossible. This was my way of proving it.

Things didn't improve after that; on the contrary. The

more concerts I gave, the more reviews I got with that hateful word. It now struck me why the word would always be there as long as I was under Father's domination. Father completely misunderstood it. To the critics it meant a failure to grasp the poetic and inner quality of a piece of music. To Father it meant playing wrong notes. The truth is, personality was lacking. The more I followed Father's instructions, the further I was from sounding like an artist with something of my own to say. I even began to see why Father put so much stress on the outer aspects of piano playing, how this very stress led in turn to a basic distortion of musical values. He had absolutely no respect for the average concertgoer. He thought of him as a man who preferred acrobatics to art. This realization didn't help me out of my blind alley. The situation steadily got worse. I began to notice how Father blundered with people the same way he did with music.

It pained me to hear him rant on about how Mr. Wagner was "cheating him right and left," and I was miserable when they broke up. I got to know and love Johnnie Evans, of Columbia Artists, who became the tour advance-man, but I couldn't forget how kind and loyal Mr. Wagner had been. From the very start he had been thoroughly sold on me as an artist. When I was eight and looked half my age, he would compliment me after a concert by saying: "You are six feet tall." For my eleventh birthday Mr. Wagner gave me a beautiful diamond pendant which I still wear today at every concert, one of the few things Father allowed me to keep, not without this acid touch:

"After all, he made enough money off you."

That was too much. "Mr. Wagner didn't have to give me the pendant," I said. "He earned every dollar that we paid him. That was his commission. He gave me the pendant because he wanted to, because he likes me——"

Wham!

That may have helped bring about his break with Mr. Wagner. I liked him and he liked me. That was enough for Father to throw the book at him—withheld fees, exorbitant commissions, faulty promotion, inadequate bookings, "stabs in the back." I loved and defended Mr. Wagner; therefore he was "cheating" us.

This curious conflict grew worse and worse in me: I could not bear the thought of living without a piano and yet I feared going before the public. It was as if each time that terrible word appeared in a review I was branded anew. It made me feel condemned, tainted. There was nothing I could do to wash off this stain of immaturity. I remember there was talk of my touring South Africa. It excited me for only one reason: perhaps at such a great distance from America and Europe, the critics might not call me immature. The inferiority complex it gave me was frightful. I began to think I was not made for music, that there was something glaringly wrong somewhere, so wrong that none of my teachers, least of all Father, could correct it.

Then one day a wild hope seized me. Maybe if I stopped playing the piano and learned to sing, I wouldn't sound so immature. Hadn't Marcella Sembrich predicted that someday I would sing? Elisabeth Rethberg had said the same thing to me twice at the Metropolitan: "Someday you may sing even more beautifully with your voice than you do with your hands." I recalled Rosa Ponselle's words that my gift would turn to song when the time came, and even Chaliapin once said that if I ever revealed a voice, I would make a fine dramatic singer because of my "natural phrasing." They were singers, of course, and for them singing was the ultimate in music. The way they thought of voice, I had thought of the piano. But the piano was bringing me nothing but pain and sorrow. So I sought this way out of my blind alley.

Father was strangely amenable to the idea. Evidently he saw no harm in trying. First he took me to Charles Panzera, a friend of Mr. Cortot's and noted lieder singer. Mr. Panzera was quite impressed by the fact that I knew languages, could sight-read a song easily, and was able to accompany myself at the piano. There was only one thing missing, he said. I had no voice. "Maybe you will develop one later; at fourteen you haven't the trace of one."

Far from deterring Father, this gave him the idea that with practice I might bring out a voice. Hadn't he done wonders with my hands? I could see that Father was already having visions of perhaps an even more spectacular career for me as a coloratura. Successful singers, he once said, outnumbered successful pianists. So my nine-hour schedule at the piano was cut to seven, the remaining two hours given to vocalizing and songs by Pergolesi and other Italian masters. What Father didn't realize was that you couldn't treat a voice the way you treat hands. Each time he brought me back to Mr. Panzera or one of the five or six other singing teachers who succeeded him, there were new cracks in my voice. Each time that happened, Father beat me for not working hard enough. Now, when he thrashed me for a mistake at the piano, I usually bawled my head off and corrected the mistake. Not when I sang, however. A fit of crying would leave my voice quavering for hours. The result was that we both tired of the business of singing. What little voice I had Father beat out of me in a few months. I don't think it was time wasted, however. The singing lessons had given me a better feeling for molding a melodic line.

The episode soured and embittered Father still more. Escape seemed more hopeless than ever. The projected tour to South

Africa fell through. Books were ceasing to be a magic carpet of flight. I was at my wits' end about the awful block that had developed in my music. I was starved for playful release of any kind. It pains me to recall the time I visited my old tutor Miss Ellinwood in Phoenix, Arizona, where she was teaching in a private school. I was a gawky adolescent of fourteen, and the first thing I said was, "Can I run, please, Miss Ellinwood?" It was all the proof Father needed of why the critics called my playing immature.

If only I had had Mother to talk to at this time. But Father had erected and maintained a barrier between us. The practicing and the tours had prevented any closeness. As a rule, Father dictated my letters to Mother. How could I feel close to her if I rarely had a chance to talk to her in private? I can't blame her if she felt the same way about me. There were so many little things she could do for Helen and Gloria while Father was away. She could buy a new coat for Helen, pick a hat for Gloria, take them both to movies and plays. This all stopped the moment Father and I were back in Paris. He controlled every movement of hers as he did mine. During all those years Father was all the family I ever knew. What makes it worse was that Mother wasn't a musician. This whole problem of mine, the conflict of ideas, the immaturity, the blind alley of my playing, was a closed door to her. My sisters would cuddle up to Mother in bed. I couldn't because I was up so early and at the piano. Mother used to bake cakes and cookies for little parties for Helen and Gloria and their friends. My only parties were with Father and the metronome. Paint sets given to me as gifts went to Gloria and Helen. What time had I for such trifles? I was Mother's daughter, but never her confidante or pal. Mother says today that because of my music I deprived my sisters of a father's natural love. She forgets that I was deprived of the natural love of a mother and two sisters. Nobody was to blame, I suppose; nobody but Father, who wanted it that way. Between my sisters and me there was an added partition: I felt like an adult; they were always "the kids."

I was in this hopeless muddle in Paris when the war broke out. Here I was all mixed up inside and suddenly everything around me was all mixed up, too. Excited huddles of people everywhere; frightening mobilization posters on walls; midnight sirens; wild flights to the cellar with gas masks; concierges urging silence for fear of using up oxygen. Who knew when, where, how the bombs would fall? I remember pounding louder and louder on the piano to pretend to myself that those things weren't really happening. You couldn't walk to the corner without wearing that ugly long cylinder containing a gas mask. Everybody had a dry gray look. People scurried about like frightened mice, all of us reduced to one common denominator—musicians, bootblacks, bakers, tycoons—all trying desperately to get out of Paris. Parisians wanted to flee to the country; country people, fearful of being stranded, wanted to get to the big city; foreigners wanted to go home. Everybody was going somewhere, or at least trying to. Frantic calls and cables were sent to speed their exit. Wires were pulled to facilitate passage on trains and ships. In this wild melee and exodus, the five Slenczynskis were seized with panic, too.

This was the last straw for Mother. The war was her clinching argument against the whole insane blunder of my career. Only a few months before she had offered to leave Father and take us back to California. But for my stubbornness, we would all now be safe in our own country. She had never liked leaving America in the first place. She had hated speaking a foreign language and sending her children to foreign schools. From the time Father took me to Philadelphia, she had felt like a deserted wife. It was my music that had forced an inhuman loneliness on her. Now here we were trapped in a country at war, all on account of two crazy musicians in the family. This was the end of the line, as far as she was concerned. I couldn't blame her. Meanwhile the family was united in one thought: how to get out.

So we queued up with thousands of others outside the steamship offices. Anxious days crawled by, till finally we got word of accommodations for the entire family. It seems I had a fan in New York, a Mrs. Franklin, wife of the president of a steamship company. A cable from her to the Paris office assuring us immediate passage had done the trick. I believe that through Mrs. Franklin Father was even able to expedite the crossing of Mr. and Mrs. Fritz Kreisler, who stood in line with us. Father had known him in his Vienna days and he and I had often crossed paths along the concert circuit. It was one more time I appreciated having a fan.

Finally the five of us were packed into a stateroom built for two, and the voyage home began. I remember how awed I was by the enormous American flags painted on the ship's sides and flooded with light so the U-boats wouldn't mistake us for somebody else. The ship was teeming. There were cots in the corridors, cots in the lounges, cots in the dining room, cots on the promenade decks, and cots on the boat deck. People even made grisly jokes about putting me to sleep inside the piano to make room in the stateroom for someone else. Children were crying all the time; people whispered and commiserated with one another. The air was thick with rumors of torpedoes and planes. We were like trapped, frightened animals till we saw the Statue of Liberty. For six whole days I didn't touch the piano. For the first time in ten years I had ceased being a pianist. I was just a terrified human being like everybody else. The music, the reviews, the trouncings had all faded in this greater nightmare.

Six hours after arriving in New York we were at Grand Central Station ready to entrain for California. Aunt Evelyn and Uncle

Phil and their two little girls were at the station with us. Suddenly I felt a new freedom and relief. My sisters and I excitedly told our cousins about the war, showed off our gas masks, envied their long silk curls, hated our own short, straight hair-dos. The five of us were romping up and down the stairs, free and gleeful, when suddenly Father reached out, and with everyone looking on shocked and embarrassed, uttered an oath and gave me a swat. All the joy went out of me in a flash. I had escaped Hitler, but not Father. . . .

BACK in Berkeley, we moved back into our two-family house on Etna Street. That proving small, Father went house-hunting, and in a few weeks we were all installed in our new home on Warring Street. My two sisters were soon enrolled in public school, where they did brilliantly and began making wonderful new friends. Again their lives took on a normal pattern. Mine slipped back into the old routine, nine hours a day at the piano with Father. New home or old home, Paris or Berkeley, the wall between me and my mother and sisters was up again. Talk of a proposed African tour was revived, but this time Mother put her foot down. She wasn't going to let us go traveling all over the Pacific with U-boats running wild. At the request of Mr. Tobin, who headed the local committee, I played a concert for Polish War Relief in San Francisco. Meanwhile my attitude toward Father was worsening daily. My early respect for him had by now completely deteriorated. I had accepted everything for years because I had found music through him. I had worshiped him. I had resigned myself to the beatings as punishment deserved for my errors. In the beginning he had been like a god to me. Now he was someone to be outsmarted and somehow eluded. More and more I saw through him as a musician. I began to understand exactly where and why he was wrong and how as an artist I was in a hopeless rut. Too often now I knew I was right and he was wrong; yet wrong prevailed. It was a form of brain-washing, but brain-washing that boomeranged. For example, the Polish concert was a great success financially and socially. Perhaps because it was a benefit, the critics were most cordial. There was one line in particular that I was sure would please Father. It said that in every respect I played like a wonderful pupil executing a well-learned lesson. Surely here was proof that I was following Father's instructions to the letter. Wasn't he proud to be the sole teacher, as he never tired telling everyone, of this "wonderful pupil"? Well, he was not.

"It's because you played like a pupil rather than an artist," he shouted.

And the idea crossed my mind, though not my lips, "If I'm supposed to play like an artist, isn't an artist supposed to think for himself, even a little bit?" How could I take complete dictation from him and be an independent artist, too? I couldn't win. But my revolt had begun. And that Polish War Relief concert proved a turning point. I had been waiting for a chance to hoodwink Father. My letters to Mr. Tobin were merely an escape; my daydreams at the piano an emotional flight from darkness; growing doubt in his judgment was only a hidden rebellion. What I wanted was a specific act of defiance in which Mother, my sisters, and I would be allied for once against Father. There was nothing unethical about the matter. It was simply this: Father had decided Mother wasn't going to have a new gown for my concert and I decided she was. As usual he wanted this to be *his* affair, not hers. He bought himself a gorgeous tuxedo for two hundred dollars. As for Mother, the last time I remembered her wearing a gown was ten years earlier when I played at tea in the Mark Hopkins Hotel in San Francisco. It was a long brown velvet affair. She had had no shoes to match, however. Father had decided that since the gown was long, Mother could wear an old pair of suède sport shoes, the only brown shoes she owned, without anyone's being the wiser. All afternoon she had kept tucking in her feet for fear of being found out. This time I wanted to be sure Mother was beautifully decked out for my concert. I wanted Mother to have a gown, a pair of shoes, and an evening wrap to put over the gown. To all our pleas, Father was adamant. One night after dinner I persuaded Mother to put on the old brown velvet dress and casually parade before Father in it. We knew Father's reaction would be an outburst of pretended ecstasy. In reply to which we had rehearsed a chorus of reproach and ridicule. Sure enough, his eyes lit up when Mother appeared. He raved about the style and material. He dwelt on the way the gown brought out Mother's figure. Actually the garment looked like a bundle of wet wash.

"How can you say that?" we jumped on him. "It's a bag and you know it!" My sisters and I were shrill. "Mamma needs a new dress for the concert. You got yourself a new tuxedo. It's only fair she should have a new dress."

Taken aback by the united front, he replied that we knew nothing about fashion. Gowns weren't stylish any more. The very best people, the cream of society, wore plain short dresses at concerts. If Mother didn't like the brown velvet gown, which was so gorgeous, she could wear one of her other dresses. She had enough of them. That was final. A tantrum was coming on, so we desisted. My sisters and I went into a huddle for our next move. The only answer was Mr. Tobin. Maybe we could borrow the money and pay him back in small installments. One Saturday afternoon the three of us managed to sneak out the house and take the train across the bridge to San Francisco. There we saw Mr. Tobin and told him why we needed seventy-five dollars so desperately. He told us not to think about it any further. Everything was going to work out all right. The following week the whole family was invited to the Tobins for tea. Shortly after we arrived, Mrs. Tobin proposed a drive for the womenfolk, herself, Mother, Gloria, Helen, and me. Our destination was a big department store where Mother was outfitted with a beautiful gown, complete with evening shoes and wrap. Mr. Tobin, of course, footed the bill, and I'm still wondering whether the very glamorous orange dress that a designer was supposed to have donated to me for the occasion wasn't also Mr. Tobin's secret contribution. There was nothing Father could do. The shopping excursion hadn't cost him a cent. Mother had her gown, and I had my first real taste of victory. I was beginning to fight back.

Despite the reservations in the reviews, Father thought them good enough to forward them to New York with the idea of paving the way for a Town Hall concert the following season. By then Father had broken off with Columbia Artists and returned to Mr. Wagner, who told me later he consented to the arrangement only for my sake. Father revolted him. Mr. Wagner agreed to the concert in New York. At first I was terrified. Then I resolved to work as I had never worked before. This might be my last chance, and I wanted to make one last attempt to please Father. I didn't care about pleasing myself. I disregarded all of Mr. Cortot's and Mr. Rachmaninoff's teachings. This time I would strain every nerve in my body to do what Father said. I think I was putting him to a final test. I toiled like a fiend at my Town Hall program. That was to take place in November 1940. Now, up to that time I had had mild attacks in my right side which may or may not have been from my appendix. They had happened on tour, sometimes during a concert. But they had subsided so quickly that I had grown used to them. Well, the night before the concert Father and I had dinner with our friends the Smadbecks in New York. For some reason, Mr. Smadbeck scented trouble ahead, maybe a fiasco. He knew Father and was concerned about the consequences for me.

"I know you want Ruth to start concertizing again," he said to Father. "I know you're an excellent musician and that Ruth will do her best. But suppose she fails. What then? Are you prepared for that?"

"It's got to be a success!" cried Father. "It will be a success! I've devoted my whole life to Ruth. She is trained to do exactly what I want her to do. She'll play beautifully because that's the way I taught her. Don't even mention the word 'failure.'"

That night, at the Ansonia, I couldn't sleep. The pain in my right side had come back. I was feeling nervous and shaky. In a flash of revelation I knew the concert would be a disaster. I knew that everything Father had told me to do was wrong, that his instructions contradicted all I had learned from Mr. Cortot and Mr. Schnabel and Mr. Rachmaninoff. Like a helpless robot, I was going to do all the very things I had been criticized for. I was going to hit the piano to get an effect of big tone; I was going to exaggerate *rubatos*, falsify phrases, distort feeling, play the fast passages even faster; I was going to play things I couldn't understand like the B-flat minor sonata of Chopin. I was going to be a circus performer, not a musician. It had gone too far and it was too late to defy him. The pain in my side was getting worse. . . . Finally I slept a brief and troubled sleep. The following morning I complained about the pain to Father. "Oh, you've had it before," he said lightly. "Take an aspirin; it will pass. Today's the big day."

It was a big day, one of the blackest and most dismal days of my life. The concert was an absolute and unqualified failure. I played badly, got murderous reviews, and deserved every one of them. I went through the music in a trance, like a complete automaton, with nothing to hang on to but Father's same old bag of tricks. It was like stealing, or perhaps like some ritual of self-sacrifice. I walked out on the stage knowing I was committing a wrong, feeling physically miserable, yet determined at all costs to go through with it for Father. I knew before Father did that the audience was cold. I knew before Father did what the critics would say. The irony of it was that he had every right to be satisfied. I was doing everything he wanted. Only at the end did he suspect that something was amiss. All he said was: "You could have done the second movement of the Chopin sonata better. The audience didn't seem to like it too much. What was wrong?" I said dully, "I don't feel well."

The next day I was disowned.

Father came in with the newspapers and handed them to me without a word. There was only this peculiar gray gloomy look on his face. I knew what it said. It was the end. There was no beating. It was beyond beating. A thrashing would have been sweet and simple compared to this deathly silence. I had been rejected once and for all, with no hope of reprieve. . . . I read the critics. They didn't spare me in the least. The worst of the reviews said I was a burned-out candle, an example of the prodigy who had blazed for a while and subsided into mediocrity. I was a warning. . . . Suddenly I realized Father was talking:

This is what he had sacrificed himself, his wife, his other daughters, his own private life for. Ever since I was born he had tried to make something wonderful and great out of me, an artist, something the world would remember. I had repaid him by bringing him shame. I had defeated him, I had disgraced him. I had left him nothing to live for. . . . This wasn't delivered in his usual loud, angry tones, but in a cold, steely, faraway voice. His eyes were hard; his lips drawn thin and firm. I know I wasn't his daughter any more. Buried deep in my own misery, I must have heard only half of it. It began in our room at the Ansonia. It continued as we walked down the street to the Automat for breakfast, a persistent monotone that only stopped for the dull, flat silences that were even worse.

On the train back to California I couldn't look people in the face. I was ashamed of myself, of my work, of my feelings, of my music. I had made a needless sacrifice, playing exactly as he wanted me to, and brought down an avalanche on our heads. I had lost respect for both him and myself. I was so torn and divided inside I could see nothing, nothing ahead for me. I didn't even dare mention the sharpening pain in my side. Nobody was there to meet us at the station when we arrived. At home Mother clasped me to her tightly, feeling perhaps closer than she had ever felt before. I don't blame my sisters for the jeers. I had asked for it. I had dismissed them as "the kids"; I had always felt superior to them and twitted them about the language their friends used. Now here was their famous sister Ruth, the talk of the family, the rage of two continents, coming back a "burned-out candle." They were so young; how could they know the pain of it, the horrible blackout for me?

And here was the appendix getting worse and worse, till five days after I had first complained to Father I was in the hospital having it out. Father had finally treated me with a laxative! I was so doubled up in agony when they brought me into the emergency operating room that the doctor said later I would have been dead in another half-hour. For several days I was a very sick girl. I dimly recall Mother and Father coming into the hospital ward to see me. The ward was my father's frugality again. Well, one day, though still very ill, I started talking with the other patients. Naturally I wanted to brag. I couldn't boast about myself because I was now a disgrace to my family. So I bragged about my father, how shrewd he was in business, what profits he made in real estate, how wealthy he was. This got back to my father in the worst possible way: in the form of an embarrassing questionnaire by the hospital officials. So the next time he came to visit me he gave me the very devil in front of everybody for opening my big mouth and making a damn fool of him. I set up a howl, had a relapse, followed by a nightmare, and an attack of hysteria when my father called again the next morning. Sobbing and trembling, I pleaded with the nurse to let only my mother in.

"Please, please don't let him near me!" I sobbed. "I don't want to see him! I don't want him! He isn't my father any more!"

At that moment he was everything in my life that stood for pain and misery and humiliation; he was the end of my music; my attack of appendix, my one and only enemy in the world. This was the end of our relationship. I had loved and worshiped and respected him. I had done everything to make him happy. I would have died to please him. I had nothing more to give. I was worthless, sick, and exhausted. I had been reduced to nothing, and I wanted no more of my father. That horrible gap never closed between us. It remained there to the end, black and unbridgeable. I think there were times when we wanted to reach out to each other, but it was beyond our capacity.

A new loneliness stared me in the face. Before I had had no one but Father; now I didn't have him either. If ever I reached bottom, it was in the empty, creeping weeks and months that followed my return home from the hospital. I wandered around aimlessly. There was no more practicing at the piano. Father didn't seem to care whether I lived or died. My sisters had their little lives of school and play and parties. Mother was busy cooking, washing, shopping. The piano was still there, and so were the piles of music. But they were like strangers, fascinating and puzzling, not comforting any more. I played a few bars listlessly, took walks, barely existed from day to day.

I ate thoughtlessly, ravenously, till I got like a little balloon. I didn't care. It was a state of complete numbness, a moral and spiritual vacuum. There was no point to anything I did. I was a vegetable, or rather a big useless healthy weed with no other function but physical growth. . . . It was a living death. All my life till then I had practiced nine hours a day. I had always had concerts to prepare; lessons to do; English teachers, German teachers, French teachers; new music to learn; tours to plan; interviews with the press; sittings with dressmakers; appointments with managers; timetables; hotel reservations to make; music to play to everyone everywhere. There had never been enough time for everything. Now all I had was time, and absolutely nothing to fill it with but the mechanical job of remaining alive.

About a block away from us in Berkeley stood a large, beautiful building—International House. Sometimes on my walks I used to see bright, smiling young people alone, in couples or in groups walk in and out of its doors. One day I worked up courage enough to climb up the steps, enter the lobby, and look around. I followed the sound of music upstairs and found myself in a long and spacious room at one end of which stood a grand piano. A door led to a smaller second room from which the music was coming. I was sixteen and it was a bright spring day. The sun flooded the large room through the high windows. Only a few people were there. Rather timidly I wandered over to the piano and played a little, just for myself, and somehow, as my hands rambled over the keys, I found myself liking what I heard. I had nobody to please now; certainly not Father, who didn't care any more. I began to think it might be fun to please myself. I had never tried that before. I hadn't even thought of myself as a person with any right to something to say of her own. Then I got up and listened to some records. Gradually a new feeling took control of me: I had become conscious of myself as "someone" who had thoughts of her own to think and ways of her own to please herself. I knew now the way out of the pit.

It was a slow, painful process coming to know myself; tearing away from all the old ideas and loyalties, finding my way back to music. I began to make sounds that pleased me, soft, sensuous tones that were not meant for anyone but me. Somehow it came back to me what one critic had said of my tone, that it was as hard as nails. I had thought of it only as strong and loud because I wanted so much to project it. My hands had come down on the keys in hard crashing chords in order to fill a large auditorium. I had brought all my child's strength down on the piano. That was the way I was taught. Now I didn't have an auditorium to fill, an audience to reach, a teacher to please, a father to obey. That spring day in the Home Room of International House, and for months and months after that, I learned to play for myself. I played all sorts of things, pieces I hadn't touched since I was a tiny girl, Rachmaninoff etudes Father had never let me play in public. The moment anyone approached the piano I got up hurriedly and left. I drew away from people like a little moth. The shame of my last New York recital still clung to me. I couldn't bear the thought of anybody's asking me questions, who I was, and so on. I couldn't play for anyone. That was odd for one so long before the public. Even stranger was the fact that I wanted to play for myself. My music was becoming a new sort of friend, all my very own, to be with only when I wanted. To do this I had to sneak music out of my house. At home I never touched the piano. I couldn't bear having Father hear me. So while the students were at school, I would march over to the piano, the music under my arm, and lose myself in this new world. It was all I lived for.

After several months of this a new desire welled up in me: to be like one of these gay, eager youngsters I used to see come into International House, youngsters my own age and older, pretty young ladies, much prettier than I could ever hope to be, handsome young men, with books tucked under their arms, going to school, having sodas in the coffee shop, laughing and joking, calling to one another, singing songs in groups and going to dances on Saturday night. That no longer seemed so impossibly out of reach.

At home the relationship between my sisters and me remained strained and awkward. The camaraderie of Paris was gone. With my New York debacle, the tables were turned. They were now the superior ones; I was the one Father wasn't speaking to, the one Mother was going out of her way to be kind to. The fact is they were ashamed of me. They were no more conscious of being cruel to me than I was of being cruel to them in my day of glory. But there it was: I was the problem child of the family. I was reminded of my weight, of the ugly way I wore my hair, of the odd way I had of walking with my stomach sticking out, of my dreadful complexion. I was told I talked nonsense and spoke in a weird voice. In short, I did everything wrong, and what I said was worse. "You wander around all day looking like a nun," I was told.

Now both Helen and Gloria were extremely bright for their age. Both were at the head of their class, both brilliant in languages and the sciences. Later Helen was recognized as the real brain of the family. I must admit I was dying for a chance to outshine her; it didn't matter in what. Well, the chance came. Possibly because she was nervous, Helen fell a little short of family expectations on her college-entrance examination. To Father anything under an "A" was a sign of illiteracy. When Helen brought home the examination form to prove how difficult it was, I took one look at it and maliciously proclaimed it a cinch.

"I bet you couldn't pass it," said Helen.

"I bet I could." The challenge and counterchallenge were taken up by the rest of the family, till Father took control and momentarily broke his silence to me:

"All right, smarty," he said. "If you can pass that entrance examination, I'll send you to college." All four of them were absolutely positive I would flunk out miserably. I knew I could pass it, and must. Promptly the next day I went to the University of California and came back home loaded with sample examinations of past years. I worked on them, studied my weaknesses, filled in the gaps, pored hungrily over dozens and dozens of books, and came through the test with flying colors. Father kept his word. I became a college freshman and poor Helen went to work. It was a case of sheer desperate determination. I attended my first day of school at the University in Berkeley in September 1941. I was still sixteen, and a very worried and uneasy sixteen. For the first time in my life I was thrown in with youngsters my own age, normal youngsters. I knew I looked and spoke differently, and I vaguely sensed I acted differently. My first class was at nine o'clock and the course was public speaking. I went into the room, glanced at the desk where the student speakers were to try their eloquence, and looked at the bright, young, smiling faces. I had the odd feeling that I was studying them from the angle of an older generation. I felt almost ancient, hardened by experience, compared to them. When they got up to speak, I thought them innocent, unworldly, naïve. How I could shock and thrill them with stories of what I had been through! They were so strange to me at first, and I must have been even stranger to them. I had no way of dressing the way they did, those lovely young girls with lipstick and sweaters and skirts and trim figures and high heels, chatting between classes about dates and dancing. What chance had I to be one of them, with my short squat look, drab wash dresses, bobby socks and saddle shoes, my short straight hair, my lack of make-up? I was sixteen, felt fifty, and looked like twelve. I could have fled a dozen times in shame and self-disgust. I didn't. Hard as it was, I was resolved to take it and like it from the start . . . and I did.

The first problem I tackled was clothes. It was useless to ask Father, so I thought I'd take some sort of job for pocket money. First, I visited my old friend Dr. Elkus, the head of the Music department, and the man who had shown such amazement at my precocity twelve years earlier as a girl of four. We had a delightful chat. He saw at once I was too advanced to enroll me as a student in the music department. Instead he recommended several excellent music books and guided me through many areas of research. Thanks to Dr. Elkus I secured my first job, as record librarian in the music department. While the pay was small, the work was easy and fruitful. I both did my homework and was within a finger's reach of these wonderful records whenever I wanted music.

Next to the record library, Dr. Manfred Bukofzer conducted a postgraduate class in sonata form. One day he knocked on my door and said: "May I borrow you for a few moments?" When he explained why, I locked the library door and followed him into his classroom. After a gracious introduction to the gathered students, Dr. Bukofzer showed me to the piano and I proceeded to illustrate his lecture on Liszt's B minor sonata. This became quite a regular routine, always with that polite "May I borrow you. . . ." Since I had quite a repertory at my fingertips, I was "borrowed" for every stage in the development of the sonata form. I astonished the class by knowing strange things like the early well-nigh forgotten C minor sonata of Chopin. At a cue from Dr. Bukofzer I would run off passages from sonatas of Haydn, Mozart, Weber, and Beethoven. It gave me a wonderful feeling of pride and importance. Word of this got around, and before long I was being "borrowed" by Dr. Elkus himself for the very fine lectures he gave on the later sonatas of Beethoven. Gradually I got the reputation of being a "brain" in the music division. In the library, classroom, or cafeteria music majors came up to me and spoke with a certain respect. The others got used to seeing me around the campus, a queer, chubby little character in outlandish clothes. My own major was psychology. I know experience is the true source of any real knowledge of psychology, but I enjoyed reading the books and going to class, and I just breezed through it all. The rest of it was a snap too, with one glaring exception.

I'm afraid the one part of college I flunked in badly was the social side. I wanted so much to be part of groups, theater groups, writing groups, social groups. I wanted to go to dances and have dates. I wanted to plunge into this whirl of college activity. But how could I when everything—my background, my appearance, I might as well own up, my personality—was against me. I looked and thought and spoke and acted wrong. I just didn't fit in. You have to picture me at sweet sixteen. I weighed 140 pounds and was less than five feet tall. I was squat and bulky in a protuberant way that had something to do with the structure of my spine. The condition is a sort of exaggerated swayback. As a child of nine or ten it might have been corrected, but Father ridiculed Dr. Leopold, who prescribed certain exercises. "What would be the ultimate value of it?" Father had asked. "When your daughter is grown up and ready to have babies, she would have an easier time of it," was Dr. Leopold's reply. Whereupon, Father blustered, "My daughter is never going to have worries of that kind; she's never even going to get married." He was furious. The result was no treatment, no exercise, and no fee to Dr. Leopold for the visit. For years Father ranted about my poor posture and the way my stomach stuck out. Yet he fed me all sorts of rich foods, bragging to people, "Look how healthy she is; look how fat and rosy her cheeks are." Then five minutes later he belted me for the size of my stomach. I would have had to be Houdini to "pull in my stomach."

I never wore make-up. I wore saddle shoes and bobby socks and owned one skirt, one jacket, and three cotton wash dresses. I wore my hair short and straight, and my skin was a mess. Beside me my two sisters looked like Hollywood queens. Helen at fifteen was quite the beauty. At fourteen Gloria was already in high heels and used lipstick, her silky hair brushed long and wavy, looking every bit of seventeen, while I looked twelve, and a fat, hefty, unattractive twelve at that. I was so short, in fact, that at seventeen I got into the movies for eleven cents as a child under twelve! This was even funnier when I married. My husband George would pay half price for me and his eleven-year-old brother, Bill, explaining to the cashier that I was Bill's girl friend! Strangest of all, Bill accepted me strictly as a contemporary. We went to the zoo together, played tag, wrestled, and pushed each other on the swing in the playground. To Bill I was just another kid like himself. . . . That's what I looked like.

Every Saturday night there was a dance at International House—"I House," as the boys and girls called it. And every Saturday night, after supper, I would wash myself spanking clean, put on one of my best-looking cotton dresses, walk over to "I House" in my bobby socks and flat shoes, pay the entrance fee of thirty-five cents, and sit by myself in a corner all evening watching the couples dance and clown and flirt. At the stroke of twelve I got up and walked back home to Warring Street.

Mother would call me to her bedside: "Ruth, did you have a good time?" and I would whisper excitedly: "Oh, a marvelous time! I danced all night!" This went on week after week, during my second and third years of college. One Saturday, when she was not quite sixteen, I took my sister Helen along with me to the dance. She put on lipstick, high-heeled shoes, and long stockings, and with her neat little figure danced all night and met the boy with whom she eloped less than a year later, becoming the first of Father's young rebels to be disowned.

Except for the little help I gave Dr. Elkus and Dr. Bukofzer in their sonata classes, I kept my piano playing to myself. There in a corner of the Home Room of "I House," I communed with myself at the keys. The door leading to the adjoining Record Room must have been open one day, for when I strode into it, after a long spell at the piano, a young man seated there looked up at me in amazement, as if refusing to believe that what he had heard had all come out of *me*. He had sat there quiet and motionless, for fear that whoever was playing would stop if they knew he was there. First we talked about music and records, then about movies in general, and finally about one movie in particular. Had I seen *Mrs. Miniver*? My heart gave a thump. I hadn't. Would I see it with him? I can still feel the cold shivers running up and down my spine. That was my first date. The jinx was off. Right after that a young man asked me to go to the ballet with him. That meant raising some extra cash for new silk stockings and high-heeled shoes. Now the University stadium was about two blocks away from us, and the big Stamford-California football game happened to be scheduled for that very Saturday. I calculated that our three-car garage was as good a way of raising the money as any. So when Saturday came and Father and Mother were downtown shopping, I stood out on the street and rented the garage for the day at three dollars a car. Thus enriched, I got myself the needed finery. Later I learned from Mother how Father reacted to all this bustle on my part.

"What does she want silk stockings and new shoes for? Nobody will ever ask her out!"

Mother told him someone had.

His only comment was: "Bah, it's somebody after her money. What a surprise he'll get!"

I went to the ballet, and to many other things, sometimes with a boy, sometimes in groups, and in time I lost that awful sense of isolation. I was no longer a freak, someone apart, but an active member of a widening social group. I was invited to join an honor society called "Tower and Flame," moved with a certain clique at the Ladies Club Rooms, lunched with a particular set of girls. I augmented my modest earnings in the record department of school by tutoring high-school students in French and working four nights a week as gymnasium attendant at Berkeley High School, checking purses and coats. This enabled me to buy extra little things to wear on dates. It was all good for my morale.

Best of all, I was finding my way back to music. It didn't matter to me what Father or anyone else thought. I was on my own. For a while the sessions at "I House" sufficed to keep me in practice. But they became irregular as my school and social schedule became more crowded. So one morning, without anyone prodding me, I got up at six, and in my nightgown, but without Father, went to the piano and ran through the twenty-four etudes of Chopin. After which I had breakfast and dashed off to school. That became my daily setting-up exercise. Sometimes it would be the Chopin preludes, sometimes the scherzos and ballades, sometimes the sonatas. Later came the etudes of Liszt and several sonatas by Beethoven. By degrees, and over a period of months and months, I reviewed everything I had ever learned. But it was like discovering a new world. I had put all my Father's tricks and distortions behind me. I had only myself to please this time. I tried to remember everything Petri and Schnabel and Cortot and Rachmaninoff and Bachaus had taught me. I studied all the annotations they had made in my scores, questioning, analyzing, searching for whys and wherefores. Why did Mr. Cortot write *crescendo* here? Why should this be faster? What did Mr. Rachmaninoff want me to express in this tableau? I was probing, experimenting, a luxury I had never enjoyed before.

Something else was happening. I was beginning to play for others at school, mostly in the clubrooms, where an admiring circle of friends would form about me and shout out things for me to play. Soon they were saying, "Why don't you give us a real concert at Wheeler Hall?" I shrugged my shoulders, as if to say it was for others to decide. So they consulted with Dr. Popper of the Music and Arts Department, and in due course there was I, in Wheeler Hall, back on the concert platform for the first time in four years, playing the twenty-four etudes of Chopin. It was 1943, I was eighteen, and for the first time in my life I enjoyed every note of my playing. I was answerable to no one but myself. Nobody was coaching and drilling and threatening me. For the first time in public, Father's shadow was not lying across the keyboard. They were all friends listening to me. It was fun all the way. Between two of the etudes I caught sight of my banished and disowned sister Helen and her husband in the third row. I almost waved to them, but refrained. I think in that split second I knew I was a concert pianist again.

That concert was something of a crisis of reappraisal and stock-taking. In my own mind I had already recovered a measure of my status. My playing was far from miraculous, but I knew it was pleasant, acceptable, valid for what it was. My ideas were certainly not those of a Horowitz or a Gieseking, but they were coming to be my own. I seemed to see clearly for the first time what it was Father expected of me and what I really was. My father had confused precocity with genius, technical dexterity with art, exhibitionism with greatness. I think for a while he really thought me greater than the great masters who taught me. It was a monstrous delusion that could only end in disaster. These college years were hammering home the difference between true art and my own poor accomplishment. I knew now I had been acclaimed and magnified because of my incredible youth. To be sure, they were phenomenal feats for a child to accomplish. But I could do them only because I was rigorously drilled to do them. Whatever had been good I owed entirely to outside forces and an early start almost without precedent. I knew now I was not yet an artist, but that I had a remarkable equipment to work with if I wanted badly enough to become an artist. The know-how had been pounded into me till it was part of my being. I knew how to create almost any effect on the piano; I knew the methods employed to make the piano sing and laugh and cry. But there was a world of difference between knowing how to do a thing and doing it. I did not yet have a true artistic conception of all it involved. It was like having a million dollars and not knowing the real meaning or use of money. There was so much, so very much, to do if I was ever to be an artist, and I wasn't sure yet that I wanted to try. The concert at Wheeler Hall at least showed me I could stand on my own two feet and like it.

ONE night I was dancing with a friend at a party in Berkeley when the jukebox broke down. Immediately somebody took over at the piano, eventually got tired, and I was asked to pitch in so that the dancing could continue. I played a few popular songs I had heard, and noticed a young man leaning over the piano with a sly, appraising look on his face.

Finally he said to me: "From the way you play, you sound as if you can handle a lot better music than that."

I said, "I can."

"How about playing for us?"

"What would you like to hear?"

So this young man thought he would stump me.

"Can you play the C major etude of Chopin, the first one?"

I said, "Sure I can."

And I just rattled it off with all the élan I could muster and he stood there dumbfounded.

"Gosh!" he cried. "What's your name?"

I said, "It's in the phone book."

"Well, what's your phone number?"

"That's in the book, too."

My date broke in at this point, but later the young man came up to me and said: "I know who you are. You played a Chopin concert not so long ago in Wheeler Hall." To which I replied, "Guilty!"

"I'm going to get in touch with you," he said.

I brushed him off with a "That's nice," but that night I told Mother someone special was going to call and that whatever I was doing, practicing, homework, bathing, she was to call me to the phone. Well, that special someone did call, and that's how my romance with George Born began. It was a whirlwind courtship of a few weeks. George expected to go into the Merchant Marine any day, and he was making me break dates with other boys. Finally, one night as we sat on our porch, he proposed. I told him I had to think about it.

"What's there to think about?" he said. "We'll have such fun together. We'll travel everywhere together. You'll play——"

"What do you mean, I'll play?"

"Why, you'll be giving concerts all the time."

"Oh no, I won't. I've given my last concert. When I get married, I'm going to make flapjacks for my husband and darn his socks and have a family, a home, a garden, and a dog, and go to other people's concerts."

George said, "We'll see about that."

And I thought to myself, "Well, *I'll* see about that too."

I was strongly attracted to George, his lovable, happy-go-lucky nature, his genuine passion for music, his easy gallantry. I liked the gracious atmosphere of his home, the light gaiety, the way brother and sisters teased and told one another everything, the French mother who delighted to speak French with me, the piano they were thrilled to have me play on for them. Up on the third floor George had a den stacked high with a fabulous record collection, and a beautiful view of San Francisco from the window. If it was all part of George's campaign to break down my resistance, he succeeded. Listening up there with George to recordings of Beethoven and Debussy and Ravel, I said to myself: "I think it would be a very nice thing to do, to marry George." Immediately the thought of Father bore down on me like a stone. The obsession was still there. "I'll have to talk it over with my parents," I said to George.

The problem wasn't easy. Except on very rare occasions, Father and I weren't talking to each other. What we had to say to each other we communicated through Mother. A thick, ugly curtain of silence hung between us at table. Yet I knew that deep down he was studying me like a thoroughly familiar object that was suddenly behaving strangely. To Mother he commented disgustedly about my practicing. How could it be otherwise than bad? I needed the guidance only he could give. Mother repeated this to me in a reproachful tone, as if I were a wayward child. Why didn't I apologize to Father? Why didn't I go to him like any normal daughter and make up? I almost did once or twice out of sheer filial need. But I just couldn't. It wasn't hate; just pride and self-respect. I had lowered myself enough for him; he had done everything to shut me off from life. He had made me the stepchild of the family, the unwanted, the unknown, the unspoken to. I was the extra one, out of it all, the burden that had once been the pride and joy. It was a hard fight back, and I was determined to make it on my own.

For a while I even thought of sharing an apartment with some of the girls at school, doing menial jobs or typing on the side for the extra money. I broached the idea to Mother, who promptly inquired at the nearest police station and warned me that if I ran away Father could get the law to bring me back. Helen had already fled, to acquire a new dignity as Mrs. James Lee and to forfeit a home and a father she had never much savored. Gloria was the real daughter now. I was a tolerated outsider, and not always tolerated. None of my friends was ever welcome, certainly not while Father was home. A boy from school called one afternoon while I was practicing. Father opened the door. When the boy asked to see me, Father took out his watch and said: "You can have exactly five minutes with her; she's working." The visitor was politely ushered into the living room and five minutes later politely ushered out, with not a single word or glance to me from Father.

I dreaded appearing before guests, never knowing what embarrassing situation might develop. Once, during my second year of college, I was asked to give a recitation before friends of Mother's. In the middle of it something must have displeased Father; maybe the mispronunciation of a word, maybe a gesture, maybe only a bitter memory. Without a word, he got up from his chair, strode over to where I was standing, and in the presence of everyone slapped me across the face and banished me from the room. I was eighteen years old and still trapped. To Mother he cited examples of other daughters who were working and bringing home nice fat paychecks. I was just a useless sponger, a parasite; who was I to enjoy the luxury of a college education? Why, I hadn't learned how to talk yet. What a deadening thing this man's bitter frustration had become. . . . Yet he never interfered with my early-morning sessions at the piano. If my concert, which he attended with the family, brought no praise, it brought no brickbats either. There was something of watchful waiting; a deep, sullen surprise that I was making the grade unaided, maybe even climbing back to music. On the subject of marriage he remained brutal, adamant. Mother was quite frank in relaying the messages. Who could possibly want me? I was a misfit, a repulsive personality, an inert lump. The boys that dated me? Bah, they just wanted to brag they had taken out a former celebrity! Or else they wanted my money. That was a laugh! I hadn't a cent to my name and never would have, not if he could help it. Where did George fit in?

I realized I had to build him up a bit. My fiancé George was only a student at the University, with a small part-time job on the San Francisco *Examiner*. He was twenty-three, had no money of his own and lived at home with his parents, like me. The idea of puffing him up to my parents didn't appeal to George one bit. He found it humiliating, saw nothing to be gained, and of course he was right. My promotion campaign only turned Father more violently against him. George was all for dropping the matter and going off to get married. When at last we decided on a day in June, I insisted on one last attempt to win Father's consent. After a sharp quarrel, George gave in. He agreed to accompany me into the house and talk to Father. Now Father, ever since the mess at the hospital, had taken to drinking by himself. George and I must have chosen a particularly unfortunate day for our peace parley. Father was in an ugly, belligerent mood, in underclothes and trousers and suspenders, when George and I broke the news to him. He blew up. It was a warm June afternoon, between four-thirty and five. The house door was still open. There stood Father, like an uncaged beast, blasting away at us in the foulest language. He looked so ludicrous in his suspenders and undershirt and tipsy grimaces. He swore in five languages. He said I was no good, selfish, ungrateful, not worth a damn as a daughter or anything else. What would a real man want with me?

"You'll find out how horrible she is when you're stuck with her," he shouted to George. "And what good are you? Just a lazy shiftless bum who'll never amount to a damn. You won't get a dime out of me, either of you. . . . *Get the hell out of my house!*"

And Father, all five feet four of him, began pushing George, who was one hundred and eight-five pounds of football brawn, out the front door, screaming the vilest epithets at the top of his voice, and George, bless his heart, calmly putting out his hand to me and saying, "Ruth, are you coming with me or staying with him?" I took his hand and went down the front steps with him. When Father bounded down after us, we broke into a run, hand in hand. Suddenly the screaming was different, plaintive and pleading, as if life itself were being torn out of this pursuing maniac. "Ruth!" he yelled down the street, "Ruth, come back! You don't know what you're doing! Come back to your father!"

I could feel it piercing my heart; but I ran on and on, my hand tightly clasped in George's. What a sight for people to behold through their windows on that sunny June afternoon! Everybody must have been in on the show for three whole blocks. Behind us the yelling had receded; the tone had changed again. In a new flash of revulsion Father knew I meant business, that there was no having me back again. Through the air came a final sickening shriek:

"You lousy little bitch! You'll never play two notes again without me!"

We could feel each other shrivel, George and I. But we never looked back. On College Avenue we caught a streetcar and sat there panting and shaking. I was soaked with perspiration, sobbing on George's shoulder, while he smoked cigarette after cigarette and kept saying, "Don't take it so hard, Ruth. He wasn't himself." To relax, we stopped off to see a movie, which turned out to be a horror film that left us even more clammy and jittery. That night I spent with George's parents, while he went off to a hotel. The following morning, June 17, we went to Reno and were married. We had known each other exactly two months. After the ceremony we rented a car and drove off to our honeymoon. For hours we sat side by side in a strained, self-conscious silence. I looked at George and it came upon me that I really didn't know too much about him. Much the same thought must have crossed his mind. He seemed awkward and distant. Then suddenly he put his arm out and said, "Come, lean your head on Papa's shoulder," and I knew that everything was going to be all right.

The elopement caused a flurry in the San Francisco papers. There were pictures of us, nice juicy headlines, and flashbacks of my career. I must say George's family wasn't exactly displeased by the fuss. I had suddenly become news again, and they were kind of proud of me. Quite solemnly I told the press my only aim in life was to be a good little wife; they even took a picture of me in an apron serving breakfast in my mother-in-law's kitchen. "No more concerts!" I repeated emphatically. When Father was asked his reaction to this by the press, he said he was "heart broken." I told a reporter: "I'm sorry my father feels the way he does, but I'm very happy. I'm never going to play the piano in public again." I was going to enjoy music just for myself and George. My life was going to center in him and in whatever career he cut out for himself. Mine was a thing of the past, a dead, unlamented past.

So I began a new life on Funston Avenue in San Francisco. Since George had taken me home to live with his parents, I came to feel more like a new little member of the family than his wife. I was made to feel very welcome, particularly by my mother-in-law, who took me on shopping tours and bragged about me to her friends.

During the first three weeks of my marriage I scarcely touched the piano. I went past it without a flutter; it kept winking at me, but nothing doing. Then one day, when I was alone, it beckoned and I succumbed. I had run away from home with nothing but the clothes I had on and a wristwatch. Father absolutely refused to let me have my music, my books, my jewelry, my clothes, even my modest savings. They were his property, he claimed. So each time I went downtown with George's mother, she bought me a piece of music. Friends who knew of my predicament began donating scores, and gradually I built up a new library. More and more George was having me play for him. Slowly he broke down my resistance to all piano composers after Brahms. Father had dismissed them all as discordant and decadent, betrayers of the great tradition of Bach, Beethoven, and Brahms. I had been forbidden to play any of this "rubbish" in public. George made me realize I had learned no new music since I was fourteen! Debussy was George's god. Like an idiot, I tried to tell him he was formless and loose. He made me listen to record after record, till I was won over. Thus prodded I studied all sorts of new things by Debussy, Ravel, Stravinsky, Prokofieff, and Bartok. A vast new world opened before me. Horizons widened on all sides. At home in Berkeley I had lacked the courage to do more than review what I had been taught to play. Now I was my own interpreter, with no one to coach or guide me.

While this was happening, George kept feeding me music and pep talk, taking me to concerts, hinting at glowing things ahead for both of us. He was becoming more and more enamored of the pianist and less and less of the wife. I was drifting helplessly into a new mould, or was it new? Again and again he urged me to resort to legal action to retrieve my belongings from Father, including the fortune in fees that was rightfully mine. He even had me put in a threatening call to Father from a lawyer's office. That was the last time I heard my father's voice. He told me I had lost my mind; that when I came to my senses and returned home I would be treated as his daughter again. In the meantime I was George's wife. I had made my bed and I could lie in it. Those were Father's last words. George and the lawyer proposed an immediate suit. I refused flatly. There was this lingering fear of Father in me that George could never quite cope with. He knew I was still haunted by that terrible street-scene and the curse Father had hurled at me. He knew I dreaded the idea of giving concerts again. But George also knew what *he* wanted, and he wasn't giving up so easily. He now began to work in real earnest. First, he and his stepfather, Mr. Earle Van Muckey, rigged up a concert for me at the Granada Theater in Reno, where George had an influential uncle. I balked strenuously, to no avail. Somehow I walked out and played. Both the public and the critics were cordial enough to fill George with fresh hopes.

Together with Mr. Van Muckey he next booked a concert for me a month later in San Francisco. This time I was petrified. First of all I was scared of Father, and said so. Mr. Van Muckey assured me a private detective would be stationed back stage. Then I was scared of the critics. I knew in my heart I wasn't a great pianist, certainly not the great artist George kept insisting I was and expecting me to be. The critics would know the truth; hadn't they before? So I walked out on the stage thinking, "Let's get this darn thing over with. George will find out for himself and he won't make me play any more." Again the public was good to me, and so, on the whole, were the critics. A healthy dose of doubt and reservation appeared here and there, but George wasn't one bit discouraged. He read the reviews the way he wanted to read them. According to him, I was on my way, or, rather, "we" were on our way. Just at that point, however, his high hopes were cut short by Uncle Sam. George went into the service. In the meantime I was urged to practice like a fiend. George's parents even went to the expense of buying a large Baldwin for me to work on, and before I knew it I was back to a rigorous routine of practice at the piano, still with no serious thought of returning to the concert stage. So far I was still being a good wife and good daughter-in-law.

And soon I was doing my little bit too. Mr. Van Muckey evidently built me up at the offices of the USO one day. The result was that I began playing in camps and hospitals three days a week all over the Bay Area and beyond. In the hospitals I played on miniature pianos that were wheeled from ward to ward. I played whatever the boys asked me to, boogie-woogie, popular songs, marches. If the piano was too small to take a given composition, I transposed the music. If the keyboard couldn't stand a difficult etude, I replaced it with some flashy composition or other. I wasn't being the concert artist; just the entertainer bringing momentary respite and distraction to those needing it. I would sense the mood of a ward and use all my ingenuity in putting a few numbers together. I was so grateful when I got smiles and applause and even an occasional mash note. In camps I was merely one in a long parade of performers, coming somewhere between the acrobats and the vocalists. There was always an element that craved serious music too. For them I played things like the "Moonlight" sonata and the Second Hungarian Rhapsody. In two years I made nearly a thousand appearances, for which I treasure a prized memento, the Armed Forces Entertainment Pin.

In between I probed deeper and deeper into this vivid world of new music that George had opened for me. I learned the preludes, etudes, and suites of Debussy; several pieces by Ravel; Spanish compositions by Albéniz, De Falla, and Granados, a rich, exotic adventure bristling with novelty and surprise and daring. My whole outlook was changing with my broadening repertory. I had also resolved to stop living off my mother-in-law. I was being pampered, and I wanted to earn my keep, buy some clothes, and share expenses. George's service pay was going into a savings account against the day when we would set up house by ourselves. So I started to teach, not as Ruth Slenczynski, but as Mrs. George Born. I began by placing ads in the *Shopping News*. My fee being only ten dollars a month for lessons, I built up a cozy little clientele among the neighborhood children. By the time George left the service, our combined savings sufficed to make a small down payment on a house around the corner from his mother's on Balboa Street.

The place was badly in need of repairs we couldn't afford, but it was a home of our own. That's when the hard times really started. George found it slow adjusting himself to the business world, and I'm afraid for a time we had to live off my earnings as a piano teacher. Meat gradually vanished from our suppers, and George still laughs over the time I gave him creamed celery on toast just once too often. We were on enforced diets. I refused to accept help from George's parents. But the bills began mounting up; first- and second-mortgage payments; electric and gas bills, clothes and movies; all supposed to come out of my meager teaching fees, plus what little George could scrape together from sporadic employment.

We were two hopeless innocents when it came to budgets. There was George's taste for antiques, for instance. If an extra bit were put aside for the next mortgage payment, George would come home with a gorgeous piece of old porcelain. It was something to have this dazzling object staring us in the face, and no meat for supper! I could have screamed the day George brought home an antique bed. But George discoursed blissfully on its history. So we made up the bed, and in the middle of the night, landed right on the floor. To each of my complaints George had a pat answer: "All right, stupid; if you only began giving concerts again, we'd be rolling in money and laughing at the bill collectors." That was one line of strategy. Then there was the technique he used when we went to hear a pianist at the War Memorial Opera House. "Can you play as well as this one?" he would ask tauntingly. "With one hand tied behind me," I'd answer back in the same spirit. "Then why should he be playing all over the place for big fat fees while you sit at home like a nice little old lady giving piano lessons to a bunch of dumb kids for chicken feed?" Finally, to get him off my neck, I said wearily, "Very well, George, if that's the way you want it, I'll give concerts. But just remember I warned you." George rubbed his hands in triumph. "I'll take that chance!"

The current was too strong for me to buck. I was being swept into it against my warning instinct of risk and danger. I wanted to wait and see. Time and again my father's words came back to haunt me: I couldn't play without him. But even Father was nothing to the other ghost that haunted me, the image of Ruth Slenczynski, the wonder child who was a "burned out candle" at fourteen. . . . Mr. Van Muckey and George went ahead with their bookings. A second concert in San Francisco, at the Geary Theater, went unexpectedly well. That was followed by concerts in Fresno and Vallejo and a circuit of smaller towns in California. Hopes were rising in George's family. I was still watchful, fearful. One day George's mother and I ran into a widely respected music critic while lunching in downtown San Francisco. "If I were you," he said, "I'd give a New York concert. You've made stupendous progress." That clinched it. A family council was held. Passionately as I fought against it, the voting was three to one in favor of a New York comeback in Town Hall. The money was raised, and I gave my recital.

It was murder. Everybody expected so much more of the pianist I had once been. The promise of a great gift had not been fulfilled. Comparisons were made between the prodigy I once was and the mature artist I was not. Just as I used to know I could never escape Father, I now knew I could never escape Ruth Slenczynski. That little ghost was to follow me about everywhere I went. She was like Father's avenging hand. The blow to George and his family was a crushing one. The emotional shock and financial loss were too much for poor Mr. Van Muckey. They undermined his health badly and, I feel certain, helped speed his death. The setback sobered George for a while. There were no more taunts about my teaching, and

oon, having lost our house on Balboa Street, we moved back in
with my in-laws. I didn't dare raise any objection. I had brought
umiliation enough to these good people. I was going to try
gain to be a model daughter-in-law. The one consolation I
ad was that now George would surely see it my way: that
oing back to the concert stage was a hopeless and brutal busi-
ess. The cards were stacked against me.

Out of a clear sky and at exactly the right time I received
a call one morning from Sister Mary de Chantal of the music
department of the Convent of Our Lady of Mercy in Bur-
ingame. This was an exclusive college for young ladies about
eighteen miles from San Francisco. It seemed a Dr. Strauss on
heir staff was leaving for an indefinite sojourn in Europe. Sister
Mary wondered whether I would take the job on a temporary
basis. Would I? I left immediately for Burlingame and stayed
on as advanced instructor of the piano department for three and
a half years. That period at Mercy was my salvation. I loved the
serenity of the place, the gentleness of the Sisters. I loved my
beautiful walnut-paneled room opening on three sides to glorious
scenery, and my two large beautiful pianos. My master classes
were attended by talented ladies from hundreds of miles around.
Every few months I gave a recital to raise funds for a charity
selected by the Sisters. And I began to play a lot of the new music
I had learned. This kept me in wonderful trim. The boost to my
morale was unbelievable. I could have gone on forever at Mercy
but for the ceaseless prodding. This came from everybody, the
sisters, the other music teachers at Mercy, my pupils, and of
course George. The truce on the concert question had ended
for George. He was baiting me again, with an oft-quoted re-
frain, "Those who can, play; those who can't, teach." Here I
was, proud of my new position, content and at peace for the
first time in my life, and there was George telling me I was
letting a great talent go to waste by burying myself away in teach-

ing studios. I was a coward, he said. By this time, I was also teaching at the San Francisco Academy of Music. Between the two jobs I was earning a rather nice salary. But George went on hounding me.

When it came to music, there was just no peace for me with the men in my life. I wasn't aware of it yet, but a pattern was beginning to repeat itself. Subconsciously I was rebelling, fighting again for my right to a normal life. I was being subjected to so many inner and outer drives that I'll never know exactly how it was that I did return to the stage. My teaching had brought a new approach to music. Through showing students the meaning of music as a language, I was able for the first time to project musical thoughts with a natural simplicity that had always eluded me. It was as if up to a certain point I had been a pitcher into which musical ideas were poured; after I became a teacher the pitcher itself became a fountain and gave forth musical expressions from a source within. The urge to return to what had been my only real world for so many years must have been strong. When I finally crossed over again for good, it was as natural as coming home. But it was a home without George, or anybody else. That was the price. This next phase must have begun with my appearing as solo pianist at the Bach Festival of July 1951, in Carmel, California. This is how it came about. I was practicing in the auditorium of the Academy of Music one spring day when a distinguished-looking stranger came up and asked me my name. I told him. The reaction was typical.

"Not the famous prodigy?"

"Well," I said, just a tiny bit nettled, "I was once considered that. Now I'm on the teaching staff here."

"Is teaching all you do? Or do you still play?"

"I give school concerts occasionally."

The upshot was that the gentleman, who was Gastone Usigli, of the Bach Festival of Carmel, California, invited me to appear as recitalist on one of the July programs. Now I didn't fancy myself a Bach specialist; indeed, scarcely a Bach pianist at all. But I accepted gladly because I was eager to reintroduce a neglected D major sonata of Bach's that I had chanced upon in my researches. Mr. Usigli liked the idea when I proposed it.

"You'll be playing in a small, intimate hall to a group of people with fine classical taste," he said. "The perfect setting for your Bach sonata."

The moment Mr. Usigli left, I sat back and thought of Father. It almost startled me that I should do so. I had come to think of him as buried way back in my past, a memory that could only flash back as a nightmare. For some odd reason I suddenly longed to see him, to tell him of this Bach concert and my Bach sonata, to reclaim him, if at all possible, as my father. At the time Father and Mother were living in Salt Lake City. Father had decided to leave Berkeley for good, because, as he put it, he couldn't "live down the disgrace" of my elopement. In that surge of yearning I forgot that and all the other ugly things he had said and done. That, I decided, was all ancient history. The chance came sooner than I had hoped. The American College of Musicians invited me to go to Ogden, Utah, as a judge in an annual piano contest. I immediately communicated with Mother, whose response was a frantic plea to stay away from Father. He wasn't well, she said; he had a heart condition; he was diabetic; his drinking was getting worse. He had sworn almost daily that he never wanted to lay eyes on me again. It might even kill him to see me. Did I want that on my conscience?

I wasn't going to be put off. Something in me cried out for a glimpse of him. I was sure if I took this first step on my own, without rancor and in a spirit of letting bygones be bygones, and perhaps even apologizing a little, we might be father and daughter again. It took courage, for the truth is that deep down under it all, I still feared him. Mother's anxiety also worried me. I didn't want this to be her responsibility at all. So I didn't let her know I was coming. After my work was done at Ogden, I went on to Salt Lake City. Wholly un-announced, I climbed up the porch of my father's house and rang the doorbell. I confess I was trembling, yet the hunger was stronger than the fright. There was no answer. I rang again, and again. I had two hours before my train left, and in those two hours Father never showed up. Where he was, what he was doing that afternoon, I never found out. Heavy-hearted, I dashed back to the station and returned to California. Two weeks later I received a telegram from Mother that Father was dead. My first thought, after the stab of pain, was that my conscience was clear. I *had* tried to see him and make up.

And now for the first time in seven years I did see him, lying in his coffin in a funeral parlor in Salt Lake City. The sad, empty bleakness of that day was awful. The only mourners were Mother, my sister Gloria, and I. We sat there far into the evening, and in all that time only two others, business ac-quaintances of Father's, came to pay their respects. What a horrible feeling it was for the three of us to realize that Father had had no friends. There was all this money he had accumu-lated, but no real personal ties, no warm connections with any-one. That night I stayed with Mother in the still, lonely house that had been his refuge from the memory of me. She told me a few last things about the hard, bitter man who had just died. Yes, he did know that I was going to play at the Bach Festival in Carmel. But he said it was useless. I would never succeed without him. She told me that a few days before he died, a picture she kept of me in my wedding dress had disap-peared from her room. "Don't bother looking for it," he had said when she asked him about it. "You won't find it." He kept recalling things about me as a child; reading out headlines and reviews from scrapbooks. He used to say that as far as he was concerned, his daughter had died when she was fourteen years old. That was the Ruth he remembered and mourned.

"He didn't really mean it, Ruth," my mother said. "Did you notice that bare corner in the living room? He never let me put a bookcase or armchair there. Do you know why? Because that was where the piano was going to be put when you came back."

So he wanted me and didn't want me. I should have cried, but I didn't. The crying had all ended the day I found out he sold the piano and my music cabinet before leaving Berkeley for Salt Lake City. There were no tears left. I tried to console Mother by telling her to look ahead and forget the past, and, if she remembered at all, to remember only the good things.

"What about you?" she asked. "Why do you still give concerts? Weren't you hurt enough? Doesn't it make you suffer to be criticized? What makes you go on?"

I told her I played the piano because I loved music. I couldn't think of myself apart from music; I had tried, but it hadn't worked out. I wasn't particularly anxious to go back to the concert stage. This concert in Carmel wasn't my suggestion, and besides, I didn't think the critics would bother writing about it, certainly not about me. So there wasn't any reason to worry about my being thrashed again in print.

"Can you really do it without your father?" she suddenly asked.

That doubt remained with her for years. It wasn't, in fact, till very recently that she gave up the struggle to keep me from returning to the stage. She is now one of my most ardent concert fans.

Three weeks later, on July 22, I played at the Festival in Carmel. My program of Bach was very warmly received. Despite the no-encore rule, I asked the audience if I might play an additional number by Bach in memory of my late father—his own arrangement for piano of the prelude to the E major partita for violin. While I played, the oddest thing happened. I had a sudden picture of my father on his last day of life, something Mother had told me about when we got back from the funeral parlor. It flashed before me now with strange vividness. It was trivial, perhaps, but it reflected a side of Father that was a legend in the family, his vaunted personal neatness. This is what Mother had told me and what I saw as I played. Knowing the end was near, with almost his last ounce of strength, Josef Slenczynski rose up from bed, shaved himself, and went back to die.

AS it turned out, Mother and I were both wrong about the Bach concert in Carmel. I had predicted the critics wouldn't review my performance; they did. Mother was positive they would tear into me, as they had in New York; they didn't. The fact is they were quite impressed. They not only welcomed the D major sonata as a happy rediscovery; they found my playing warm and spirited, gentle and lacy—all the things, in fact, that Bach should be and so seldom is.

"Miss Slenczynski made an extraordinary effect on her audience," said Alexander Fried of the San Francisco *Examiner* of July 23. "She has retained the great keyboard facility of her prodigy days, but a new spirit has mellowed and deepend in her Bach. Her playing was uncommon, and full of imagination. It had quiet, insight, restraint. Her preludes and fugues and C minor toccata actually created a spell."

Overnight I had become a Bach specialist to reckon with. If I was flabbergasted, how am I to describe George! The man was just hopping proud. "We've got to act fast on these reviews. People are going to hear about this everywhere. The time for you to get back to where you used to be is right now. Ruth, we're really on our way this time, believe you me!"

I still couldn't see it. George kept hammering away at my complacency; needling me about my "cozy teaching rut"; trying to rouse my envy of successful pianists he swore were my inferior. The appeal was often directed to my self-indulgence:

"Ruth, you don't have to slave for a living. With your hands we could live like royalty. All you have to do is go out and give concerts the way you did when you were a little girl. It ought to be even easier now that you're grown-up." When I balked, he said: "Would you rather scrub floors and polish silver?" Another jibe was this: "You gave two thirds of your life to your father. You gave concerts to please him. I'm your husband. Don't you want to please me?"

That was it! George was Father all over again, egging me on, not with "magic sticks" and leather belts and coarse oaths, but with taunts and pleas and all sorts of reminders of my duty to myself, to my music, and to him.

George could be vehement, pressing, irritated, but seldom sharp, really, and never nasty. Actually he was the gentlest soul alive. But he had become a man with a fixed idea, a vision. And I was naïve enough to want him to love me for myself alone, just as I had always wanted my father to love me. They just refused to see me as anything more than a pianist. If their aim was to make me see myself as such, they succeeded. This campaign continued for three weeks, through the first part of August. Then at breakfast one morning the phone rang. It was the same Mr. Fried, the critic who had never lost faith in me. Could I be ready to play with the San Francisco Symphony in their Art Commission Series later that month? George was right. It had started again. The concert was to be the last of the series and Arthur Fiedler, of the Boston "Pops" Orchestra, was to conduct. The current was too strong to resist. Mr. Fiedler and I talked on the phone, and we decided that I should play both the "Capriccio Brilliant" of Mendelssohn and the "Totentanz" of Liszt. Later when I met Mr. Fiedler for the first time, or what I thought was the first time, he said:

"You won't remember me, but I heard you when you first came to Boston as a little girl. I came backstage and congratulated you and your father. You were magnificent!"

"I hope I don't let either of you down," I said.

"Either of us . . .?"

"You and that little girl you heard in Boston," I said.

The concert was a sensation. A crowd of ten thousand packed the Civic Auditorium, this being the closing program of the series, always a big event in San Francisco. The ovation after my Mendelssohn and Liszt numbers almost alone persuaded me that George might be right, after all. When the reviews came out, there was no holding the man; he fairly leaped and bellowed with joy. I wasn't exactly unhappy about it myself. Here were words like "mature" and "musicianly" and "taste" and "personality," words that had never cropped up in any of my notices during those painful adolescent years. One critic even called me "a female Horowitz." George was just beside himself, poring over reviews, jumping out of his chair, pacing back and forth, reading out words and phrases like magic incantations.

"The most celebrated of twentieth-century prodigies proved that she has developed into a formidable pianist indeed. This was evident not only in her dazzling technique, but also in her beautifully modeled phrasing, glowing, vigorous tone and mature musicianship."

"Right you are, Mr. Hagan of the *Chronicle!*" panted George, after reading the paragraph in one excited breath. "And if you don't believe the *Chronicle*, Ruth, listen to Fried of the *Examiner*."

That was good reading too: how the onetime child prodigy was now ready to grip the attention of the big concert public on a new high level; how even at five my keyboard flash and accuracy had been amazing; how I still retained my old technical wizardry, but was now "maturing into a pianist of keen taste, thought, and personality."

"Ruth, darling," said George, "aren't you convinced? What more can they say?"

"I don't know. I'm still kind of scared, George. You just don't know what it's going to mean to the two of us if it really gets going again. It's going to mean a great change."

"Rubbish!" cried George. "We'll be closer than ever. You can't stop now! Why, you've got our whole future in your two little hands!"

Like it or not, the thing was gathering momentum, almost as if I had again become a helpless automaton controled by a stronger will than mine.

By way of personal compliment Mr. Fiedler gave me a standing invitation to be his soloist any time I cared to come East or wherever he might be conducting. Well, offers began pouring in. I accepted one to play in Honolulu, and on my return gave a concert in Dallas, where that glorious word "mature" once more soothed my eyes in the following day's reports. Another new acquisition was the term "communicative." Both were very, very precious to me because I had waited so long to see them. Finally George decided the time had come for me to try my luck in the East. My heart sank at the thought. But I dutifully wrote to Mr. Fiedler, who wrote back setting a date for me at Symphony Hall in Boston. A conflict with my teaching schedule was smoothed out and George and I emplaned for Boston. I was so nervous at the first rehearsal that once out on the street, just beyond Symphony Hall, I burst into tears.

"George, please take me back home. I can't play. I'm not fit to play. I'm not a pianist. I don't want any of this. I want to go home and teach and keep house for you."

George gave me a withering look.

"If you're going to talk that way, I won't walk with you."

Whereupon he veered off and went into a café by himself, leaving me to walk the streets of Boston alone, crying and muttering and getting more and more scared of the concert. I told myself I was psychologically unfit for the life of a pianist. I didn't want to go through that ordeal all over again. Why couldn't I be like everybody else? Why wasn't I allowed to do what I wanted, to sew and cook and clean house and entertain friends like other wives. My father's words came piercing back again: "You won't play two notes without me!" Of course Father was right! Cravenly, I retreated into that thought. I'm afraid I was giving poor George a bad time of it, but it wasn't exactly a bed of roses for me. At the hotel a calm and masterful George opened the door.

"I'll speak to you," he said, "if you promise not to carry on like a baby."

I thought him heartless and cruel, not at all like my father, but, in his own insistent and patronizing way, a tyrant just the same. What I have to do to please these men, I thought. But I needed the treatment. Without the faith and persistence of that lovable nag of a husband, I could never have made it. At the concert all I could think of as I sat there in my little yellow dress, playing Mendelssohn and Liszt, was this: "I'm playing for myself. I don't care what anybody else says or thinks. If nobody likes the way I play, that's just too bad. I'm going back to teaching, with or without George."

George must have been right. The performance went splendidly and I received seven or eight curtain calls. News of the performance eventually reached Marks Levine, then head of NCAC (National Concert and Artists Corporation) and that did it. On his next trip West, Mr. Levine offered a contract, contingent on the outcome of a concert he would book for me in Carnegie Hall that December. It was a tall order. The very thought of New York gave me the shivers. Now that I was near this new crossing, the comfort and security of a teaching career seemed more attractive than ever. The Carnegie Hall concert meant giving that all up for the kind of practicing I hadn't done in years. I didn't relish the loss of a good income in exchange for what might well be a fresh harvest of slashing notices. I wanted so much to say no to it all. But George fussed, nagged and scolded, and finally threatened:

"All right, you're going to give up teaching and I'll ask Mother to sell the piano. I won't have it both ways. Either you go into this concert business hook, line, and sinker or you give up music completely."

He painted a picture of what was in store for me as his wife if I persisted in being a fool. I would live with him in a shabby little apartment and wash dishes and mop the floor till I became old and gray and cranky. There wouldn't be any music because he wouldn't take me to any concerts and there wouldn't be a piano around the house to play it on.

"I'm not going to have a piano in the house for you to moon around on," he said.

I tried to reason with him. I told him if he had any idea what the life of a concert pianist was like, he'd be more against it than I was. I told him about the constant traveling, the tiny hotel rooms, the attack of jitters before concerts, the tears, the disappointments, the bad reviews, the physical discomforts, the mock tinsel, the backstage drabness, the spells of loneliness. . . .

"We'd never be together, George," I pleaded.

This meant nothing to a man who thought being a concert artist was the most elevated form of living. Never a musician himself, he had worshiped musicians from childhood. At twelve, when he was confirmed, he took the middle name of Leopold, after Leopold Stokowski. During our first months of marriage we used to go to sleep to recordings of Stokowski and Toscanini and Rachmaninoff and Horowitz. The exalted concert career he couldn't have himself, he wanted to have through me. In that way, too, he was like Father. Through me he aspired to live on that high plane of his heart's desire. Where it left me as a wife, I knew, just as I had known where it left me as a daughter. I finally gave in to George. Tearfully I turned in my resignation at Mercy College, where I had spent the most tranquil three years of my life. It was what George wanted. The Boston concert had taken place in June 1952. Now there was just one person I wanted to play for before going East. That was Artur Rubinstein. I felt I could count on both his judgment and the friendship we had enjoyed in my Paris days as a prodigy. Early in July I let Mr. Rubenstein know through a mutual friend that I would be on vacation in the area of Beverly Hills sometime in August. Would he let me come to see him on a matter of great importance to me? The reply was prompt and cordial. He would be happy to see me. So a few weeks later I went up to his lovely home on Tower Road, and there at the door was Mr. Rubenstein with an outstretched hand.

"I see you still have that marvelous hand," he said, "just like mine, square, powerful, elastic. Do you still play as well as you did?"

I said, "Well, that's for you to say."

"Don't you know?"

"I want you to tell me, Mr. Rubenstein."

Still holding my hand, he led me into a large, beautiful room in which there were two pianos, a concert grand and a seven-foot grand. Bowing, he pointed to the concert grand and said:

"Go right ahead. Play anything you like."

I played something by Chopin.

"Play me another Chopin piece."

I played it.

"Play me some Bach."

I did.

"Play some Debussy . . ."

"Play some Beethoven."

I did.

"Play some Liszt . . .

"Now play me another Chopin piece."

I played the "Etude in Thirds," after which Mr. Rubenstein came up to me and said:

"Do you know, you play that better than I do."

"You're fooling," I said.

"I'm not, and I'll tell you why. Because you obviously practice all those things, and I don't. Why should I at my age? You're young. You've got the vigor to do it, and all the time. Now what is your problem?"

I told Mr. Rubenstein about my Carnegie Hall concert in December and the qualms I had about going back to the stage.

"Nonsense," he said. "Go to Carnegie Hall. Open your program with Bach and close it with Liszt. In between play the twenty-four etudes of Chopin. If you play the way you played just now for me, you'll be a sensation."

I was so overwhelmed all I could say was, "Thank you, Mr. Rubenstein."

"Don't say, 'Thank you.' That's all right for a child. I'm not telling you anything as a favor. Allow me, instead, to thank you for playing for me."

If only I had listened to him. By the time I returned to San Francisco, all my doubts had swept back. I told myself it was too risky to play so much Chopin and wind up the program with a rousing Lisztian finale. Fearful of overreaching myself, I picked a mollycoddle program that included shy, different things like the F minor variations of Haydn and a bloodless toccata by Paradies.

Later that autumn I went to Carmel. For three solid weeks

I practiced in peace for my Carnegie Hall recital. A devoted pupil of mine cooked and kept house while I worked away and took walks on the sand and looked wistfully at the sea. Already the separation from George had begun. This was what he wanted and this was what it was going to be. At the end of three weeks, I made one last desperate effort to squirm out of the New York appearance.

"George," I announced, "I'm just not ready for the big test."

"What you need is a psychiatrist," was his far from playful comment.

I took him up on it. For thirty-five dollars I learned several things I already knew: that I felt secure and respected as a teacher; that I feared losing this security; that I shouldn't allow George to pull me in any other direction; that my father had planted a frightful inferiority complex in me.

"Mrs. Born," said the psychiatrist, "you have accepted your husband as a substitute for your father."

That wasn't news either, but it was a jolt to have it put to me so bluntly, and it certainly didn't help my concert in Carnegie Hall. The one good thing I came away with was a prescription for nerve-calming pills which I was to take three times a day for three days before the concert. By this time my nerves were completely shot. For the first time in my life I began to worry about things that had never bothered me before. For no reason at all, I wondered if my memory would play me false in the middle of a particular composition. I suddenly thought all my ideas of interpretation drab and commonplace. Worst of all, I started to doubt the very technique that had always been my bedrock of confidence.

One day, while alone, I screamed out hysterically:

"*I can't play!*"

Father had told me so. The New York critics had repeated it time and again. Why should they change their minds now?

I wept over my resignation from Mercy College. I cursed George for burning this last bridge behind me. This Carnegie concert was a do-or-die proposition. Failure meant the end of music and teaching and piano, and a weird, uncertain future with George. If only Father had taken me out of circulation when Mr. Rachmaninoff advised it; if only he had listened to Mr. Downes and Mr. Taubman. . . . I could still feel the sting of my last New York notices, and the ones so many years before that had pronounced me dead as a prodigy. How many more obituaries did I need? There was something nobody seemed to understand, least of all George. I was fighting a ghost. If only my name were Tillie Jones, a pianist without pretensions and without a past of wild acclaim and sensation, of meteoric rise and fall. If I could somehow have found a new name and identity, a plastic surgery of mind and body and soul that would once and for all destroy that other . . . I was haunted by the ghost of a little girl who had borne my name.

Well, I was prepared for the worst. The closer we got to the concert, the more jittery and despondent I became. The stakes were too high; the challenge too much for me. All of it seemed so senseless and illogical; the obstacles so insurmountable; the sacrifice of job and money and peace of mind so needless. December finally came. For three days I took my psychiatrist's pills, and walked out on the stage of Carnegie Hall and into a nightmare. Between groups I could scarcely hold the glass of water George gave me. My hand shook like a leaf. At intermission Mr. Levine came backstage to tell me I wasn't making any impression on the crowd. "You play as if you were half asleep. Snap out of it and give them something. I know you have it in you." I walked through that program in a complete haze. I had no taste at all for it, only a dull deep sense of futility. And what a namby-pamby program—except for the

Bach and Schumann—to pick for a comeback, Haydn variations, miniatures by Béla Bartók, a sheaf of *morceaux* by Debussy, good little fillers and encores, every one of them, but nothing of real bulk and body. There was just too much alkaline and too little color; it was shadow and miscellany, rather than substance. If only I had listened to Mr. Rubinstein and played the music that was really my music, that was part of me. What made me do it? I suppose the dread of reading that my tone was harsh and granitic if I played the bigger things. I wanted to sneak back on tiptoe. No wonder Mr. Levine thought me half asleep. Probably the audience was, too. Yet here was George full of smiles and good cheer, hands on my shoulders, almost pushing me back onstage:

"Go out there and do your stuff. You can play rings around the best of them. Ruth, don't let me down. . . . *Don't let your father down!*"

I'll never know why I didn't scream at that and run out into the street, away from Carnegie Hall, and New York and Mr. Levine and George—and Father. I never hated myself as I did at that moment, for all the years of submission to the will and whim of others. How I reached the end of that program I'll never know. At George's insistence we waited in Toffenetti's on West Forty-third Street till the early morning papers came out with the reviews. I knew I would be annihilated. I couldn't care less. I'll say this for George: he never gave up. Nothing dampened his hopes. Well, we finally read the reviews, and I couldn't believe my eyes. The critics hadn't slashed me. The New York *Times* was far from complimentary in its comparisons with past glory. But there were one or two nice little touches about my "sweetness and gentleness" and "wistful charm" in small pieces that gave me a lift. I had, it seemed, developed into "a serious young woman." The review I hugged to me was that of Francis Perkins in the *Herald Tribune*. It contained something I was waiting for someone to say: that there was indication in my playing that my "ultimate artistic reputation" would not depend mainly on my brilliant career as a prodigy. The evil spell was broken. If I could go through a program in a trance without being guillotined by the New York critics, what would they say when I played my best? I decided to try, if Mr. Levine would have me.

Mr. Levine would have me. The contract was drawn up the next day in his office, and when he signed it, he gave it to me straight. The critics hadn't raved, he said, but at least they hadn't made mincemeat of me.

"There was something wrong with you and the program last night," he said. "I know you can play. But you have to grow up. You have to practice harder than ever."

"Should I study with somebody?"

"No. You're already formed. I like a pianist who develops himself. Rubinstein didn't have a lesson after he was fourteen. I think you know what you want and what you need. You've had the best training in the world. Go out and develop what you have. Become a personality. People don't want to hear pupils; there are too many of them giving concerts. They want personalities. I know you've got the makings."

Mr. Levine handed me the contract.

"Now before you sign it, go somewhere and read it with your husband."

Over at Child's Restaurant across the street, George and I talked it over. Before you knew it, I was in tears again. I didn't want to sign it. I again described to George the miseries and discomforts of concertizing. I told him I would have to tour Europe and live in damp hotel rooms and speak a different language every six hours and open my suitcase in the middle of the night in drafty trains, scurry around for cleaners and laundries, write innumerable letters to managers—alone and worried and far from home.

"That's what it's like, George, when you're a concert artist who isn't in the major league yet."

George listened without moving a muscle. He merely pushed the contract gently across the table and said:

"Here it is, Ruth. You don't have to sign it if you don't want to. If you don't sign it, you're through with music. You've no job to go back to. The piano will be sold. And what's more, I'm not going to take that kind of wife."

"But what kind of wife will I be the other way? We'll be apart for months. I'll be a wife in name only. George, I'm warning you. Don't let me go back. This might be our last chance."

"I'll take that chance."

I signed the contract, knowing full well that if I became the success George was dreaming about, it would mean the end of my being Mrs. George Born. George would have to become second to my music. I knew I could only give myself completely to one or the other. George knew it, too, and he risked it gladly. The funny thing is that he is happier now that he has proved his point. I am back on the concert stage and like it. I am Miss Slenczynska now, but it took me a long time to get used to it because I couldn't give George up so easily. I wanted so much to be Mrs. Born, to have a little house and garden and a small circle of friends, and it hurt me terribly to know that wasn't the way George wanted me. It was the pianist or nothing. For a while I fed on his pride and faith in me. If that was how it must be, I was determined to justify his confidence; I wanted to please my husband. In a way a new personality was born. I even used a new name. The "a" at the end of Slenczynska, which proclaims to all the world my pride in being a feminine artist; not my father's daughter or my husband's wife, but a personality in her own right.

So George went back to California and I stayed on at my Aunt Evvy's in Brooklyn, pulling myself together as an artist, weighing and sifting my ideas, taking stock of my strengths and weaknesses, resolved to grow and deepen and broaden as best I could. All, at first, with the idea of pleasing George. It was the old pattern again. As time and distance lengthened between us, George Born because Josef Slenczynski in my mind, and I his meek and will-less daughter. While in Europe later that year, on my first overseas tour in fourteen years, I felt a pang every time I got a letter from George addressed to "Miss Ruth Slenczynska." When he wrote, phoned, or cabled, he was communicating with a pianist, a protégée, a child to be disciplined, anything but a wife. On my first tour I kept begging him to let me come home. I told him of the cold wet season in Europe, of going on stage with a fever and aching muscles, of going without sleep or proper food, or playing encore after encore when all I could think of was a nice warm bed. . . .

"Please take me back," I wrote to George from Holland, where I had fainted from exhaustion and canceled a concert. "I want to cook for you; I want to darn your socks; I want to scrub your floors. Sell the piano; do anything; but let me come home."

George punished me by not writing for three weeks. It was my father once more, holding the threat of his displeasure over me. I had the feeling of being hounded and chased. I did not yet have the consolation of feeling that my work was good enough to stand up and be rewarding in itself. I had yet to convince myself that temperamentally, psychologically, artistically, I was fitted for this business of playing the piano night after night in city after city. A certain something was missing; I think I had to know that I was doing it for others, not just for George or for me. . . . I had been too obsessed by myself, my problems, my fears, my relations with George. In my blindness I had overlooked the people who took the trouble to come and hear me play. *They* were the ones to please, to communicate to. This was the awakening I needed; and it came to me when I crossed the French border into Germany and played at Cologne. . . .

Bright, cheerful Aunt Evvy accompanied me on that trip, giving me confidence in my blackest hours. Without her I would have returned to America after my first week in Europe. The first jolt came when we raised the blinds of our *wagon lit* as we approached Cologne. Before us stretched a vista of havoc and rubble. "Gosh, Aunt Evvy," I said: "These must have been munition factories." Then we came to a bombed-out station that looked like a horrible skeleton, around which huddled streets upon streets of smaller skeletons. Finally, Cologne itself, a nightmare of naked walls and jacked bricks and twisted metal. There was no station; only tracks. You got off the train and that was the station. The whole center of the city, acres and acres of it, was rubble—stones and weeds and barbed wire, and once in a while a piece of street. Only the cathedral stood intact amid that chaos. The people were shadowy, gray-black figures. Suddenly I turned to Aune Evvy:

"What are we doing here? These people don't want a concert. What good will it do? Chopin and Beethoven aren't going to clothe and feed them and take their minds off this horror. They don't want entertainment."

In the shock of what I saw I felt so futile and purposeless. I was a pianist in a graveyard. At the hotel on the outer edge of town, I met the local manager, a Mr. Gustav Finemann, who greeted us warmly and invited me to look over the piano I was going to use and the place I was going to play in. "Tell me the truth, Mr. Finemann," I said. "Is there any real interest in my concert?" He looked at me in surprise: "Why, of course; a concert is a big event to these people."

The hall was in a cold, drab building at the rear of the Martin Luther Church, large enough to seat some six hundred people. On the platform was a rebuilt Steinway piano that turned out to be the very best piano I played on throughout that tour. The place was freezing cold. Mr. Finemann asked me if I wanted to stay there alone and practice. I said I did. It was ten in the morning. Left to myself, I started running through technical passages to warm my hands. I felt the loneliness of that empty, bleak hall. My dejection was growing every minute. What possible interest could these gray, sallow people have in me? I was so inadequate and insignificant. Presently, as my fingers limbered up and flitted easily across the keys, it came to me. I knew why I was here. I was on a mission to bring a few moments of beauty and solace into the lives of the six hundred men and women who would be seated in this grim hall in a few hours. God knows they had little enough to be thankful for. I would try to fill these empty hearts and souls with something precious and personal the very memory of which would keep them warm. There was suddenly hope and excitement in me. I must give them the emotional experience of being lifted to a higher plane through my music. That was my responsibility as an artist. That was all that counted. I *could* do that; I had to do that. These people needed it. And my need was to satisfy them. So I practiced passages and phrases with that one thought of communication in mind. I played as I had never played before. A long-hidden spring of freedom and love and beauty was suddenly revealed to me. It was eight o'clock when I raised my hands and sat back with a sigh. I had been at it ten hours! There was just time enough to hurry back to the hotel, reassure an anxious Aunt Evvy that I hadn't fallen into a bomb crater, slip into a concert dress, gulp down some food, and dash back to the hall behind the Martin Luther Church. I was ready to leave a little bit of me in Cologne. And I believe I did.

When I walked out again on the stage that evening, the first thing that caught my eye, after I had bowed and sat down to play, were the rows and rows of people who had brought copies of the music with them. I had somehow forgotten that German audiences were that way. They give you, or rather the music, the absolute attention of following it with an open score in their hands. Just as you might hear a cough or a chair squeak somewhere else, in Germany you are likely to hear only the rustling of pages turning in unison. Now my first thought, as I beheld all those heads bent over scores, was that I must touch these people. I must somehow take them out of their chairs and their gaze off their music. There they sat, gray and still and absorbed, in a cold, damp auditorium, by turns eying me and eying their music. And there was I in a white dress in front of a black piano playing music they could scrutinize for the slightest flaw. What I wanted to do was to make them forget where they were and who they were listening to, forget everything but the wings on which this music could carry them. I wanted them to forget the music in their hands and think only of the music in mine.

I began with the "Chromatic" fantasy and fugue of Bach. It was in the soft opening measures of the fugue that I first missed the sound of the turning pages—and that I believe I first became an artist. I was saying things of my own and saying them with conviction. There was a message for me to deliver and somehow it got through to them. I'm positive it did. Much has happened to me since, and much had happened to me in the years gone by, but nothing has ever quite equaled that thrill of triumph. It was a triumph over myself. I no longer had doubts. I knew I would never again have doubts. I had found my true self at last. The ghosts of Josef Slenczynski and his fabulous automaton had vanished for good. I pledged myself to perfect this new gift of communication wherever I played, to small audiences or large, so that I might always leave something worthwhile behind me.

That night I could feel the new excitement mounting in me like a live current. With every note I knew I was on the right track at last. I had the feeling I was casting some sort of spell and tried not to breathe too loudly for fear of breaking it. I was resolved to keep this up, and I believe I did to the very end, when those grave, dark figures rose from their shabby wooden chairs and cheered me. I felt I had succeeded in making them listen to the music as it should be listened to and as I wanted them to. I was proud that I could take this responsibility on myself. There was no father in the wings waiting to scream at me for playing a passage too slowly or too softly; no Mr. Cortot to point out where the expression might have been strengthened; no Mr. Rachmaninoff to pat me indulgently on the back. There was no praise or blame from anyone to whom my life and my music were accountable, and George was too far away for new prophecies of the rosy vistas of high living ahead. This much I knew: the piano and I were now bound for life, partners, companions, mates. Nothing and no one would ever be quite that important again, not husband, not home, not family, not good reviews, not bad reviews.

I had made contact with my listeners! The consciousness of that was like a taste of heaven. It made up for the hardships and sacrifices and bitter humiliations. In that new-found rapture of communion, everything else paled to a shadow. It is what I live for now—the need and urge to reach others through my music. The road has been long and hard, full of turns and blocks and detours, and a still longer road lies ahead. But I have glimpsed the goal and I know which way I'm headed. I feel deeply privileged to serve those who come to hear me, to share with them a few handfuls of the gold we call music. For that privilege the cost was none too high. All of it is paid for and forgotten.

That day in Cologne, behind the Martin Luther Church, had done it—the cold, damp hall, the makeshift dressing room, the huge black piano, and no one but the audience and me and the music we had dreamed together. And oh, how it sufficed! Deep down, I knew I would never need anyone or anything else again. I had reached a point where instead of absorbing from others, I could make others absorb from me. So long as there were others to receive, I knew I had something to give. That was challenge enough for the future and a squaring of accounts with the past. The stinging taunt of Father's last words was not even a faint memory. I *could* play two notes without him or anybody else. I was completely on my own, and somehow, somewhere, whatever the personal sorrows and rebuffs still in store for me, there would always be a piano for me to turn to. My future was in my hands.